NIMROD
the
EMPIRE BUILDER

ARCHITECT OF SHOCK AND AWE

DOUGLAS PETROVICH

NIMROD THE EMPIRE BUILDER: ARCHITECT OF SHOCK AND AWE
by Douglas Petrovich

First published in 2023 by
Ancient World Publishing, Richmond, TX

Front cover illustration: mingling of the Mask of Sargon and the Stele of Sargon, painted by Oliver McRae

Back cover illustrations: Stele of Sargon (Louvre Sb 1: Sides A and B, Sargon of Akkad with procession) and Stele of Sargon (Louvre Sb 1: Side C, vultures feasting on corpses), drawn by Oliver McRae

ISBNs: 978-1-962605-00-7 Paperback | 978-1-962605-01-4 E-Book

Ancient World Publishing
Richmond, Texas, USA

NIMROD

the

EMPIRE BUILDER

ARCHITECT OF SHOCK AND AWE

DOUGLAS PETROVICH

ANCIENT WORLD PUBLISHING
RICHMOND, 2023

For my grandparents: Andrew Petrovich (1910–1990), who loved studying the Bible and gave me his only set of the ISBE, and Stella Petrovich (1911–2011), who loved the first journal article I published

"Truth is unkillable!" – Balthasar Hübmaier

NIMROD'S BIOGRAPHY

GENESIS 10:7–12: 7The sons of Cush *were* Seba, and Hawilah, and Sabtah, and Raamah, and Sabteca, while the sons of Raamah *were* Sheba and Dedan. 8Now Cush sired Nimrod. That one acted irreverently, in order to become powerful on the earth. 9He became a powerful slaughterer in the sight of He-who-is, on account of which it is said, ". . . as Nimrod, a powerful slaughterer in the sight of He-who-is." 10Now the starting point of his kingdom was Eridu, and Uruk, and Akkad, and all of them *were located* in the land of Šumer. 11From that land, he went out *into* Assyria, and he built up Nineveh, and Rehoboth City, and Kalhu, 12and Resen—*being located* between Nineveh and Kalhu, which is the great city.

– Author's translation

[Italicized words were added either because they are inferred in Hebrew or for contextual clarity in English.]

CONTENTS

ACKNOWLEDGEMENTS

THE AUTHOR IS INDEBTED TO MANY PEOPLE for the completion of this book on biblical Nimrod, not all of whom I can recognize here. Yet *Nimrod the Empire Builder* would not have been completed without their contributions. The first person to thank is Dr. David Deuel, one of my professors when I was a student at The Master's Seminary during the 1990s. He always has maintained a balanced love for God, for people, and for the study of the ancient historical world of the Bible. Not only did he teach me biblical Hebrew and introduce me to numerous scholars in the field of ancient Near Eastern history, but he oversaw my Old Testament History course that would thrust me headlong into the cognate fields of Egyptology, Assyriology, and more.

The next person whom I need to thank is Professor Timothy Harrison, my Ph.D. advisor at the University of Toronto from 2009 to 2016. Dr. Harrison served for two terms as the president of the American Schools of Oriental Research, the world's premier academic society for the study of the ancient Near East. He is an outstanding archaeologist and historian, who constantly challenged me to be a better learner, thinker, and writer. Probably his greatest legacy in my life is pushing me to broaden my interests related to ancient history and archaeology, both geographically and temporally. I entered my Ph.D. program with a strong interest in the Holy Land of the 2nd millennium BC, yet with a mild interest in that region during the first millennium BC. I left the program with a love for the entire ancient Near East, of *all* periods of antiquity.

Dr. Harrison pushed me to study the archaeology of Mesopotamia, the northern Levant, Anatolia, Egypt, and Nubia. One story behind this push demonstrates how the present volume never would be in print apart from his involvement in my learning. During the spring before my last year of Ph.D. coursework, we had agreed that I would study the archaeology of the southern Levant of the Late Bronze Age in the format of an independent study. Two or three days before fall classes were to begin, I met him in his office to iron out the details of the course. When I asked him how he wanted to construct the plan, he essentially said, "You know, I think it would be far better for you to take an archaeology course in the classroom, under the guidance of one of our professors in the department. Professor Clemens Reichel is offering a yearlong course in Mesopotamian archaeology. I prefer that you take this course with him over doing an independent study with me."

With all of the excitement that had been building in me over the previous summer to study the archaeology of the Holy Land of the Late Bronze Age to a far deeper degree than I previously had studied it, Dr. Harrison's words initially caused my heart to sink. Afterward, I called Dr. Bryant Wood, my archaeology mentor, to ask his advice on how to handle this situation. He said, "Doug, just do whatever your advisor asks of you. When you graduate, you can study the archaeology of Canaan of the 2nd millennium BC until your heart is content." I heard nothing but wisdom in his words. I went into the class a bit hard hearted, but soon I was thrilled to be learning so much about ancient Mesopotamia, the cradle of civilization, which I never imagined I could enjoy. I ultimately came to trust that this redirection in my coursework is God's doing.

I also want to thank Dr. Reichel for such a fascinating course on the history and archaeology of Mesopotamia. Without taking his course, there is no way that I would have written this book on Nimrod, because it was in this course that I dove deeply into the biographies of the great rulers of Mesopotamia, which allowed me to ask the question as to whether one of them might be the equivalent of the Bible's great imperialist who lived before the lifetime of Abraham. In this course with Dr. Reichel, we also studied the expansionary movements of people from Mesopotamia, which enabled me to equate one of them with the outward movement of people from biblical Babel (Genesis 11). If God allows, I will articulate all of this in great detail in a future book entitled, *The Forgotten Era: Illuminating Biblical History before Abraham.*

Another individual whom I want to thank is Dr. Oliver McRae, the artist who produced the images on the front and back cover. Oliver is a retired art history professor who taught at the university level. Some months before the manuscript of this book was complete, Oliver wrote to me and said that he is excited about my work and would enjoy assisting with any illustrations that might be needed for my publications and presentations. When the time came to select someone to produce the needed images related to Nimrod's reign, I remembered Oliver's gracious offer. The images he drew are simply fabulous, exuding both vibrancy and warmth. I am extremely grateful for his effort to bring the book's covers to life, as his contribution adds a visual element to the story that I certainly do not have the talent to produce.

I am thankful to publish *Nimrod the Empire Builder* with Ancient World Publishing, which hopefully will be publishing many more non-fiction books in the future that relate to the ancient Near East and biblical history, as well as historical fiction. I also am extremely grateful for the typesetter, Benjamin Kelley, who has shown great patience and kindness to me. He provided many excellent ideas and improved the layout in ways that I never would have considered. Benjamin turned a raw product into a beautiful piece of work, and he knows his craft well. This is the second book that Benjamin has typeset for me, with the first being *Origins of the Hebrews: New Evidence of Israelites in Egypt from Joseph to the Exodus*. Thanks also go to several anonymous people who proofread the final manuscript for me. They corrected my errors and found mistakes that slipped through my own proofreading passes. Any flaws remaining in the manuscript are purely my own.

Lastly, I would like to express my gratitude for the students whom I have been privileged to influence over the years, including the ones in the courses that I have taught online for Brookes Bible College in St. Louis recently. They have been a joy for me to teach, and we have developed a wonderful comradery and bond that is rare to experience between professor and students. We studied both the history and the geography of the ancient Near East, and the experience was special for all of us. My enthusiasm became their enthusiasm, and their enjoyment of learning about these matters has filled my heart and given me the desire to learn and share with others even more.

On a final note, as long as I am able to fulfill this offer, I want to extend the opportunity for you to buy a signed copy of this book directly from me, whether for yourself or as a gift for someone else. Given that several of the many books I own bear the author's signature, and that those books carry with them a deeper sentimental value, I want to pass that chance along to my readers. Look for me on Twitter (now X), where you can send me a direct message: https://twitter.com/PetrovichDoug, or on my academia. edu webpage, which you can access by searching with any internet browser (Douglas Petrovich + academia.edu), and where you can find my e-mail address. By the time you read this, I hope to have a video or two on Nimrod uploaded to my YouTube channel: Illumining the Path.

INTRODUCTION

WHEN I WAS A BOY IN MIDDLE school during the late 1970s, my favorite teacher was Mr. Haas, an energetic and insightful man of German descent. His two greatest passions that rose to the surface while teaching us at Jennings in Akron, Ohio are history and geology. On more than one occasion, he took those of us who had developed a budding interest in geology to gem and mineral shows that came to our area. I was truly a kid in a candy store at these shows, as I fawned over the colors and shapes of the spectacular rocks and gemstones that were displayed by dealers who were there to show and sell their incredible objects of natural beauty.

Probably the most memorable purchase I made with the money my parents gave me to buy a few mementos is a piece of petrified dinosaur dung. I suppose that this is what would fascinate a boy of junior high age more than almost anything else there, as any physical remnant of a dinosaur would bring to life the age of those behemoths that roamed the earth in a bygone era. Yet for all of the wonder produced by seeing and touching tiger's eye quartz, a geode, or a multi-colored agate stone, I was captivated even more by the study of human history.

Mr. Haas truly had a gift for bringing the events of the past to life, and I would hang on his every word when he spoke about the French revolution, the American Revolutionary War, or the war to end all wars (i.e., World War I). The most fascinating topic that can be treated in a history class for a boy growing up in the 1960s and 1970s, though, almost undoubtedly is World War II. This was the freshest global war at the time, and indisputably the most devastating and destructive war in history, as it spread far beyond Europe. After all, World War II also was fought in Africa, the Soviet Union, China, Japan, throughout many of the islands of the western Pacific Ocean, and even in North America.

Accordingly, Mr. Haas told us about many of the most fascinating moments in World War II. In March of 1938, Hitler annexed Austria and symbolized his wealthy acquisition by driving into Vienna in a Mercedes. In September of 1939, the German war machine captured Poland, even using armored vehicles against cavalry forces on occasion. The Nazi blitz-krieg into France during May and June of 1940 not only netted them the occupation of the French nation but also the Netherlands, Belgium, and Luxembourg. December 7, 1941 became an infamous day for the United States, as Hitler's Japanese allies attacked the naval base at Pearl Harbor in the Hawaiian Islands. The list of such significant events during the war is extensive.

When we finished studying World War II, Mr. Haas gave our class an exam, which was old school: long and detailed, with true and false statements, multiple choice, fill in the blank, and essay questions. In total, the exam consisted of six pages, with questions on both the front and the back of the page. Although I wrote this exam too long ago to remember how long it took to write, the time must have seemed like an eternity. One detail I do remember, though, is my score: a 100(%). That score forever cemented in my mind the reality that I have an inescapable fascination, perhaps even a magnificent obsession, with history.

This obsession took a bit of a detour during my years in high school. While a junior higher, I had repented of my sin, confessed that Jesus is the son of God, and believed in my heart that God raised him from the dead, as the first of many to be resurrected to eternal life on the new earth. My Christian conversion truly changed the course of my life, even as a boy of 14 years old. In light of this, my high school years were a combination of learning more about the Bible and the Christian life, and learning more about other fields, such as astronomy, geometry, advanced mathematics, and English grammar and literature. Only when I was studying in my first master's degree program did my love for history truly come to the forefront again.

I did take a Western Civilizations course as an undergraduate student at a community college in southern California, but this put a bad taste in my mouth, because our atheistic professor seemed preoccupied with undermining our belief in biblical historicity, as an unstated but undeniable part of his agenda. Years later, God used a Christian seminary with a high view of the Bible to rekindle my passion for history, which had turned primarily to ancient—rather than modern—history. What amplified my excitement was studying history in the context of God's revelation of himself in the pages of the Bible, a completely error-free writing as originally written, because the Spirit of God bore along the inspired authors (2 Pet 1:21). In this context, I took a New Testament History course while working on my Master of Divinity degree, and I followed this up with an Old Testament History course in my Master of Theology degree program.

Unfortunately, I took the latter course as an independent study (i.e., without a professor who taught in a classroom setting), because there were not enough M.Div. students who wanted to take Old Testament History as an elective course. I could not wrap my mind around their lack of interest in history. After all, my seminary staunchly advocated for the grammatical-historical method of interpretation, which became a foundational component in the academic life of the church during the Reformation of the 16th century. This reflects a hermeneutical approach with a sharp focus on the matters of (1) grammar and syntax of the original biblical languages in which the text was composed and (2) the historical context surrounding the people and events described within any given biblical passage.

This independent study exposed me to the formal study of ancient Near Eastern peoples such as the Šumerians, Akkadians, Amorites, Egyptians, Assyrians, and Babylonians, among others. A year later, after having moved to Russia to help found a seminary from scratch, I was tasked with creating a curriculum for a divinity program, starting with a blank sheet of paper. This was a chance to put my money where my mouth is, so I chose to require students to take a New Testament History course and an Old Testament History course alongside numerous required courses in the biblical languages.

The teaching of these history courses, which none of my colleagues on the faculty at our budding seminary desired to teach, is what God used to show me that this should be the focus of my Ph.D. degree. I had been taught all three biblical languages extremely well as a student, along with the exegesis of the biblical text as a whole, so my desire with a Ph.D. program was to break new ground by strengthening my weaknesses in the area of grammatical-historical hermeneutics, rather than strengthening my strengths and avoiding my weaknesses. I knew then that I could count on one hand—with fingers to spare, even—the number of biblical scholars who were trained extremely well in both the biblical languages *and* in biblical history, which includes subfields such as archaeology, epigraphy, iconography, and chronology.

I understood that the field of biblical history was ripe for harvest, meaning that the potential was there for exciting contributions and discoveries that had yet to be made. However, I had no idea that God would lead me to stumble into major discoveries that would necessitate the rewriting of the history books and biblical commentaries, which were awaiting me in my Ph.D. program, and I certainly did not enter the program with any such ambitions. The yearlong course I took in Mesopotamian archaeology led me to discover the timing of the post-Babel dispersion and the ancient city in Genesis 11 that God renamed dysphemistically as *Babel* (i.e., "Confusion"). A dysphemism is the use of a derogatory term in place of an inoffensive term, which is the opposite of a euphemism (e.g., "passed away" instead of "died," or "woman of the night" instead of "prostitute"). An example of a dysphemism is calling mail sent via the postal service, "snail mail," in order to contrast it with the speed of communicating electronically with e-mail.

The minor of my Ph.D. is Egyptology, which allowed me to study Egyptian archaeology and three years of Middle and Late Egyptian (hieroglyphics). While I was preparing for my comprehensive exams in January of 2012, I stumbled into published animal remains from the site of Avaris, the city where Jacob settled his family after leaving Canaan due to the intensity of the famine there. These burials consisted of the four types of animals that (1) are dated precisely to the reign of the exodus pharaoh (i.e., Amenhotep II) and (2) are documented in Exodus 11 and 12 as coexisting with the Israelites and Egyptians at the time of the first Passover (i.e., sheep, goats, cattle, and dogs). Moreover, these animal burials fit exactly with what would be expected of the animals at the time of the first Passover, which was observed in Egypt just before the exodus.

This discovery then presented me with a research question: if these odd burials are evidence of Israelites in Egypt at the time just before Moses led his people out of Egypt, confirming the biblical date of the exodus (1446 BC) if the numbers are taken literally, is there corresponding evidence of Israelite residence at the site for the previous 430 years that the Bible describes as the length of the Israelite sojourn in Egypt (Exod 12:40–41)? Further research led me into one goldmine of discovery after another that attest to this extended residence in Egypt, which is documented in my book, *Origins of the Hebrews: New Evidence of Israelites in Egypt from Joseph to the Exodus* (Nashville: New Creation, 2021).

In turn, these discoveries led me to the unplanned and unexpected understanding that Joseph's two eldest sons, Manasseh and Ephraim, invented the world's first alphabetic script, and that Hebrew is the language behind the original alphabet. This pictographic script was developed by taking 22 hieroglyphs from among the 800+ pictographs in the Egyptian sign list and connecting the first letter of the pictographic meaning of the image to a corresponding word in the Hebrew language that comes to mind for the Hebrew speaker who looks at that image. This method for creating the world's first alphabetic script utilizes what is called the acrophonic principle, because—for example—the drawing of a house would connect the Hebrew mind to the *b*-sound, given that the absolute form of the Hebrew word for 'house' is *bayit*. All of this, along with 15 fully-translated early alphabetic Hebrew inscriptions, is detailed in my book, *The World's Oldest Alphabet: Hebrew as the Language of the Proto-Consonantal Script* (Jerusalem: Carta, 2016).

One other discovery that came as a result of my time studying at the University of Toronto is the historical identity of the biblical figure known to Moses as *Nimrod*, which is the focus of the present volume. During my Mesopotamian archaeology course, I became convinced about the identity of the Mesopotamian ruler who equates to biblical Nimrod. So, in 2013 I published a peer-reviewed article in the *Journal of the Evangelical Theological Society* that attempts to persuade the academic community that Nimrod can be connected to this ancient ruler with great confidence. Nimrod's biography that is recorded in the Bible, which I have translated from Hebrew and put on the page just after the dedication page above, is somewhat cryptic.

This biographical brevity for Nimrod has led to no shortage of ideas as to which historical person or divine being was meant by Moses when he composed the 10th chapter of Genesis. I have been surprised at how mesmerizing the identity of this obscure biblical character is to those who enjoy biblical studies. The clearest sign of this that I have seen derives from the number of hits on my own academia.edu webpages, to where I uploaded this article on Nimrod. Out of all of the journal articles, unpublished papers, chronological lists, textual variant resolutions, teaching materials, and other documents I have uploaded there, the one that exceeds all of the others in how many times it has been accessed is the journal article about Nimrod.

For some unknown reason(s), this minor character in the Bible whose story is hidden away in a small corner of the massive book of Genesis has captivated the interest and imagination of countless readers, obviously creating within them an insatiable curiosity to know just who he is, beyond the elusive name that Moses gave to him. Apart from the two times that Moses refers to Nimrod (Gen 10:8, 9), his name appears only twice more in the Hebrew Bible. First, the writer of Chronicles names him in Cush's genealogy (1 Chr 1:10), representing a portion of the postdiluvian (i.e., after the universal flood of Noah's day) genealogy that this later author summarized from Moses's account in Genesis. Second, Micah the prophet refers to Assyria as "the land of Nimrod" (Mic 5:6), given that Nimrod expanded his kingdom into Assyria (Gen 10:11) after having established his domain in Šumer (i.e., southern Mesopotamia).

This limited information about Nimrod is enough to understand the type of ruler that he was and how he acquired his empire. In 1996, a military strategist named Harlan Ullman coined the term, "shock and awe," which he used to describe the strategy of using a rapid and repeated show of excessive force to pressure the enemy into ceasing from hostilities. On 19 March 2003, the United States military implemented the strategy of shock and awe by continually bombing Saddam Hussein's military infrastructure in Iraq, with the intent of disorienting his troops and forcing a surrender. This quick-strike approach led to the seizing of Baghdad on 5 April and a U.S. declaration of victory on 15 April. Ancient conquerors lacked the technology for this exact form of blitzkrieg, but Nimrod certainly applied an early version of shock and awe to devastate his enemies.

Since the annals of extra-biblical (i.e., sources outside of the Bible) history do not record the exploits of a powerful ruler named Nimrod who built an empire by a campaign of shock and awe, this presents a bit of a challenge to anyone wishing to connect him with a historical figure. However, the task is not impossible, and it certainly does not mean that God never intended for people of later times to attempt to identify just who this king is. Such a discovery-repressing approach would be a terrible philosophy to embrace, and ultimately it spawns far more from laziness than from piety or virtue. The possibility of pinpointing the identity of Nimrod does exist, but only if sufficient evidence can be compiled to construct a persuasive case.

The burden of responsibility for anyone who connects Nimrod with a known historical figure is to prove beyond reasonable doubt that he is indeed that very person. The most popular options that scholars have presented for Nimrod's identity will be presented and evaluated in this book. These options include (1) Ninurta, the god of war, (2) Gilgamesh, the king of Uruk, (3) Amenhotep III, an Egyptian pharaoh of the 18th Dynasty, (4) Sargon of Akkad, the first king of the Akkadian Empire, and (5) Naram-Sin, the Akkadian king who was Sargon's grandson. The present writer is convinced that one of these individuals is the same person as Nimrod of Genesis 10, rendering the other four candidates as erroneous choices.

Purposefully, *Nimrod the Empire Builder* is written for a general audience of people who just love the Bible, not for professional scholars or experts in the field, so no formal citations of sources are included. Anyone who desires to study the sources that the author consulted for the preparation of the manuscript can consult his scholarly article of 2013, which is much shorter in length and scope than the book. The dates listed for kings and rulers, unless otherwise noted, are regnal years that signify the exact or estimated years during which they ruled. Any capitalized year appearing for a specific king signifies a given year of his reign as king.

For example, if Year 4 is attributed to Ur-Nammu of the Third Dynasty of Ur, this refers to some event that occurred in the fourth year of his reign as king. All translations of biblical passages within this book are those of the present writer unless otherwise noted, because a translation of relevant verses that is both precise and ideal is vital to achieving a proper understanding of minute details that must be nuanced precisely, as well as to arriving at proper conclusions. In short, as a teacher of all levels of biblical Hebrew, the author is compelled to use his own carefully composed translation of the biblical verses that are treated within the book.

This volume includes no maps, drawings, or photographs, apart from the drawings on the front and back cover of the book. Sufficient resources of this kind can be accessed nowadays on the internet by using the search field on one of the standard web browsers available on any personal computer or tablet. Such images obviously would be viewed better on a large screen of one of these electronic devices than on a smartphone. The other option, of course, especially for those who prefer books to electronic devices, is to consult a general encyclopedia (e.g., *Encyclopedia Britannica*) or a set of volumes that focuses specifically on ancient history (e.g., *Cambridge Ancient History*).

Numerous abbreviations appear within this book, and they are noted within the next three paragraphs for the reader's reference. The metric system is used for distances, with "kilometer" shortened to "km" and "meter" abbreviated to "m." The words "also known as" are abbreviated to "a.k.a." here. Several Latin phrases commonly used in abbreviated form appear occasionally: (1) e.g. for *exempli gratia* ("for example"), (2) et al. for *et alia* ("and others"), (3) etc. for *et cetera* ("and so forth"), and (4) i.e. for *id est* ("that is, . . .").

Although virtually all of the English translations of passages from the Bible are those of the author, occasional references will be made to published translations. These translations will be abbreviated as such: (1) KJV for the King James Version (1611/1769), (2) NASB for the New American Standard (1977), (3) NASU for the New American Standard updated version (1995), (4) NIV for the New International Version (2011), and (5) NRSV for the New Revised Standard Version (1989). The archaeological period in the Levant known as the Early Bronze Age will be abbreviated to the EBA.

The Amarna Letters of the 14th century BC are coded by the two initial letters EA, which stands for El Amarna, the Egyptian site from where these Akkadian tablets derive. The ancient Near East, which is abbreviated to ANE here, is the primary term that scholars and historians use for the westernmost part of Asia and some surrounding lands. Although there are no strict boundaries offered as to what does and does not fit within the parameters of the ANE, the term most often is used of Anatolia (a.k.a. Asia Minor in New Testament times, and Turkey in modern times), the northern and southern Levant (i.e., ancient Syria, Phoenicia, and Canaan/Israel), Egypt and Sinai, and Mesopotamia.

SECTION I

BACKGROUND TO NIMROD'S IDENTITY

CHAPTER 1

Pinpointing Moses's Motivation

BACKDROP FOR NIMROD'S STORY IN GENESIS 10

A VITAL LITERARY CONVENTION OF MOSES IN GENESIS

A GREAT DEAL OF STUDY AND WRITING has been invested not only in the content of what ancient writers composed, but also in how they composed their writings. These authors often chose a particular literary style, such as narrative, poetical, or didactic (i.e., for teaching, usually in the form of an epistolary letter) literature. Samuel the prophet wrote what is called the *Book of Samuel* (one book in Hebrew) in narrative form, while *Ecclesiastes* is a poetical book presumed to have been written by Solomon, and an unnamed author composed the *Epistle to the Hebrews*. Beyond the simple matter of literary style behind a composition, many authors of antiquity chose to follow specific literary conventions of the day, or at times to create their own conventions.

For example, most writers of Hebrew narrative text used a versatile conjunction called a *waw* (named after the Hebrew consonant that makes the *w*-sound) to move along the successive historical events recorded in their accounts. The *waw* conjunction is so versatile that it can be translated as any coordinating conjunction (e.g., and, but, or) or any subordinating conjunction (e.g., then, when, after, because). The context alone helps the translator to know which option is best for rendering the word into English. For another example, when writing the book of Genesis, Moses—who wrote about the reigns of Egyptian kings of his day, particularly Thutmose III and Amenhotep II—followed the standard Egyptian practice of the day by leaving enemy kings unnamed in historical writings such as the royal annals of war. Historical details such as this repulse the critics who suggest that Genesis was composed after the Babylonian invasion of Judah in 587 BC, rather than between 1446 and 1406 BC, as a literal understanding of biblical chronology requires.

The story of Nimrod is nestled about 20% of the way into Genesis. Essential to understanding an author's particular literary conventions of choice is identifying just who that author happens to be. Unfortunately, the scholarly community is at odds over the identity of the author who wrote Genesis. Probably it is fair to say that the majority of biblical scholars today, whether they profess to be Christian or non-Christian, reject the time-honored position that Moses authored the book. Historically, Judaism and Christendom have stood in agreement that Moses is the author. The Pentateuch, which consists of the first five books of the Bible, has been understood historically by these two faith traditions to be a single literary unit.

Although no claim as to authorship is recorded within the Pentateuch, unlike Paul's typical claim at the beginning of most of his letters (e.g., "Paul, an apostle of Christ Jesus . . ."), numerous internal statements infer Mosaic authorship. For example, Deut 31:9 states that "Moses wrote this law [Torah] and gave it to the priests, the sons of Levi who carried the ark of the covenant of He-who-is" (with *He-who-is* being a more accurate translation of the tetragrammaton, the masculine, singular participle that the ancient Hebrews used as their covenant-name for the God of Abraham, Isaac, and Jacob). If Moses wrote the law, and the law is contained in the Pentateuch, then Moses authored the Pentateuch.

The text of Exod 24:4 states that "Moses wrote all of the words of He-who-is, rose up early in the morning, and built an altar below the mountain *with* 12 pillars, according to the 12 tribes of Israel." If Moses wrote all of the words of He-who-is, and the Pentateuch is littered with statements that are attributed directly to God during Moses's day, then Moses wrote the Pentateuch. In Exod 34:27, mention is made that "He-who-is said to Moses, 'Write these words, for in accordance with these words I have made a covenant with you, and with Israel." If Moses wrote down Israel's covenant with God, and the Pentateuch records that very covenant, then Moses composed the Pentateuch.

External witnesses in other biblical books also allude to Mosaic authorship of the Pentateuch, including the reference to "the book of the law of
Moses" in Joshua 8:31, which in the initial decades after Moses's death can
refer only to the first five books of the Bible. When Jesus asked the Pharisees what Moses commanded regarding divorce (Mark 10:2–5), they said
that Moses permitted the Israelites to write a certificate of divorce (Deut
24:1–4). In this encounter with the Pharisees, Jesus clearly attributed the
authorship of Deuteronomy to Moses. If all of these biblical writers and
speakers—including the only-begotten son of God, no less—were convinced of the Mosaic authorship of the Pentateuch, any objective person
should be content with this reasonable conclusion. On these grounds, Moses
is accepted in the present volume as the author of Genesis.

Yet can the existence of Moses as a historical person be accepted
when so many critics have doubted its validity? For several millennia, no
extra-biblical writings were known to attest to the historicity of Moses. Stun-
ning extra-biblical confirmation of Moses's existence came to light when
the present author published a groundbreaking book in 2016 called, *The
World's Oldest Alphabet: Hebrew as the Language of the Proto-Consonantal Script*, a book that identifies Hebrew as the language used for the extant
writings that are universally accepted as representing the world's oldest
attested alphabetic script. On a stone inscription from Serabit el-Khadim in
southwestern Sinai called Sinai 361, which dates to 1446 BC by a combination of ceramic evidence and biblical chronology (although there is no date
inscribed on the stone), the text reads, "Our bound servitude had lingered.
Moses then provoked astonishment. It is a year of astonishment because of
the Lady" [i.e., Hathor/Baʿalath, the patron (i.e., chief) goddess of the tur-
quoise mining site at Serabit el-Khadim].

With the argumentation in favor of Mosaic authorship having been
presented and the historicity of Moses having been affirmed by contemporary extra-biblical inscriptional evidence, a vital literary convention that he
employed in Genesis must be discussed in order to ensure that no confusion
exists over the correct position of Nimrod's life on a timeline with absolute
dates. This is important, because many scholars and laypeople alike have
concluded uncritically that Nimrod lived before or during the events related
to the tower of Babel (Gen 11:1–9), and possibly even led the charge or par-

ticipated in the selfish corruption that took place at Babel, simply because Nimrod is discussed one chapter earlier than the events at Babel appear. The reality is that Nimrod lived long after the events that unfolded at Babel, but before this can be proven in the biblical text (see Chapter 2), the assertion that an event recorded in Genesis 10 can date to a time after the major event at Babel that is recorded at the beginning of Genesis 11 must be justified.

One literary convention that Moses often employed in Genesis is the composition of a broad, panoramic timeline that carries the narrative from one relatively distant time earlier in history to an opposite relatively distant time later in history, then—after writing this general account of events over that larger timespan—composed a more detailed but temporally more limited story that fits within that broader timeframe. A modern historian writing in this way could compose a brief and general account of U.S. history of the 20th century, including events such as the sinking of the titanic, World War I, the roaring 20s, the great depression, World War II, the cold war, the hippie movement, the landing on the moon, and so forth.

Then, the historian could start a new chapter immediately afterward, going into great detail about the cold war between the Soviet Union and the United States, including the campaign of Senator Joseph McCarthy in the 1950s to expose alleged communists within the State Department, followed by an in-depth discussion of the Cuban missile crisis of 1962, and so forth. With this example, the historian would paint the general backdrop of the overall century before putting the cold war under a microscope and discussing it in finer detail to ensure that the readers know all about this event on which the historian wants to expand. First, the greater context is established. Second, the historian drills down into the details related to a single, vital topic within that greater context.

The first biblical example of this literary dynamic in Genesis comes from the contrast between the two narratives about creation, one in Genesis 1 (plus 2:1–4) and the other in Genesis 2 (minus 2:1–4). Many university professors exploit the opportunity to accentuate this contrast by attempting to undermine the validity of both chapters simply by asserting cavalierly that these are two conflicting accounts of creation. "After all," they decry, "the biblical story is internally unreliable, given that these differing accounts contradict one another." This criticism, however, is weak and misses Moses's point entirely. No contradiction whatsoever exists.

The narrative in Gen 1:1–2:4 documents all six days of creation in chronological order as a sequential account of every event deemed to be important enough to mention. Apart from several introductory details to prepare for what is at the heart of chapter two, Gen 2:5–25 describes in more detail the creation of mankind, consisting of male and female. The inception of human life occurs on Day 6 of creation, which fits within one of the consecutive days of creation delineated in the broader context of the previous account. A crucial note is added about how humans are God's regents on earth, as they were given the responsibility to guard and tend the earth. If these two chapters are so vastly different in how they describe creation, how do they not contradict one another? The answer to this question is abundantly clear and extremely compelling, demonstrating how even highly educated professors can be guilty of reading the Bible in a purely cursory fashion.

Genesis 1:1–2:4 focuses on the *order* of creation (i.e., Day 1, Day 2, Day 3, etc.), while Gen 2:5–25 concentrates on the *pinnacle* of creation (i.e., mankind, the one and only lifeform on earth that bears the image and likeness of God [Gen 1:27]). The first chapter flies the plane at 30,000 feet as the flight attendant points out the major features that can be seen above the clouds, as it were. These strictly-chronological six days feature the creation of the empty universe, the earth, the conglomeration of elements that formed the building blocks that would fill the universe yet initially provided light on the earth, the objects and lifeforms that would fill the earth, the (earth's) sun, the (earth's) moon, and the innumerable stars. Day 6, the 24-hour period that places the creation of humans under a microscope in chapter two, is treated similarly to the other days within chapter one: just hitting the high points.

The second chapter represents a trip at ground level through the jungle that is led by a forester, who meticulously points out the plants and animals that inhabit the landscape, as it were. This includes the mist that watered the ground, the garden in which mankind was placed, the tree of the knowledge of good and evil, the four rivers that spawned from the river that watered the garden, and the origin of mankind. The chapter begins with the preparation of the environment for mankind's arrival, then concludes with an extensive exposé on the responsibilities mankind bears on the earth, along with the relationship between the man and woman. Therefore, chapter one acts as the overall timeline that takes the reader from the beginning to the end of creation, while chapter two only zooms in on one dot plotted within that timeline and positions it under the microscope for a more thorough study of the details.

A second example of Moses's tendency in Genesis to compose a panoramic timeline first, then to tell a detailed story of some event(s) that transpired within that timeline, is related to Genesis 5 and 6. Genesis 5 primarily consists of a genealogy that sweeps through a vast amount of time, in a fashion that is similar to Genesis 1, covering Adam, Noah, and every male in the genealogy between them. In fact, the purpose of the chapter is to provide a complete, purely-human chain from the first man to the only man from the antediluvian world (i.e., before the universal flood of Noah's day) to survive the global flood, not counting his immediate family. The beginning of Genesis 6, running counter to chronological order, does not pick up the story during or after the lifetime of Noah.

Instead, the beginning of Genesis 6 takes the reader back to a time earlier in the antediluvian period, when evil angelic beings who were called three different titles (i.e., sons of God [6:2], fallen ones [6:4], and powerful ones [6:4]) corporealized themselves into fully-human form and attempted to corrupt the purely-human line of mankind that was intended to extend from Adam to Messiah by forcefully interbreeding with females of Adam's line. In fact, Gen 6:4 speaks not only of the time when these evil spirit beings performed this heinous act, but of a time when these fallen ones first were on earth, as the text states that "the fallen ones were on the earth in those days [i.e., before the forced sexual activity] and afterwards also, when the sons of God were going into the daughters of mankind and sired *offspring* to them."

Therefore, with Moses's episode about the corruption of the evil spirit beings, he took the reader back to a much earlier time than the end of the timeline that acts as the outer bracket of Genesis 5's genealogy. Just as with the relationship of Gen 1:1–2:4 to Gen 2:5–25, here Moses drew out the extended timeline in Genesis 5, then with the episode in Gen 6:1–6 went back to a single point in that timeline and put one set of events under a microscope, effectually zooming in on it by presenting a detailed account—blow by blow—for his readers. These two examples demonstrate the validity of this proposed literary convention employed by Moses and provide persuasive precedent for gaining a proper understanding of the order of events in Gen 10:1–11:9, namely as to why the narrative of the (chronologically later) story of Nimrod *precedes* the story of the (chronologically earlier) tower of Babel in the flow of Genesis. Numerous other examples could be cited.

Conveniently, the genealogy of Genesis 10 acts as a virtual mirror-image of Genesis 5, except that the second genealogy pieces together the human connection from Noah to Peleg, rather than from Adam to Noah. Genesis 10 actually serves to accomplish something that goes beyond anything Genesis 5 has to offer. This chapter not only connects a man on one end of a timeline to a man on the opposite end of that timeline, but it actually provides three genealogies: the sons of the initial man, namely Noah. The bloodlines of Shem, Ham, and Japheth are traced with extreme care, because the interactions, flaws, and fates of all three of their family trees will be crucial for understanding the flourishing of the Israelites in Canaan, onto whom Moses will shine the spotlight after Jacob has fathered all of his children.

Genesis 10's genealogy of Noah's three sons documents multiple generations for each of them. The line of Japheth appears as the first of the three, undoubtedly because his offspring play the least significant role in the daily lives of the future Israelites. Ham's descendants emerge second, as they are not part of the line that eventually leads to Abram but will interact more with the people of promise than will Japheth's line. The line of Shem is reserved for last, given that his family tree leads directly to Abram. This resembles how some people eat food that is on their plate: the unimpressive consumables, such as green beans and beets, are eaten first, leaving the tasty garlic-flavored mashed potatoes and fillet mignon to be enjoyed afterward, without interruption from the mediocre vegetables. What is of crucial importance for understanding the relationship between Genesis 10 and 11 is where Shem's lineage stops in chapter ten.

The final three individuals in that family tree are a father and his two sons: Eber, then Peleg and Joktan. Peleg is the son through whom the line would pass to Abram, but only Joktan's sons are named here, all 13 of them (Gen 10:26–29). Peleg's prodigy is omitted here because the spotlight will shine directly on them in the latter part of Genesis 11, when Moses meticulously traces the family line from Eber to Abram, through Peleg. The significance of Eber's role cannot be overlooked, because his Hebrew name is the equivalent of the Akkadian word *Habiru*. When Moses wrote of Abram in Gen 14:13, he referred to the great patriarch as "Abram, the Hebrew." The point of this appositional ethnic descriptor is that Moses was emphasizing to his readers how their Hebrew ethnicity is tied to Eber/Heber, the father of the Habiru. The word *Hebrew* is simply the Hebrew equivalent of the term *Habiru*, which is used of an ethnic group that is found throughout the ANE at the end of the 3rd and into the 2nd millennium BC.

Back to the task at hand, Peleg essentially is the last man in the family tree of Genesis 10 who is a direct ancestor of Abram, who will come into focus in Gen 11:26. All of this prepares the reader for the connection of Genesis 10 to Genesis 11. The narrative about the tower of Babel in Gen 11:1–9 represents another moment under the microscope, and the point at which it ties into the greater timeline of Genesis 10 is in the lifetime of Peleg. After all, Moses stated conclusively in Gen 10:25 that Eber's son was named "Peleg [i.e., "Division"], because in his days the earth was divided." This parenthetical statement about Peleg is offered here as a micro-spoiler for the crucial story in Genesis 11 about a global division in communication that stymied collaboration. In support of this conclusion, Moses earlier had noted that the peoples of the coastlands who derived from Japheth through Javan and his sons "were separated into their territories, each man according to his language, according to their families (Gen 10:1–5).

Disappointingly, some enthusiasts of the Bible have attempted to interpret the division of Peleg's day to the breaking apart of Pangea, the prehistorical (i.e., the era before the advent of writing) supercontinent (German: *Urkontinent*) that existed before it split into the seven recognized continents of modern geography. However, this interpretation has no scriptural merit and should not be entertained with any seriousness. The view represents an overzealousness with connecting modern geological science to the biblical narrative, as Moses was no primitive geologist who studied continental drift or visited the continents as an explorer who mapped out their contours and discovered that they fit together as puzzle pieces. Instead, the division of which he wrote is connected *directly and unambiguously* to the first event that comes just after the end of Genesis 10's fascinating genealogy. The division to which Moses eluded in Gen 10:25 is the physical separation of the people groups of the ancient world—along familial lines—when they completely lost the ability to communicate with one another in a common language (Gen 11:1), causing full-scale division among them.

At this point, the soil has been prepared for the needed disproving of the uncritical assumption of many that Nimrod lived *before* the calamity at the tower of Babel, rather than *after* this set of events. Given that the story of Babel's demise contextually fits back into the timeline of Genesis 10 at the point where the line from Noah to Abram stops (i.e., at Eber and his son, Peleg), the question remains as to where the story of Nimrod fits on that same timeline. Most importantly, it must be remembered that Genesis 10 consists not of one timeline, but three timelines. The author intended for the reader to follow the lineage of all three of Noah's sons who survived the flood by riding on the ark with him.

In light of this, the three genealogies must be viewed independently. The point at which the story of the tower of Babel is plugged into Shem's genealogy has nothing to do with the chronology of the genealogies of Ham or Japheth. Correspondingly, the point at which Nimrod's biography is plugged into Ham's genealogy has nothing to do with the chronology of the genealogies of Shem or Japheth. In fact, it will be proven in Chapter 3 that the Hebrew text of Gen 10:8 does not require Nimrod to have been the direct, biological son of Cush. Therefore, the position of Nimrod's name early in Ham's genealogical tree is completely unrelated to how soon Nimrod came onto the scene after the life of Cush. Without doubt, the events surrounding the tower of Babel, including the post-Babel dispersion, long preceded Nimrod's life.

This makes complete sense when studying both accounts, because Gen 11:4 clarifies how Babel is the first city that was built after the global flood, given that the people in Šumer (Hebrew: *Shinar*) said, "Come on! Let us build for ourselves a city, and a tower, with its top in the sky." Confirmation comes in Gen 11:5, where it says that "He-who-is came down to see the city and the tower that the sons of mankind had built." What made an occupational site a true city in the ancient world is the advent of urbanization: a strong central administration (i.e., governmental authority), urban planning, public works, civil security, a marketplace economy, and a massive labor force that worked to create and sustain the city's infrastructure and monumental architecture. Without these components of urbanization, an ancient site simply is less than a full-blown city.

In stark contrast to the city-less landscape that existed before the events that begin with Gen 11:1, Gen 10:10–12 states that Nimrod's kingdom consisted of at least seven cities: Eridu, Uruk, Akkad, Nineveh, Rehoboth City, Kalhu, and Resen. The whole point of the Nimrod story is to document the utter evil that can be unleashed when a city appoints a king, who—when he gives himself over to a lust for conquest—can invade other sovereign cities, decimate innocent residents through warfare and bloodshed, then incorporate those cities into his own dominion that was pieced together by a craving for unlimited power.

It must be considered completely illogical to propose that a story with *many* urbanized cities on earth took place before a story with *one* urbanized city on earth. Such a model simply would not spawn from anyone with training in ancient history. Embracing such a self-contradictory conclusion as true would require the willful suspension of disbelief, similar to how fans of Star Trek or Star Wars simply ignore the impossibility of space travelers walking about their spaceships freely, as if earth-like gravity were present on the ship while flying through outer space. The building of the tower of Babel and the post-Babel dispersion clearly preceded the lifetime and conquest-laden reign of Nimrod as a king who founded a kingdom and subsequently built an empire of captured cities. Babel was the *first city*, while Nimrod was the first inter-regional conqueror of a *multitude of cities*.

CONTEXT FOR NIMROD'S STORY IN GENESIS 10:7–12

For Jews and Christians alike, Genesis is the first book of the Bible, and it contains 50 chapters. The central theme of this book can be summed up in just one word: beginnings. Among other subjects, Genesis records the beginning of (1) the empty expanse of the universe, (2) the earth (i.e., the first object created within the empty universe, whatever any astronomer or biblical critic may say to the contrary), (3) celestial light, (4) the stars, (5) the moon, (6) earth's atmosphere, (7) earth's waters, (8) plants, (9) animals, (10) mankind, (11) marriage, (12) human sin/evil, (13) enmity/conflict with God (14) shame, (15) sacrifice, (16) childbirth, (17) death/murder, (18) people groups, (19) intimacy with God, (20) rainfall, (21) covenant, (22) law, (23) division of universal language into multiple languages, (24) faith, and (25) prayer.

Moses authored Genesis, and the reasons for accepting this position were discovered in the preceding section. From all indications, he wrote the book from the plains of Moab, a desolate patch of land that is located in Transjordan (i.e., modern Jordan), across from Jericho (Num 22:1; 26:63), while Israel was poised to traverse the Jordan Rift Valley and enter Canaan from the east. The Israelites were about to cross into the Promised Land that would flow with milk and honey, as long as they would remain faithful to God (Exod 3:8; Deut 6:3), who was about to unleash a judgment of catastrophic wrath against the wicked Canaanites (Gen 15:16; Exod 23:23).

In Abram's day (2166–1991 BC), God considered that the wickedness of the Amorites and other inhabitants of Canaan was not yet complete (Gen 15:16). By the time that the Israelite conquest of Canaan was carried out under Joshua (1406–1400 BC), however, God must have determined that their wickedness had become complete. Yet he knew that his covenant people would not eliminate the wicked peoples of the land utterly and completely, as he had instructed them to do (Deut 7:1–2).

Therefore, He-who-is furnished the Israelites with Genesis 1–11 as a vaccination against the adverse effects that would occur as a result of their constant exposure to the poisonous worldview that the Canaanites embraced, in order to allow his chosen race to live skillfully and successfully among peoples with a lifestyle that is antithetical to a God-centered worldview. He-who-is expressly warned the nation of Israel in reference to the wicked Canaanites, "For they will turn your sons away from following me to serve other gods. Then the anger of He-who-is will be kindled against you" (Deut 7:4). God, out of kindness and the desire to prevent his people from falling away from him and being subject to his fury, thus provided his people with a God-centered worldview, so that they could thrive among the godless peoples who would continue to live among them in Canaan for many centuries to come.

One of the lessons that Moses taught the Israelites is how sin entered the world (Gen 3:1–19). God enabled a snake—which was possessed by Satan and given a voice to speak, with which it distorted the truth—to persuade Adam and Eve that God had deprived them of having their eyes opened, since eating the fruit of which God instructed them not to eat would enable them to be as God is: one who understands the difference between good and evil (Gen 3:5). With this temptation as a carrot that was dangled in front of them, the man and woman disobeyed God. While eating a forbidden fruit is not even close to the worst possible offense they could commit, the point is that they disobeyed the only prohibition God established for them, and he who fails at just one of God's commands is indeed guilty of every possible offense (Jas 2:10).

Of equal importance, the root of this sin is the exaltation of self to a position reserved for God alone. Their free will became their enemy when they utilized this faculty to produce perpetual enmity between God and themselves. The most difficult part of theodicy (i.e., the problem of evil) to resolve philosophically is how evil could have entered into the created universe and the human race when (1) God created the entire universe, with no outside source having created any part of it, and (2) God exists as a completely holy being, unable to participate in immoral activities or be tainted with evil in any way. If God truly is holy, and he actually did create everything, he cannot be responsible for the creation of evil. This problem is unaddressed in the Bible but was resolved best philosophically by Augustine, who proposed that evil is the privation of love.

For Augustine, evil is not an entity that can be counted among the components in the universe, such as mankind, animals, plants, or celestial bodies. Instead, evil is the corrupting of something already created: love, which is an inanimate object. One way to picture this is as if God were emitting ray after ray of love at Adam and Eve. The correct and God-ordained response to the receiving of these rays of love would be for them to send those rays of love back to God, which establishes an endless loop of selfless love. When they chose to disobey God by attempting to take for themselves something that was forbidden, in an entirely selfish act, in essence they circumvented the love-rays loop by pointing those rays back at themselves, rather than at God. With this act, they transformed selfless love into selfish evil. They did not *create* something new in a universe that God alone created (John 1:3), along with all of its component parts, but instead they *corrupted* something pure that was in existence already, which God introduced into the universe for a holy and benevolent purpose.

The love-corrupting act performed by Adam and Eve introduced evil into the created order, a fate from which the present earth and the universe cannot escape. In Rom 5:12–14, Paul noted that through one man sin entered into the world, and death through sin. The man of whom he was speaking is Adam, since Paul went on to state that death reigned in this world from Adam to Moses, even over those who did not commit exactly the same sin that Adam committed. The evil that entered the world through Adam increased on the earth so greatly that by the time it found its way to Nimrod, he carried out a plan to conquer cities and nations as he expanded his kingdom northward through Mesopotamia and into Assyria, among other directions.

Adam's and Eve's evil act of eating a forbidden fruit quickly was outdone by one of their very own children, as mankind's sin dramatically worsened from simple disobedience to the murder of one's own sibling (Gen 4:1–16). When their sons, Cain and Abel, had become of sufficient age, Cain became jealous after God looked at his brother's offering favorably but looked at his offering without any favor at all. This jealousy caused Cain to become "exceedingly angry" (Gen 4:5), which in turn drove him to the brink of uncontrolled rage. Having seen this transformation due to Cain's inner turmoil, God asked him a riveting question: "Why is *your anger* kindled for you, and why has your countenance fallen? If you do *that which is* right, will it not be accepted? Yet if you do not do *that which is* right, sin is crouching at the door, and its desire is for you. But you, yourself, must be master over it" (Gen 4:6–7).

God so deeply desired for Cain to avoid committing a terrible crime against Abel, his own flesh and blood, that he personally communicated with Adam's son in a last-minute effort to deter him from committing a horrifically evil deed. Actually, God laid out what would become a timeless principle for millennia to come when he informed Cain that Cain, himself, is responsible for mastering the inner urge to bring great physical harm to his brother out of jealousy. If God placed the onus squarely on Cain, then Cain possessed *all* of the inner faculties to master his sin nature, even though this occurred at a time in human history long before the permanent indwelling of the Holy Spirit, which began at Pentecost during the 1st century AD (Acts 2:4). Cain had everything he needed to resist the temptation to surrender himself to evil's lethal grip.

Instead, Cain rose up against his brother and killed him while they were out in the field together (Gen 4:8), obviously implying that Cain chose a time and a place when no one would be there to see him or stop him from carrying out his dastardly plan. To Cain's shame, when God came along afterward and asked him where his brother is, he answered, "I do not know. Am I my brother's guardian?" (Gen 4:9). Cain attempted to cover up his crime when he boldly lied to God by declaring that he had no idea where Abel is. Since Abel's life was extinguished by his own brother, obviously Cain would have known that his brother's body was lying exactly where it went limp at the moment of the murder. God's displeasure and judgment of Cain is seen in how he cursed Cain from agricultural success (Gen 4:11), the very area of his own profession (Gen 4:3). Within one generation, the manifestation of evil worsened exponentially by going from disobedience about the eating of a particular food to the murder of one's own blood brother.

Moses did not document a great deal about the lives of people in the generations soon after Adam's children, but a story is recorded about Cain's great-great-great-grandson, Lamech. A young man somehow wounded him, whether this implies a physical or an emotional wound, and for this, Lamech killed him (Gen 4:23). The placement of this story in the narrative, between the recounting of Cain's killing of Abel and the birth of Seth to Eve as a replacement for Abel (Gen 4:25), is Moses's way of informing his readers that the acts of extreme evil committed by people within mankind's first six generations reflect the way in which humanity quickly was spinning out of control and heading for a destructive crash. With no law to regulate relationships or protect the sanctity of human life, along with no repercussions for evil deeds, there were no restraints on the sin nature. A world tainted by perpetual sin proved unable to sustain itself without any law.

God clearly took notice of this increase in wickedness on the part of mankind. Moreover, he also implicated the evildoers of the spiritual realm in Gen 6:1–4, when evil spirit-beings were allowed to take on human flesh. These debased angels then forced themselves on the women who had descended from Adam's line, creating offspring with the intention of corrupting the purely human line that God intended to continue all of the way down to the Messiah, whose bloodline was to pass solely through the line of the first woman (Gen 3:15). As noted above, Moses referred to these angelic beings in corporeal form with three terms: sons of God, fallen ones, and powerful ones. This vile sin effectually became the straw that broke the camel's back, as God determined that his only course of action was to restart the human race afresh.

Due to how sin was so rampant among mankind and creatures on earth, the course of action that God chose is to destroy not only the entire human race in a global flood, except for Noah's family, but every living creature, except for marine animals and those that he preserved in the ark that Noah built (Gen 6:1–8:22). One clue as to why the animal kingdom on land is known to have been equally guilty of causing great harm to mankind is found in Gen 9:5. There, in the passage that presents human history's first law, known as capital punishment, animals and mankind would be held accountable for killing people. The text states of those who kill humans that God "will demand it [i.e., the creature's life] from the hand of every living thing," just as he would demand "the life of the man from the hand of mankind, from his fellow man."

In other words, not only was God requiring that any person who takes the life of another person be put to death by fellow human beings, but any non-human creature (i.e., animal) that takes the life of a person was to be killed by the people who apprehend that creature. For this reason, wildlife experts in India today correctly believe that taking the life of a tiger that kills human beings is essential, because this animal will be prone to killing people again if it is allowed to live. If this law was instituted in Gen 9:5 to protect against animals and humans who kill people, then the reason for introducing the law is that this act of evil was commonplace in the antediluvian world. Such murder seemingly was a routine event, with little or no retribution or deterrence. God offered the law of capital punishment to mankind as a way to protect the sanctity of human life, because mankind uniquely bears the image and likeness of God within (Gen 1:26–27).

God's way of ridding the world of the effects of humans and wildlife that were committing acts of uncontrolled wickedness—and of evil angelic beings that were attempting to taint the purely human line that had to pass from Adam to Messiah (Luke 3:23–38)—was to unleash a global flood on the earth. The text specifies that the rain lasted for 40 days and 40 nights, and that the underground aquifers of the earth released their waters onto the surface of the earth, as "all of the springs of the great deep burst, and the windows of the sky were opened" (Gen 7:11). How devastating was this flood on earth?

The Bible says that "all flesh perished: the thing crawling on the earth, along with the bird, the animal, the living things, and every swarming thing that swarms on the earth, along with all mankind. Everything that in its nostrils was the breath of the spirit of life, from all that were on dry land, they died" (Gen 7:21–22). No person who was not on the ark with Noah escaped, along with no creature from the animal world, whether one that flew or one that crawled on the ground. The flood took no prisoners, and it did not discriminate among its victims. If this flood actually was a local one—as some interpreters have concluded—rather than a worldwide one, then the miraculous nature of the event is all the more impressive, because a local flood simply does not have the destructive force to rid the world of every living creature that does not reside within a body of water.

With the end of the global flood that devastated all life on the earth, the landing of the ark represents a fresh start for mankind and the animal kingdom. Many theologians have called Noah the 'new Adam' for this very reason. At the same time, not enough attention has centered on the traumatic effect that the annihilation of humanity must have had on Noah and his family. The emotional weight of this catastrophe undoubtedly wreaked havoc on the man who had spent his whole life living in the antediluvian world, and perhaps this immense amount of stress contributed to Noah's surrender of himself to the intoxicating wine that he produced after he became a man of the ground and planted a vineyard (Gen 9:20–21).

Moses's recounting of what happened during one of Noah's episodes of drunkenness has indirect but potentially profound implications for the present study on the life of Nimrod (Gen 9:18–29). During Noah's intoxicated stupor, he uncovered himself inside of his tent (Gen 9:21), implying that his clothes were removed and that he was standing in the nude. When Adam and Eve recognized their nakedness after they ate of the forbidden fruit of the tree of the knowledge of good and evil, they sewed fig leaves together and covered their private areas to hide their nakedness from one another (Gen 3:6–7). This demonstrates the inner shame that comes with being naked in the presence of others, a natural sense that would have been dulled in Noah's case, given that he was under the mind-numbing effects of the alcohol in the wine.

What happened next seemingly left a lasting legacy on numerous races of people. Noah's son, Ham, was the only person who gazed at his father's nakedness when the patriarch was walking around in the nude while inside of his tent. What course of action did Ham take? He walked outside of the tent, tattled on his naked father to his two brothers, Shem and Japheth, and let them troubleshoot the problem on their own (Gen 9:22–23). Ham's action led to a fascinating result that has intrigued interpreters for ages. Rather than discussing any potential impact these actions had on Ham, Moses simply noted that Noah's response to these events was to curse Ham's son, Canaan, who was not the one directly responsible for his father's handling of the drunken foolishness of his grandfather. Why did Moses curse Canaan, and not Ham?

After all, Ham evidently is the one who committed the wrongdoing, at least in Noah's eyes. The only mistake that the story seems to imply is that Ham broadcasted his father's shame to his two brothers rather than discreetly covering up his father's shame. Moreover, he left the two of them to deal with Noah's shameful state of nakedness rather than solving the problem on his own. Truthfully, Shem and Japheth never even had to know about their father's compromising situation, as Ham should have kept the indiscretion to himself and taken care of it before his brothers even entered the tent. Now the focus can be brought back to why Moses describes Noah's cursing as being on Canaan, and not on Ham, the actual perpetrator.

The beginning of the answer to this question is rooted in why Moses would have singled out Canaan for attention. The Israelites were on the verge of entering the land of Canaan at the time that Moses wrote Genesis, and they knew that God intended to judge the Canaanites for their utterly wicked deeds by using God's chosen people to annihilate them completely, as well as any living thing within their cities (Deut 20:16–18). Moses knew that his countrymen needed to understand the divine rationale for carrying out the utter devastation of the people of the land that they were about to dispossess. Moses also wanted them to understand why they should not embrace the deities, worldview, or practices of the Canaanites whom they would spare, in obvious disobedience of God's categorical commission to exterminate every last one of them.

With all of these personal connections that the Israelites were about to have with the Canaanites, Moses wanted to inform his readers how Canaan, the ancestor of the Canaanites who lived in the land that the Israelites were about to acquire, had received the terrible curse placed on him—and thus on his descendants—by Noah. What exactly is the curse placed on Canaan? Noah said that "Canaan is being cursed. A servant of servants he will be to his brothers. . . . May He-who-is go on being blessed, God of Shem, and may Canaan be a servant to him. May God enlarge to Japheth, and may he live in the tents of Shem, and may Canaan be a servant to him" (Gen 9:25–27). Therefore, the curse on Canaan is that his descendants would act as servants for the descendants of Shem and Japheth.

At this point, many people object that the curse on Canaan is unfair, given that Ham committed the improper act against Noah. In reality, though, Moses never stated that Ham was *not* cursed, only that Canaan *was* cursed. For all anyone knows, Noah also may have cursed Ham, which Moses simply did not see the need to record, or his source simply did not know. Therefore, the notion that a curse was placed on Ham also is absolutely plausible. Another possibility is that Canaan somehow participated in the crime, or perhaps reacted to his father's indiscretion in a disrespectful or inappropriate way, such as mocking or laughing at his grandfather. A third possibility is that out of mercy, God prevented the curse from being extended to all of Ham's line, limiting its impact to only one of Ham's sons. Considering all of these possibilities, one should not object to the validity of the curse on Canaan, especially since Moses omitted so many elements of the story.

Another event that occurred before the Nimrod story is the narrative in Gen 11:1–9 about why different languages are spoken on the earth, which is due to how Babel's residents conspired together to exalt themselves and make a name for themselves. The text notes that all of the earth had (i.e., spoke) one language at this time, as the words they used were common to one another. "It came about with their moving from the east that they found a plain in the land of Šumer, and they settled there" (Gen 11:1–2). The land of Šumer is located in the southernmost part of Mesopotamia, just to the north(west) of the Persian Gulf.

A Šumerian myth called *Enmerkar and the Lord of Aratta*, which was composed in the neo-Šumerian period of the Third Dynasty of Ur (i.e., the 21st century BC), describes how Enki, the god of the sweetwater Apsu (i.e., the earth's underground freshwater aquifers), changed mankind's language. According to Thorkild Jacobsen's translation, "Enki, . . . lord of Eridu, changed the languages in their mouths, as many as he had put there, the languages of mankind, which were one." In other words, an extremely ancient extra-biblical text from the culture recognized as the birthplace of civilization describes how the singular language of mankind that all of the people of the world spoke ended when the patron deity of Eridu "changed the languages" that were "in their mouths." This astounding account, which attributes the altering of languages to the wrong god, attests to an earlier time when one universal language actually existed, affirming Moses's later claim that "all of the earth had one language" (Gen 11:1) before God stopped the builders from completing the tower.

By using brick for stone and tar for mortar, the residents built for themselves "a city, along with a tower, with its top in the sky" (Gen 11:4). One commonly held view is that the entire population of the earth gathered themselves together at this city. However, the text simply does not support this view, and there is no reason whatsoever to embrace it. All that the text states along these lines is that "all of the earth had one language" (Gen 11:1). The fact that all of the earth spoke one language cannot be extrapolated to infer that all inhabitants on the earth moved to one particular residential site. Most English translations add that these events "came to pass with their [i.e., mankind's] moving to the east" (Gen 11:2), but the Hebrew text instead states that people traveled "from the east," seemingly implying westward movement. During the process of mankind's migration, some of the descendants of Noah settled on a plain in the land of Šumer. However, there is no reason to doubt that descendants of Noah's also migrated to the north, to the east, and to the south.

Moreover, the text never even states that all of those who migrated to the west came to the site of this city and its tower. Its location simply is one site where people settled and built a city (i.e., an urban center). Of course, the city must have been impressive, because building it and its tower required many of the components of urbanization. Allegedly, the people built the city so that they would not "be scattered over the surface of the entire earth," and they built the tower so that they could "make a name for" themselves (Gen 11:4). The urbanites' mantra directly violated God's instruction for Noah and his descendants not only to "be fruitful and multiply" but to "swarm on the earth" (Gen 9:7). In other words, they were instructed to spread out over the surface of the earth, which is the opposite of crowding themselves into one concentrated location.

Building the tower to make a name for themselves not only implies that people in other cities, towns, and locations would be impressed with their achievement while visiting, but that the builders were obsessed with the glory that would come with their feat. These characteristics are rooted in selfish pride, much along the same lines as Adam's and Eve's sinful desire to be like God, who knew the difference between good and evil, and to make themselves clever (Gen 3:5–6). In a fascinating statement, the people of the city expressed the fear that they may "be scattered over the surface of the entire earth." The object of their fear was not only in direct violation of God's command to spread out over the surface of the earth, but God's subsequent punishment involved the fulfillment of the very consequence that they dreaded if they had not built the city.

After He-who-is "came down" to view the city and the tower that the sons of mankind had built, he said, "Notice, *these* people are one, and the language is the same for all of them. Since they have begun to construct this *tower*, so now nothing will be impossible for them *in* all that they plan to do. Come, let us go down there and confuse their language so that *every* man will not understand the language of his neighbor" (Gen 11:6–7). God's ultimate issue with these people was that they ignored his command to spread out on the earth, and that they desired to make a name for themselves, as opposed to making a name for God. Given God's reservation with their residence in an urban environment while speaking the same language, since that would increase the pride that would be gained through their further accomplishments, he ultimately compelled them to obey his command to spread out over the surface of the earth.

By dividing them into groups that would not know the languages of other groups, God reduced the potential for innovations that lead to greater pride and the exaltation of self. This should not be viewed as an elimination of mankind's tendency toward self-exaltation through acts of pride, but rather a mitigation of the level of damaging acts that spawn from pride. According to the text, He-who-is indeed scattered them from there over the surface of the entire earth, and they stopped building the city.

Therefore, he called the city *Babel* (i.e., "Confusion") because there he confused the language of the entire earth, and from there he scattered them over the surface of the entire earth (Gen 11:8–9). The construction of the city and the tower came to a halt when God supernaturally changed their languages. This would have caused enormous stress and confusion among every nationality, inciting the people to anger, which undoubtedly led to resentment, then outright violence. The only way to escape the emotional stress and chaos that ensued was to pack up and leave the city.

Since people-groups spoke unique languages during the historical period, after the advent of writing, God undoubtedly changed the pre-historical peoples' languages according to family trees. The other sign of the certainty of this deduction comes from the naming of Abram's ancestral people group as Habiru/Hebrews. During the childhood or youth of Peleg, the "earth was divided" with the events at the city of Babel (Gen 10:25). Peleg's father was Eber, which can be deduced properly in Akkadian as Heber, so the family line whose language was created on that day is named after their progenitor, Eber/Heber. Since Babel *was not* the only place where people lived, this changing of languages must have occurred not only to the people living in this city, but to people living all over the earth, as far as they had migrated since the landing of the ark.

The story surrounding the events that took place at the tower of Babel—most notably the segregating of people on the earth according to languages, which forced them to live apart from one another in separate locations as a general rule, with exceptions—thus sets the stage for the appearance of Nimrod, who invaded city after city and slaughtered great numbers of foreign-language-speaking populations during a later period. With this as a background, one task taken up in this book is to discover what lesson God intended to teach Israel through the story of Nimrod's biography, to prepare the nation and its leaders to live successfully within their own land and—in the anticipatory foreknowledge of God—the eventual leadership by an earthly king (Deut 17:14). Nimrod's story documents the world's first empire builder, someone who had no regard for the sovereignty of national borders or a king's right to rule the city where he served as its official monarch.

CHAPTER 2

PIN THE TAIL ON THE DONKEY

BLIND GUESSES AT NIMROD'S IDENTITY

HAVING STUDIED THE FLOW OF EVENTS IN biblical history leading up to the passage about Nimrod, the time has come to survey some of the errant theories for connecting him to a historical figure in antiquity. He is thought by some to be heroic, while by others to be devious. He is considered by some to be a mere mortal, though by others to be divine. While the goal of the book is to determine—if at all possible—whether Nimrod's biography can be matched confidently with any known figure from antiquity, the goal of this chapter is to sift through numerous options that have been presented as attempts to pinpoint the identity of this enigmatic figure, and to demonstrate why they have failed. In order to accomplish this endeavor, both tasks will require a careful look at relevant exegetical data in the biblical text, and at the archaeological record that serves to inform the field of ANE historical studies, a vital cognate to biblical studies.

NIMROD AS NINURTA, THE GOD OF WAR

The first opinion on the identity of Nimrod is that he was Ninurta, the patron god of Lagash, whose name (*Nin Ur*) means, "god of war." Ninurta, son of Enlil (the Šumerian king of the gods) and Ninlil (Enlil's consort), was the Šumerian god of the southerly wind, and as such he was the god of war, who destroys rebellious lands. The oldest myth in which Ninurta acts as a divine warrior is *LUGAL-E*, which describes Ninurta as a great and powerful warrior-king who vanquished a mighty monster in the mountains that were located to the east of Mesopotamia. As Brian Colless suggested, "It amounts to this: NiMRoD can derive from NiNuRT," and "the warlike god Ninurta, associated with Sargon's city of Kish, was a counterpart to Sargon the Great as a young conquering hero."

According to Šumerian religion, Ninurta also served as the great hunter, who was thought to protect the land in and around southern Mesopotamia from all forms of beasts and demons. Following the reign of an Assyrian king of the 9th century BC named Ashurnasirpal II, Ninurta was worshiped in Assyria as a major deity, particularly in relation to his purported role as hunter and god of war. Due to these alleged connections with Nimrod, scholars such as Peter Van der Veen, Uwe Zerbst, Karel van der Toorn, and Pieter van der Horst have proposed that Nimrod's identity as Ninurta is highly probable.

Colless certainly is correct about the possible linguistic correlation between the names *Nimrod* and *Ninurta*, and the possibility does exist that Nimrod's Hebrew name derives from Ninurta's Mesopotamian (technically, Šumerian) name. Theophorics, human names that bear one or more elements of a divine name, often were assigned to people in the ancient world when it came time for them to be named. Linguistically, a N→M nasal shift, as in Colless's NiNuRT to NiMRoD proposal, is attested among ancient languages, as these letters produce similar nasal sounds that vary from language to language. Colless's suggested T→D dental shift also is attested, as these two letters produce dental sounds and vary between *t* and *d* in antiquity.

Even modern German uses a pronunciational D→T dental shift when a *d* comes at the end of a word. So, certainly the possibility exists that Nimrod's name, as such, derives from Ninurta's name. Nonetheless, this plausible connection does not imply that they are one-and-the-same person, as perhaps *Nimrod* was a personal name that derived from Ninurta's divine name, which Colless also suggested as a possibility. Nimrod's fame undoubtedly could have led future generations to connect him to the Šumerian god of war so closely that he took on that name, or a version close to it, postmortem. However, associating Nimrod, a biblical king, with Ninurta, the Šumerian god of war, as the same individual possesses two fatal flaws.

The first fatal flaw regarding the theory that Nimrod is Ninurta relates to actual exploits. Nimrod was seen to possess a human kingdom, over which he ruled and commanded an enormous number of warriors, which neither

Šumerian, Akkadian, nor Assyrian mythology ever asserted as being true of Ninurta. Moreover, Nimrod's kingdom included specific cities over which he maintained control, but these were cities that Ninurta never controlled, even if cult centers devoted to him were located in one or more of them over the course of history. Ruling over a city and being worshiped in a city as a god are two completely different matters.

The second fatal flaw regarding the theory that Nimrod is Ninurta relates to genealogical background. According to Genesis 5 and 10, Nimrod was fully human, having derived ultimately from Adam, through Ham and Cush. Ninurta was a Šumerian, Akkadian, and Assyrian deity, with no genealogical tree. As the apostle Paul categorically declared, there is no such thing as an idol that actually exists as a living being in the world, because there is no god but one (1 Cor 8:4): the exclusive creator of the universe who is eternal and omnipresent. Therefore, while there are numerous general similarities between Nimrod and Ninurta, this Mesopotamian god of war, a mere concept of a being that never lived existentially, fails at more than one biographical requirement. In order for a candidate to remain a legitimate option for being equated with Nimrod, he must fulfill *all* of the biographical requirements that are recorded in Genesis 10.

NIMROD AS GILGAMESH, A KING OF URUK

Some people have equated the legendary Mesopotamian hero Gilgamesh with Nimrod. Controversy long has surrounded the question of whether Gilgamesh is a historical personage or a mythological figure, since he is depicted as a semi-divine hero in several Šumerian epics. He also has been attributed with possessing superhuman strength, as he allegedly built the city walls of the southern Mesopotamian city of Uruk to defend his people from danger, and he travelled to meet a sage who had survived the global flood. However, the *Šumerian King List*, an ancient document that sequentially lists the reigns of the kings of Šumer, claims that Gilgamesh maintained kingship over Uruk, as he is listed as the fifth king of the First Dynasty of Uruk.

For this reason, most scholars now consider him to have been a historical personage, even if his career has been embellished through literary exaggeration. For David P. Livingston, the biblical archaeologist who founded the Associates for Biblical Research (https://biblearchaeology.org/) in 1969, the parallels between Nimrod and Gilgamesh were enough to persuade him that they are one and the same person. Gilgamesh certainly exercised tyranny, controlled territory by his own strength, opposed deity, and did his utmost to convince people to forsake that deity.

Livingston even called Gilgamesh "a type of early city founder" and contended that the Gilgamesh hero set out to kill Huwawa (a.k.a. Humbaba), the monstrous giant who is said to be the perpetrator of the universal flood. After all, Gilgamesh took his legendary friend Enkidu—a figure whom some have called a monstrous wild-man—with him on the long journey to Cedar Mountain in order to find and destroy this culprit who unleashed the flood onto the world. Gilgamesh found Huwawa and eventually cut off the creature's head. Finally, Livingston took issue with Gilgamesh's statement to Enkidu, when Gilgamesh declared that he would make a name for himself if he were to fall in battle while attempting to slay the giant.

While Gilgamesh bears many characteristic traits and qualities in common with Nimrod, many other figures in ancient Mesopotamian history likewise possess similar traits (e.g., Ur-Nammu, Shulgi, Amar-Sin, Hammurabi), so there is no reason to prefer Gilgamesh on this basis. Another notable flaw with this view is that there are no historical inscriptions attesting to Gilgamesh, so the veracity of his historicity cannot be established conclusively. A third notable flaw with this view is that Gilgamesh is not known to have founded any cities or built smaller settlements into great cities, as did Nimrod. Gilgamesh was the king of Uruk, if the *Šumerian King List* is correct, but there is no record of his conquest of any Šumerian cities, let alone his subjugation of the cities of northern Mesopotamia and expansion of building operations there. History judges Gilgamesh as a king who did not amass an empire, even if he actually is a historical figure who ruled as a king.

A fourth notable flaw with this view is related to Gilgamesh's alleged attempt to find and kill the individual who is responsible for having sent the flood to destroy all life on the earth. While the record of this event is no more than a mythological account, even if it were taken as reflective of the truth about Gilgamesh's character, this does nothing to connect Gilgamesh with Nimrod any more than it would connect any other candidate to him.

The biblical account knows nothing of Nimrod's attempt to lash out at God for sending the flood that wiped out mankind, apart from Noah's family. In short, Gilgamesh cannot be considered a plausible option for Nimrod's historical identity, since the weaknesses of this view far outweigh any perceived strengths that are put forward to support it.

NIMROD AS AMENHOTEP III, A PHARAOH OF EGYPT

An Egyptologist of the 20th century named Kurt Sethe identified Nimrod with Pharaoh Amenhotep III (*ca.* 1407–1370 BC) of Egypt's 18th Dynasty. This pharaoh was known for his great hunting expeditions, and according to Sethe, he also boasted of extending his rule to the Euphrates, although there is no historical evidence to substantiate that he controlled any territory in Asia beyond the southern Levant and the coastal region of the northern Levant. One attractive element about this view is that it avoids the 'Cush problem,' meaning that many scholars are more comfortable with assigning Africa, and not Mesopotamia, as the location to where Cush moved his family immediately after the universal flood of Noah's day.

Traditionally, many have proposed that biblical Cush was located immediately to the south of Egypt, in the region that ANE scholars refer to as Nubia (i.e., modern Sudan), but which has been referred to in the Septuagint (i.e., the Greek translation of the Hebrew Bible) as Ethiopia (Greek: *Aithiopia*). Actually, most of Cush's descendants listed in Gen 10:7 seem to have settled in Mesopotamia and Arabia, not in Africa. Given that the story of Nimrod's life was set in Mesopotamia, and not in Africa or anywhere west of the Euphrates, the notion of an African Cush should be considered highly suspect at best.

The connection of Amenhotep III with Nimrod actually creates more problems than it solves. The first insurmountable flaw with this view is that it ignores vital aspects of Mesopotamian geography that are integral to Nimrod's biography. The geographical context of the story of Nimrod's life is undoubtedly Mesopotamia, as Moses refers to a king who had ventured from Šumer (i.e., in southernmost Mesopotamia) to Assyria (to the northeast of the Tigris River). Moreover, no Egyptian king ever controlled this land between the two rivers (i.e., the Euphrates River and the Tigris

River) or Assyria. Amenhotep III never even controlled northeastern Syria, let alone extended his domain to the Euphrates River or beyond.

The closest that any pharaoh came to controlling part of Mesopotamia is when Thutmose III (*ca.* 1504–1450 BC), the great-grandfather of Amenhotep III, advanced as far as the Euphrates River in Year 33, crossed the river in pursuit of attacking his enemies from Mitanni, and destroyed the cities and towns along the Euphrates by putting them to the torch, events that are described on the Gebel Barkal Stele. Therefore, no Egyptian pharaoh is a viable candidate for a conqueror and controller of vital Mesopotamian cities, let alone key Assyrian cities to the northeast of the Tigris River.

The second insurmountable flaw with connecting Nimrod to Amenhotep III is that according to proper biblical chronology, Moses died in the very year after Amenhotep III took the throne. As argued comprehensively in the author's 2021 book, *Origins of the Hebrews*, the correct year for the exodus is 1446 BC, which is substantiated by a literal and proper reading of the term "480th year" in 1 Kgs 6:1 and by extra-biblical records such as the Jubilee cycles, the Tyrian King List, and the Parian Marble. The year 1446 BC coincides with Year 7 of the reign of Amenhotep II, the only candidate for the exodus pharaoh from Egypt's 18th or 19th Dynasty who meets all of the measurable biographical requirements of the exodus pharaoh.

Since (1) Moses lived until his death at 120 years of age (Deut 34:7), (2) Moses departed from Egypt when he "was fulfilling 40 years of age" (Acts 7:23), (3) Moses experienced the burning-bush incident only "after 40 years had passed" (Acts 7:30), and (4) the Israelites wandered in the desert for 40 years under Moses's leadership before entering the Promised Land (Num 32:13), the year in which Moses died and the Israelites crossed into Canaan had to be 1406 BC. Not only was Amenhotep III the grandson of the exodus pharaoh, but his reign did not begin until 1407 BC, which is within one year of Moses's death. Not by any stretch of the imagination could Amenhotep III have completed all of the conquests listed in Gen 10:10–11 within one year, let alone provide Moses with time to document these victories in the book of Genesis before his death.

Due to these two major flaws, Sethe's view that identifies Nimrod with Pharaoh Amenhotep III must be rejected emphatically. It goes without saying that Kurt Sethe (1869–1934) is one of the leading Egyptologists of the 20th century, but his choice for a historical figure with whom to identify Nimrod is fully unjustifiable. Sethe certainly can be commended for his selection of a human candidate for biblical Nimrod, but the view's main selling point is merely that it avoids the alleged 'Cush problem,' which even if viewed as a solution to an actual problem hardly overcomes the flaws that the view possesses. Nimrod and Amenhotep III are not the same person, even though this view was proposed by one of the top scholars in his field.

SECTION II

NIMROD'S IDENTITY IN GENESIS 10

CHAPTER 3

CONNECTING THE PERSONAL DOTS

NIMROD'S BLOODLINE AND BLOODTHIRSTINESS

NIMROD'S GENEALOGICAL BACKGROUND

MOSES OFFERED NIMROD'S GENEALOGICAL BACKGROUND IN GEN 10:7–8a. Oddly enough, a number of studies specifically devoted to the identification of Nimrod do not even include Gen 10:7 as one of the applicable verses when they list the passage in Genesis 10 that is devoted to Nimrod's biography, instead opting for Gen 10:8–12 as being sufficient. Yigal Levin admitted that the received text of Genesis attaches Gen 10:8–12 to the genealogy of the sons of Ham in Gen 10:6–7, but he also declared that the Nimrod-narrative was affixed to the genealogy of Ham by the J source, probably because it is too difficult for him to accept the tradition that links Nimrod to Cush. Levin's use of the term "J source" is a reference to a hypothetical writer called the Yahwist/Jahwist, who supposedly wrote a part of the Pentateuch. According to this higher critical view, Moses was not the author, and these first five books of the Bible were not composed by 1406 BC, as biblical chronology and the internal evidence within the Bible require.

The concept of a Yahwistic author is part of the Documentary Hypothesis that originally was proposed by Julius Wellhausen in 1883. Wellhausen dated the alleged composition of J to the 10th or 11th century BC, but critical scholars of modern times have downdated the timing of J's alleged authorship either to the Babylonian captivity (587–537 BC) or to the time after the Medo-Persian Empire (539–334 BC) conquered the Neo-Babylonian Empire in 539 BC. However, the concept of hypothetical, non-Mosaic authors of the Pentateuch should be evaluated as an arbitrary assertion that is rooted in pure speculation. Without any textual evidence disconnecting Gen 10:8–12 from the genealogy that traces Nimrod to Cush or Ham, and without any inscriptional or archaeological evidence for a J source or its elusive author, Levin's opposition to leaving these verses in their present position is unconvincing and unacceptable.

ABSENCE OF NIMROD AMONG THE SONS OF CUSH

According to Gen 10:6, Cush is listed first among the four *bane* ("sons") of Ham: Cush, Mizraim, Put, and Canaan. Gen 10:7 lists male descendants for only two of Ham's offspring: Cush (Ham's biological son) and Raamah (Cush's biological son). In fact, Cush is listed as having five sons of his own: Seba, Hawilah, Sabtah, Raamah, and Sabteca. The two sons attributed to Raamah are Sheba and Dedan. Therefore, Moses lists two generations that descended directly from Cush, with Sheba and Dedan being his grandsons.

Both of the father-son relationships are denoted with *ben* ("son") in this verse, just as in Gen 10:6, where four sons are listed as having been born to Ham. Of crucial importance to the proper position of Nimrod in his family's genealogical tree, his name is conspicuously absent from the list of Cush's sons and grandsons in Gen 10:7. This detail becomes crucial in Gen 10:8, where the text states that Cush sired Nimrod. Nimrod's displacement from the list of Cush's biological children in Gen 10:7 infers that when Moses wrote the next verse, Nimrod almost certainly is not being counted among Cush's children or grandchildren, a conclusion that becomes completely understandable after studying the Hebrew words that Moses used in these instances.

NIMROD AS A REMOTE DESCENDANT OF CUSH

While the verb *yalad* ("beget, bring forth, sire") most naturally refers to a mother who bears a child, it also is possible for a man to be in view, and thus a father who has sired a son. Therefore, here Cush is said to have sired Nimrod. For two reasons, however, Cush should not be viewed as the biological father of Nimrod: (1) Nimrod is not listed among the five sons of Cush in Gen 10:7, a list that should be viewed as comprehensive for male offspring. What is more, Nimrod is not even listed among the (two) grandsons of Cush who are named in this verse. Clearly the author is inferring that Nimrod is not a near descendant of Cush. (2) The contrast between bəne ("sons of") from Gen 10:7 and *yalad* from Gen 10:8a functions as a marker indicating a qualitative difference between Cush's position as the father of his sons and the grandfather of his grandsons versus Cush's siring of Nimrod.

Nimrod thus should be understood only as being a remote descendant of Cush, clearly beyond even the possibility of his being a grandson, given that Cush's noteworthy grandsons already are named as sons of one of Cush's sons. If Moses had intended to communicate to his readers that Nimrod was a son or grandson of Cush, he would have included Nimrod in the proper list of sons and grandsons that he just had enumerated. Moreover, as Victor Hamilton has observed, the table of nations listed in Genesis 10 uses the word *bəne* to emphasize the ancestor, whereas it deploys *yalad* to accentuate the descendant. Therefore, while Gen 10:8a focuses the reader's attention on Nimrod, as a remote descendant of Cush, the text offers no indication whatsoever as to just how distant of a descendant he is.

There should be no objection to Cush's 'siring' a remote descendant, since this concept is not exclusive to the Cush-Nimrod relationship. The cognate noun *yeled* ("son, child, descendant") is used of a wide range of progeny, including later descendants, and the use of a term of close kinship to refer to a distant descendant is not foreign to biblical authors. In Isa 29:23, the prophet records the words of God, who states that "when he [Jacob] sees his children, . . . they will sanctify my name." Since Isaiah lived over 1000 years after Jacob, there can be no denying that descendants are the children in view, not biological sons or daughters.

An example from the Greek New Testament is the use of "son of David" in the gospels as a designation for Jesus (Matt 9:27; Mark 10:47; et al.), which was used to demonstrate that Jesus's lineage traces back to David, who predated him by roughly 1000 years. A second example from the New Testament, again without the use of the Hebrew word *yeled*, is when Luke traced Jesus's lineage back to the origin of mankind, where he wrote, ". . . the son of Seth, the son of Adam, the son of God" (Luke 3:38). In a non-biological sense, Adam is considered the son of God here. Yet in Deut 32:18, Moses declared that the people "neglected the rock who bore you and forgot the God who gave birth to you." Therefore, here Moses calls remote 'descendants' of God those whom he bore, although they had their own biological fathers and were far removed from God genealogically, per Luke 3:38.

In summary, Moses describes Nimrod's genealogical background in Gen 10:7–8a in a way that makes him a remote descendant of Cush, although the text offers no indication whatsoever as to just how generationally distant of a descendant he is. Moses's use of Hebrew terminology and his clear avoidance of listing Nimrod among the sons and grandsons of Cush signals clearly to the reader that Nimrod cannot be counted among the male heirs of the first two generations immediately after Cush. For all that anyone can deduce from the text of Genesis 10, Nimrod easily may have lived centuries after Cush's lifetime.

NIMROD'S MORAL CHARACTER

Having completed the genealogical introduction to the life of Nimrod, Moses turns his attention to the topic of Nimrod's character. The question has been asked whether the Bible portrays Nimrod as a godly or an evil person. The subsequent text of Gen 10:8b–9 answers this question adequately enough on its own, but a clue might exist in the meaning of Nimrod's name. The name *Nimrod* may derive from the Hebrew verb *marad*, meaning "to rebel" (often against God). Some commentators agree with connecting his name to this verb, noting that his name means, "We will rebel." Others merely attribute the Midrash (i.e., ancient Jewish commentary on the Hebrew Bible that dates to the 2nd century AD or later) with making this association.

Scholarship is at a loss to explain why Nimrod would be called, "We-will-rebel," although Moses's choice probably does not reflect his given name or the name that he used of himself. Moses most likely chose to name Nimrod with a dysphemism, just as God changed the name of the city of Genesis 11 to *Babel* after he stopped its inhabitants from building a great tower to make a name for themselves. Another option, of course, is that Nimrod's name is a personal name that is a play on Ninurta's divine name (NiNuRT to NiMRoD), as Colless suggested, which amounts to a variant cognate of the attested form of the name of the god of war. However, ultimately the evidence is insufficient to be conclusive on the meaning of Nimrod's name.

NIMROD AS DISTINCT FROM HIS ANCESTORS, CONTEMPORARIES, AND SUCCESSORS

With no *waw*-conjunction used to connect the statement in Gen 10:8b with the previous one in Gen 10:8a, a new independent clause begins with the demonstrative pronoun *hu'* ("That one"). This word cannot be a relative pronoun that connects the former clause (Gen 10:8a) to the latter clause (Gen 10:8b), because the Hebrew relative pronoun is *'ašer* ("who, that, which"). Yet the NIV nonetheless opts to use a relative clause: "Nimrod, who grew to be . . . ," despite the clear formation of the Hebrew grammatical structure within the verse. When more precision *can* be used to translate from Hebrew, more precision *should* be used.

The subject of the Hebrew independent clause (*hu'*) should not be equated with the subject of the last clause: Cush. This is the case not only because the pronoun refers to the nearest antecedent ("Nimrod"), but because—as Hamilton correctly pointed out—the emphasis with the noun *yeled* is on the descendant, not the ancestor. The demonstrative pronoun is employed for an emphatic purpose, marking out Nimrod as distinct from among his ancestors, his contemporaries, and his successors. In other words, an interpretive rendering of the text could read, "THAT ONE, in contrast to all of those who came before him or after him, acted [in such-and-such a way]."

NIMROD AS ONE WHO ACTED IRREVERENTLY

The verb *halal* ("begin, profane") in Gen 10:8b presents a difficulty, because when it appears in the Hebrew Hiphil verbal stem, as here, the possibility for its meaning is quite varied. Moreover, no option perfectly suits how it fits within the clause syntactically. Gary Long considered that, "let be profaned, begin, make invalid," are all viable options for the Hiphil stem of this verb. Peter Van der Veen translated the verb, "became," but this meaning is not an established or accepted rendering for *halal*, despite this translation's appearance in the NASB and NASU. This translation would be suited better for the verb *hayah* ("be, become"), which is used in the subsequent infinitive construct *lihyot* ("in order to become") and as a verb in Gen 10:9, where van der Veen's translation fits perfectly ("he became a powerful conqueror").

Yigal Levin opted for translating Gen 10:8b in this manner: "he began to be a mighty man on earth," which follows the KJV and the NKJV for the rendering of the verb. While this translation is acceptable for the Hiphil's range of meaning, it does not suit the context at all, because an infinitive construct with a *lamed*-prefix, denoting purpose or result, immediately follows the main verb. This would render the translation, "he began in order to be . . . ," which is a nonsensical rendering, because there is no indication of what Nimrod had begun. Certainly "began" is not the ideal option when formulating a translation that suits the context syntactically, let alone suits the authorial intent fairly.

A better option is found in Gary Long's "let be profaned" translation, as he went on to stress the concept of a division between the holy and the profane that was perceived within the Old Testament world. The concept of profaning in the Hebrew Bible often has a moral significance, as a person could offend or insult someone else, especially when the object of the profaning is the name of He-who-is or that which is holy to him. In light of this, and the context that follows, the best understanding of the verb *halal* in Gen 10:8b is, "profaned." Due to the vagueness of this word in the context of the story, however, probably a better alternative for rendering the verb into English is, "acted irreverently."

PURPOSE OF NIMROD'S IRREVERENT CHARACTER

As mentioned above, *lihyot* in Gen 10:8b is an infinitive construct with a *lamed*-prefix, which in this case was attached to denote purpose. The reason that Nimrod acted irreverently, or profaned, is because he set out to become powerful on the earth. However, most English translations and biblical scholars fail to render the *lamed*-prefix and its denotation of purpose here, including the following: the KJV/NKJV ("to be"), the NIV/Livingston ("grew to be"), the NASB/NASU ("became"), and the NRSV/Levin/van der Veen and Zerbst/van der Toorn and van der Horst ("was"). These translations, although undoubtedly well intended, lack precision in their rendering of the infinitive construct.

The adjective *gibbor* (adjective: "mighty, powerful, brave, valiant"; substantive: "hero, despot") in Gen 10:8b and 10:9 presents a great deal of variety in its meaning. The root word emphasizes power and strength, and often excellence or superiority also, while the adjectival form is used of an individual who possesses the kind of power that surpasses ordinary strength, or with which someone accomplishes a great feat. The most common use of the word in the Hebrew Bible is in texts dealing with military personnel, such as the elite, royal bodyguard of the Judahite king (1 Kgs 1:8, 10).

These bodyguards were the strong and courageous fighters who lived in the "house of the heroes" during David's reign, a building that remained in place during Nehemiah's governorship of the post-exilic Jews within the Medo-Persian province of Yehud/Judea (Neh 3:16). In this vein, van der Toorn and van der Horst projected Nimrod as "the first on earth to be a hero," choosing to translate the adjective substantivally. Van der Veen and Zerbst, who agreed with this analysis, referred to Nimrod as a great hunter, a notion that will be discussed below, during the treatment of the phrase in Gen 10:9. Suffice it to say here that no positive connotation such as being a skilled hunter is warranted in relation to the character or deeds of Nimrod.

The positive connotations with English words such as "mighty" and "brave" seem to have enticed many scholars to impart positive characteristics to Nimrod, which frankly is unjustified. Not every *gibbor* in the Hebrew Bible actually is a good hero. The "sons of God" (Gen 6:4) also were *gibborim* "powerful ones" (i.e., the plural form of *gibbor*), but they were fallen evil angels who had incorporated human flesh in order to corrupt the purely human line that was to extend from Adam to Jesus and give mankind the hope of redemption, as promised by God (Gen 3:15). Their angelic origin made these sons of God powerful ones on the earth, yet their power was not devoted to justice and righteousness, but to subversion and self-will.

For this reason, after Jesus's physical death on the cross, he proclaimed to these imprisoned evil spirits of Noah's day that he had conquered sin's grip and overcame their plot to corrupt the Messianic line (1 Pet 3:19–20). In the same way, as will be seen in Chapter 4, Nimrod's power was rooted in violent, tyrannical rule. Perplexingly, the vast majority of translations (KJV, NASB, NASU, NIV, NRSV, etc.) and translators render the adjective as "mighty" in Gen 10:8 and 10:9. This translation is not incorrect per se, but since "mighty" carries with it a positive connotation in standard usage (e.g., David's "mighty men" [2 Sam 23:9] or God's statement that "Abraham surely will became a great and mighty nation" [Gen 18:18]), and since Moses communicates nothing positive about Nimrod's character, "powerful" is a far better translation in these verses.

The nominal form *ṣayid* ("[edible] provision, food supply, hunter, [animal] slaughterer") provides another challenge for anyone attempting to understand the story of Nimrod's life accurately. Most basically, *ṣayid* refers to something that is eaten, whether grain/bread, fruit, vegetables, food-offerings, or travel-rations. However, given that "powerful food" is not a viable option for Moses to describe the kind of person that Nimrod became, a more realistic option must be sought for this specific context in Genesis 10.

The same noun appears in Gen 25:28, where Moses notes that Esau had a taste for game, the food that is provided via the hunt. This passage most likely has drawn interpreters and translators *en masse* to render *ṣayid* as "hunter" in Gen 10:9, since this rendering is found virtually across the board in the standard translations (KJV, NASB, NASU, NIV, NRSV, etc.). The danger with the precarious practice of cross-referencing, of course, is that one can be guilty of reading too much of one passage into another passage when translating or interpreting, with the result that meaning is being imported improperly from one text to a completely unrelated text.

Scholars who attempt to identify Nimrod also seem to support "hunter" almost unanimously. The notion of Nimrod as a mighty hunter is extremely attractive to ANE scholars. According to Emil Kraeling of Union Theological Seminary, the militant hero of ancient times was usually a hunter, and the chase of the lion, wild ox, or boar was the next best excitement to war. The kings of the Levant especially were interested in hunting lions. When surveying the translations and commentaries on Gen 10:9, one discovers that the amount of resistance to the "hunter" rendering, and number of alternatives offered, is extremely limited.

The wording around *ṣayid* actually does not favor the use of "hunter" here at all. This notion appears completely out of context in the Nimrod story. In Gen 10:8, the text describes how Nimrod had become a powerful man on earth, and in Gen 10:10 it reveals the impressive list of city-states that he subjugated during his conquests. It would be incomprehensible for Moses to sandwich a casual detail, such as Nimrod's being a mere hunter on safari in his spare time, between two headlines that distinguish this barbaric man as virtually unique in human history, at least up until that point in time, as well as uniquely sinister. A better translation than "hunter" simply must be chosen if one desires to do justice to the text.

Thankfully, a viable option appears with the help of a foreign cognate of the Hebrew verb *ṣayid*, which relates to the addition of the Ugaritic word *zbḥ* ("sacrifice"). The Hebrew substantive *ṣayid* finds a direct cognate with the Punic construction *zbḥ ṣyd* ("sacrifice of slaughtering"). The ANE concept of this term thus either can focus on the food presented as a sacrifice, or on the slaughtering of the—most conceivably—animal that is offered as a sacrifice.

This means that the nominal form of the ANE word can refer to the person performing the slaughtering, who slaughters living creatures, such as a butcher. Therefore, given that the context of Gen 10:9 rules out "hunter" as a plausible translation, and that the use of *gibbor* to describe Nimrod probably connotes violent, tyrannical power, the best translation seems to be "slaughterer" or "butcher," making Nimrod one who powerfully slaughtered a plethora of living human beings.

CHAPTER 4

MOWING DOWN ALL COMPETITION

NIMROD'S EXCEPTIONAL EXPLOITS

HAVING COMPLETED HIS DISCUSSION OF NIMROD'S CHARACTER, Moses turns his attention to Nimrod's exploits in Gen 10:10–12. The majority of the narrative of his biography describes exceptional feats and noteworthy accomplishments. While this demonstrates Moses's intent for his readers to direct the majority of their attention to Nimrod's actions, the connection between the character of the man and the deeds of the man should not be downplayed. His evil actions are the natural outworking of a depraved character. Moreover, the consistency between the two should compel any reader to conclude that the true nature of Nimrod's character, revealed already to be a devious one, is reflected in the nature of his deeds. In other words, Nimrod's exploits were neither heroic nor entrepreneurial, but defiant and dastardly.

NIMROD'S KINGDOM IN ŠUMER AND AKKAD

ŠUMER AS THE LAND WHERE NIMROD'S KINGDOM BEGAN

The translation and syntactical use of the noun *re'šit* ("beginning, starting point, first [fruits]") is fairly simple, especially in Gen 10:10. Moses informs his readers that Nimrod's kingdom had a starting point, a place of origin. This does not imply that Nimrod necessarily hailed from any of these places on the list, not even the first site mentioned, but merely that his kingdom's inception can be traced back to one of them. The reason for the lack of a definite article prefixed to the noun (i.e., "starting point" rather than "the starting point") is that nouns in construct form (i.e., in a grammatical relationship, known also as a bound construction) cannot take a definite article. The site that Moses is about to name represents the starting point for Nimrod's kingdom, despite the lack of a definite article with the noun.

The prepositional phrase *mamlaktu* ("of his kingdom") in Gen 10:10 answers the question of what starting point is being identified for Nimrod. The verbal nominative *mamlakah* ("kingdom, dominion") refers to the institution or the functional system of *melek*-rule, or royal rule by a/the king. Therefore, by definition of *mamlakah* and according to all of the locations about to be defined as a part of Nimrod's kingdom, this descendant of Cush became a king with a vast dominion. Whoever Nimrod was, he must have been a king, and one with an extensive kingdom in the three-dimensional, physical world.

The prepositional phrase *bə'ereṣ šin'ar* ("in the land of Šumer") technically belongs at the end of the clause in Gen 10:10. For both logical reasons and clarity's sake, however, it will be treated here. This qualification serves as the overall sphere that is defined as the starting point of Nimrod's kingdom and defines the boundaries within which all of the cities of Nimrod's "starting point" are located. Therefore, Eridu, Uruk, Akkad, and possibly Calneh all are located within the land of Šumer. Moses contrasts this land, often referred to by biblical scholars as "the land of Shinar," with Assyria in Gen 10:11. Therefore, there are two distinct geographical regions that comprise Nimrod's kingdom, and the first one is defined as the land of *Shinar*, if the form of the word merely is transliterated from Hebrew into English.

The next matter to solve is the identification and extent of the land of Shinar. The cities listed here in Gen 10:10 provide the Bible's best picture of this land's parameters, as it includes Eridu (Hebrew: *bavel*), Uruk, and Akkad. As van der Veen and many other scholars before him have stated correctly, biblical *Shinar* is to be equated with ancient Šumer. Technically, Eridu and Uruk originally were part of southern Šumer in the 3rd millennium BC, while Akkad was the capital of the land of Akkad at the northern extremity of Šumer several centuries later. Eridu and Uruk were located in southern Mesopotamia, but at least to date, the location of Akkad has not been identified by archaeologists or historical geographers.

Since the present writer does not equate either the Babel of Nimrod's kingdom (Genesis 10) or the Babel of the tower of Babel (Genesis 11) with later Babylon of the Old Babylonian Empire and the Neo-Babylonian Empire, it is worth noting that Daniel mentions Nebuchadnezzar's removal of the Temple's vessels to his god's temple in the land of Shinar (Dan 1:2), meaning that the Babylon of the Neo-Babylonian Empire was included in Shinar. Therefore, Shinar refers to southern Mesopotamia/Babylonia, with later Babylon—in central Babylonia— Akkad acting as a northern extremity of sorts. Šumer and Akkad essentially were united under the Akkadians, which often was the case continuing into the 2nd millennium BC, thus leaving Moses and Daniel to consider the entire plain of southern Mesopotamia to be Šumer.

ERIDU AS THE FIRST AND SOUTHERNMOST CITY IN NIMROD'S KINGDOM IN ŠUMER

The first Šumerian city listed in Gen 10:10 as part of Nimrod's kingdom is Eridu (Hebrew: *bavel* "Babel, Babylon, Eridu"). With the employment of this Hebrew proper noun, Moses begins the listing of toponyms that will comprise a number of the more outstanding cities of Nimrod's kingdom, although there is no reason to believe that this list is comprehensive. The general designation of cities moves in a northerly direction, beginning in southernmost Šumer. Scant few kings of the ancient world ruled kingdoms that encompassed all of southern Babylonia, let alone extended far into Assyria. For that reason alone, the kingdom controlled by Nimrod was a vast and impressive one, and it began with *bavel*. Most scholars uncritically associate the *bavel* of Gen 10:10 with the Babylon of the Old Babylonian Empire (*ca.* 1894–1595 BC) and the Neo-Babylonian Empire (*ca.* 638–539 BC).

According to Paul-Alain Beaulieu, however, an inscription on a limestone plaque preserved at Yale University suggests that this Babylon is attested first as a small settlement during the Early Dynastic IIIA Period (*ca.* 2400–2350 BC) and grew under the shadow of the powerful city of Kish, which was located about 15 km to the east. Babylon later served as a provincial capital during Ur's Third Dynasty (*ca.* 2111–2004 BC), but there are conflicting opinions as to whether the city was described as having been built up at the time of Sargon of Akkad (*ca.* 2320–2265 BC). Either way, archaeology offers no evidence whatsoever of any occupation of Babylon as early as Sargon's reign, not to mention the much earlier time of the tower of Babel, which was abandoned during the Late Uruk Period (*ca.* 2670–2625 BC).

No evidence of pottery from the Early Dynastic Period or earlier has been discovered at Babylon, due to the site's high water table. Even surface surveys at unexcavated sites invariably yield pottery from all periods of occupation, so this acts as a significant reason to doubt the equating of Nimrod's Babel with traditional Babylon. Even if later Babylon was occupied during the time of Sargon of Akkad, despite the lack of physical evidence for it, undoubtedly it existed only as an insignificant site at the outset of his kingdom that sprang up in central Mesopotamia. Since the *bavel* of Gen 10:10 is listed before the city of Uruk, which is located far to the south of Daniel's Babylon, and since the *bavel* of the days of the tower of Babel is described as having been built in "a valley in the land of Šumer" (Gen 11:2), the same city probably is in view in both chapters.

Both of these qualifications fit Eridu, which was occupied long before the time of the tower of Babel that was constructed in the Late Uruk Period, but neither one fits Babylon. The story of the tower of Babel describes the early part of this city's occupational history, the world's first urban metropolis, so undoubtedly Nimrod reigned over the city in a later historical era. Therefore, since the Babel of Genesis 10 almost certainly is the Babel of Genesis 11, Nimrod's Babel probably was in existence as early as the time of the tower's use, pre-dispersion. All of these considerations virtually eliminate traditional Babylon from being the Babel that began Nimrod's kingdom in Šumer.

Another major weakness in equating Nimrod's Babel with Daniel's Babylon is the order in which Moses lists these toponyms. It would be extremely awkward and unlikely for him to present these toponyms haphazardly, such as choosing his first site (i.e., Babylon) in central Mesopotamia, followed by several sites down in southern Mesopotamia (i.e., near the Persian Gulf), then cite cities even further northward than central Mesopotamia—which would require 'passing back through' Babylon along the way—that are located in Assyria (i.e., north of central Mesopotamia) to conclude his listing of toponyms.

Moses demonstrated precise northerly order in first grouping and naming sites in southern Mesopotamia (i.e., Šumer), then grouping and naming sites in northern Mesopotamia (i.e., Assyria). He displayed similar order and precision by plotting sites in consecutive order—compass-point by compass-point, and site by site—when outlining the borders of the Promised Land: southern border (Num 34:3–5), western border (Num 34:6), northern border (Num 34:7–9), and eastern border (Num 34:10–12).

One hardly can be expected to believe that Moses conversely used such imprecision and an erratic approach when listing toponyms in the story of Nimrod's biography. If, however, the *bavel* of Nimrod's day—and that of the tower of Babel's day, in similar fashion—was located at Eridu, then Moses's precision is preserved. The case for locating the original *bavel* of Genesis 11 at Eridu requires a detailed and comprehensive set of arguments, and certainly this volume is not the place to attempt it.

However, the present writer will make the case elsewhere for equating the Babel of Genesis 11 with the city of Eridu in the currently uncompleted book, *The Forgotten Era: Illuminating Biblical History before Abraham.* Eridu, the southernmost and oldest of the ancient seats of power in Šumer, is located just to the southwest of Ur, and to a slightly greater distance to the southeast of Uruk. The earliest occupation at Eridu dates to the Ubaid 1 subphase, which is within the Early Uruk Period, and the site was occupied continuously until the Late Uruk Period, which is the final subphase of the Uruk Period.

URUK AS THE SECOND CITY IN NIMROD'S KINGDOM IN ŠUMER

The second Šumerian city listed in Gen 10:10 is Uruk (Hebrew: *'erek*). Only here and in Ezra 4:9 does this toponym appear. Undoubtedly, the citation in Gen 10:10 refers to the well-known city of Uruk. The ancient site of Uruk, often referred to in modern scholarship as Warka, was occupied from early in the Ubaid Period until the 3rd century AD. During the Jemdet Nasr Period, which follows immediately after the time of the confusion of languages and the post-Babel dispersion, Uruk was the most important city in Mesopotamia and included two major religious centers.

World history's earliest evidence of full-blown writing was discovered in Uruk's temple of Eanna, dating to the Jemdet Nasr Period. During the

Early Dynastic I Period, the city covered 400 hectares, and some scholars have estimated that its population was about 40,000 people, causing Beaulieu to suggest that Uruk may have become the largest human agglomeration in the world at this time. The city of the Early Dynastic I Period was surrounded by a defensive wall, and afterward Uruk remained an important religious center during much of Babylonian history. Uruk also was a formidable city during Nimrod's reign.

AKKAD AS THE THIRD CITY IN NIMROD'S KINGDOM IN ŠUMER

The third Šumerian toponym listed by Moses in Gen 10:10 is Akkad (Hebrew: *'akad*), which can be associated securely with the central Mesopotamian city of Akkad, the capital of the Akkadian Empire (*ca.* 2320–2121 BC). Yet Akkad, which also can be spelled *Akkade* or *Agade*, still remains unidentified and archaeologically unexplored, and ongoing political instabilities in the region make it unlikely that Akkad will be discovered in the near future. The successful locating of Akkad would solve an enormous number of mysteries related to Mesopotamian history of the second half of the 3rd millennium BC.

Beaulieu proposed that the city of Akkad probably lay in the lower Diyala valley or along the Tigris River near the point where the Diyala River empties into the Tigris, while most scholars consider that its location could not have been too far from traditional Babylon. Some scholars consider that Akkad and Babylon were the very same city, although this definitely is unlikely to be the case. The majority of what is known about Akkad comes from works of art of diverse provenance that were uprooted from their original context at the site as booty and relocated elsewhere, such as to the cities of Elam to the east of Šumer.

SUMMARY STATEMENT FOR THE CITIES OF
NIMROD'S KINGDOM IN ŠUMER AND AKKAD

The Masoretic text's rendering of *kalneh* ("Calneh") in Gen 10:10, if read as such, presents a complicated dilemma. The Masoretic text (i.e., the best-preserved manuscript tradition for the Hebrew Bible, primarily based on a manuscript dating to just after AD 1000 that is known as the Leningrad Codex), has been accepted as the standard text of the Hebrew Bible for many centuries. There is no such site as Calneh near or north of Akkad's presumed location—if assuming a continuation of Moses's orderly south-to-north orientation—that lies within the land of Šumer or Akkad. A tradition preserved in the Babylonian Talmud, found in Yoma 10a, identifies the supposed Calneh with "Nopher Ninphi," which is thought to be a reference to Nippur.

However, even if this attribution is correct, Moses once again would be guilty of a disorderly arrangement of the toponyms. Southern and central Mesopotamia is divided into two regions: Šumer in the south and Akkad to its north. Šumer extended from Eridu to Nippur, while Akkad extended from Abu Salabikh to the northern edge of the alluvial plains. Therefore, if Calneh is equated with Nippur, the list of toponyms would vacillate in its direction: from Eridu in the extreme south, northward to Uruk, northward to Akkad, southward to Nippur, then northward again into Assyria. This arrangement in Moses's listing of cities within Genesis 10 that Nimrod conquered is highly unlikely.

Unless one were to accept the inferred attribution in the Talmud and Moses's disorderliness, the only two options that remain are that (1) Calneh is a city that mysteriously remains unattributable but is located somewhere to the north of Akkad, or that (2) the Hebrew wording preserved in the Masoretic text does not represent what Moses originally wrote. The former option would require the willful suspension of disbelief, as Ephraim Speiser keenly noted that there is scarcely room for a freak such as Calneh in such company as Babel, Uruk, and Akkad. The second option would not require an emendation of the inspired text, but only a rearranging of the non-inspired vowel pointings. The original Hebrew text of the inspired biblical writers not only was devoid of vowels, but it was written in *scriptio continua* ("continuous script"), a Latin term for how certain early forms of writing had no spaces between letters or words, plus no punctuation of any kind.

If the reading of Gen 10:10 in the Masoretic text is not pointed correctly, the text probably would have read *wəkulanah* ("and all of them") originally. William F. Albright first suggested the emendation of the non-inspired vocalization of the inspired consonantal structure *wklnh* from *wəKal-neh* to *wəkullana*. A near-match with this variant vocalization is found in 1 Kgs 7:37 (*kullahena*), with the only difference being a *qameṣ-he* vowel used here instead of the *qameṣ* vowel found in Gen 10:10. This suggestion has become so attractive to many that they consider it to be the standard translation (e.g., the NRSV: "all of them"). If Albright's reading is correct, which certainly is plausible if not even probable, then there is implied predication between "all of them" and "in the land of Šumer." In this case, *were located* or *being located* can be supplied in italics to provide a smoother translation into English.

Another compelling reason to accept the reading "and all of them *were located* in the land of Šumer" over the "and Calneh, in the land of Šumer" reading is related to geography and the most important canon of lower textual criticism (i.e., the field of study that seeks to establish the original reading of the biblical author when at least two ancient textual witnesses conflict with one another). This canons states, "Prefer the reading that best explains the rise of the other reading(s)." In other words, the correct reading should explain the rise of the spurious reading(s), while conversely, the spurious reading(s) invariably has no viable way to explain the rise of the correct reading. There are two clear references to Calneh in the Hebrew Bible.

(1) In Amos 6:2, the prophet asks the Judahites and Israelites who feel secure to go over to the cities of Calneh, Hamath, and Gath, in order to see the misfortune that befell those kingdoms at the hands of the Neo-Assyrians. Amos served in Israel during the reign of Jeroboam II (793/2–753 BC), and his ministry dates to about 760 BC. The rise to power by Adad-narari III (810–783 BC) in Assyria marked the return of Assyrian intervention in the Levant. The king of Arpad led an alliance in 805/4 BC, which likely included the Kingdom of Patina/Unqi, whose capital was located in the Amuq Plain and known to the Neo-Hittites as Kunulua. This capital city had a variant spelling used by the Neo-Assyrians, which is *Kullania*, whose tri-consonantal root was replicated by Amos as "CaLNeh." However, this Calneh was located in western Syria, not Šumer.

(2) In Isa 10:9, the prophet Isaiah asks rhetorically if Calno (= Calneh) is not like Carchemish, if Hamath is not like Arpad, and if Samaria is not like Damascus. Isaiah served in Judah from the reign of Uzziah (791/0–740/39 BC) until sometime during the reign of Manasseh (697/6–643/2 BC), and thus from *ca.* 745–695 BC. A boundary stele along the Orontes River to the southwest of Antioch hints at a decisive downturn in the political

fortunes of the Kingdom of Patina/Unqi, which includes of the city of Kunulua/Calneh.

The inscription describes the transfer of the lands and settlements of an unknown city to Atarshumki of Arpad, apparently at the expense of Zakkur of Hamath, and the realignment of the border between the two kingdoms to the Orontes River, likely the result of action taken during the Assyrian campaign of 796 BC and associated with the events recorded on the Aramaic stele of Zakkur, found at Tell Afis. In the inscription, Zakkur accused Bar-Hadad of Damascus of having induced a coalition of northern kingdoms, including that of Unqi, to attack Hamath and its ruler, Lu'ash.

These biblical references to the city of Calneh all refer to the capital of a kingdom that undeniably was located in the Amuq Plain of western Syria, as confirmed by the detailed records of Assyrian kings in their conquest lists. Since this city is located far from Mesopotamia and the cities of Šumer that Moses listed, most likely a later scribe who recollected the Calneh of Amos's and Isaiah's texts aligned the vowel pointings in Gen 10:10 with those for Calneh, in order to 'fix the mistake' that he found in the text of Genesis 10. Yet since the original vowel pointings were added many centuries after Moses's original composition, perhaps the memory of the correct reading in Gen 10:10 simply was lost to these later scribes. In any event, the reading of "Calneh" in Gen 10:10 almost certainly is erroneous, and Albright's proposed correction should be followed as representing the proper reading of Moses's original text: ". . . and Akkad, and all of them [Hebrew: *wəkulanah*] *were located* in the land of Šumer."

NIMROD'S KINGDOM IN ASSYRIA

ASSYRIA AS THE LAND TO WHERE
NIMROD'S KINGDOM EXTENDED

Gen 10:11 begins with the transitional statement that Nimrod proceeded *min-ha'areṣ hahiw'* ("from that land"), which obviously implies that he entered into a land outside the confines of the land of Šumer. With this statement, the author delineates the existence of two separate regions that comprise Nimrod's kingdom. Moses does not indicate the direction in which Nimrod traveled to reach the new region of his kingdom, but the previous context clearly suggests that the movement was to the north, and the subsequent context confirms this as true.

The text in Gen 10:11 specifies that Nimrod's kingdom continued to the north, adding that he went out into Assyria (Hebrew: *'aššur*), although there is neither a preposition (*bə* or *el-*) for "into" nor a directional-*he* at the end of "Assyria," as is normally the case when a preposition is absent and movement is made toward/into a place (cf. *miṣrayemah* "[into] Egypt" in Gen 12:14). This grammatically unexpected wording suggests that *'aššur* is the subject of the sentence, given that the word also can signify a person's or a god's name, and thus "Asshur went out" and built up the cities of Assyria. Since Asshur is the son of Shem (Gen 10:22) and seemingly attributed with founding Assyria, one could suggest that the presence of Asshur in Gen 10:11 is the result of an intentional scribal change that created an error designed to 'correct' the text, as Nimrod otherwise may be credited 'wrongfully' as the architect of Assyria.

However, given that there is no textual evidence supporting the reading of "Nimrod" for "Assyria/Asshur" here, there is no solid ground on which to build a case for taking "Nimrod" to be the proper reading. This leaves the association of the word *'aššur* with the location of Assyria as the best option, since the biblical text is replete with references that pinpoint this place geographically as ancient Assyria (e.g., 2 Kgs 15:29; 17:3; 19:35; 23:29; etc.), especially due to the Neo-Assyrian Empire's (934–612 BC) conquest of Israel (723 BC) and attack on Judah (701 BC). The only question that exists is whether this particular reference is to Assyria as a region, or the individual city of Ashur. While both options are possible, context favors the region of Assyria as being more plausible here.

The city of Ashur, after which the region of Assyria is named, was situated on a rocky spur overlooking the Tigris River. The site, occupied since at least 2400 BC and now known as Qalat Shergat, yielded Early Dynastic styles found in the Ishtar temple, meaning that the site predated the arrival of Sargon of Akkad into Assyria. In the early 2nd millennium BC, merchants from Ashur established colonies in Anatolia. During the Middle Assyrian Period (*ca.* 1300–900 BC), Assyria expanded under Ashur-uballit I (*ca.* 1363–1328 BC), and Ashur became the capital of a kingdom that stretched from the Euphrates River to the mountains of Iran.

Given that Ashur overlooked an important crossing of the Euphrates River, sat on the edge of the dry-farming line, and lay on a vitally important and ancient trading route, this site acted as the gateway in and out of Assyria. For all of these reasons, the city always was vulnerable to incursions from pastoral nomads living on the steppe (i.e., plains of grasslands devoid of trees, yet removed from lakes and rivers). The possibility thus exists that Moses's reference to *'aššur* was not a regional designation, but the citing of the name of the strategic city of the same name, which granted access to Assyria's heartland. Yet in the end, assuming that *'aššur* is not the subject of the clause, the region of Assyria is the more secure option to favor, especially since the city of Ashur did not rise to prominence until after the lifetime of Moses.

NINEVEH AS THE FIRST CITY IN NIMROD'S KINGDOM IN ASSYRIA

The Hebrew verb *banah* ("build, build up, rebuild, fortify") is used of building cities, walls, gates, altars, high places, and houses. While this verb certainly can be used of the building of a city on virgin soil, it also can be used of rebuilding a preexisting city, such as Gezer (1 Kgs 9:17), Jericho (1 Kgs 16:34), and the cities of Benjamin (Judg 21:23). Gezer provides a perfect example of such rebuilding of a previously inhabited city, because the Bible itself attests to its occupation before Solomon rebuilt it (1 Kgs 9:16). Many translations reflect Solomon's rebuilding of Gezer by rendering the verb "rebuilt" in 1 Kgs 9:17 (NASB, NASU, NIV, NRSV), although other translations prefer to use the more generic form "built" (KJV, NKJV).

This wide range of meaning for the verb *banah*, which includes the building up of previously inhabited cities, helps the reader to understand better what Nimrod may have accomplished when he left his native land of Šumer in southern and central Mesopotamia and ventured into Assyria. He undoubtedly did not travel there to found new cities on virgin soil in order to assist the native Assyrians in improving their economy, or to facilitate their plans for civic improvement.

Instead, Nimrod traveled into Assyria to conquer cities—sparing the ones that he overtook, whenever possible—to build up existing cities to more impressive sizes, and to incorporate cities and towns of all sizes into his empire. These building projects would have allowed for the exploitation of local resources, given him access to commodities along the trading routes that went through these regions, and helped to fuel the engine of the empire, all in order to accelerate its potential for expansion to even more distant places. Archaeology bears out this model, as will be seen shortly.

The first Assyrian city of Nimrod's kingdom listed in Gen 10:11 is Nineveh (Hebrew: *nineweh*, written with a prefix as a direct object marker). This site is the first Assyrian city named as part of Nimrod's northern holdings that he built up. There is no reason, exegetically or archaeologically, to conclude that this is not the same site to which God later sent Jonah in order to proclaim repentance to Nineveh's inhabitants (Jonah 1:1) during Neo-Assyrian times. Nineveh was occupied as early as the Hassuna Period, which even predates the construction of the city at Babel and its famous tower, and certainly this is reason enough to conclude that Nimrod did not build the city on virgin soil. An amazing total of 75% of the mound consists of prehistorical remains, and during the Uruk Period its development was related close to that of southern Mesopotamia.

In the 2nd millennium BC, Nineveh was an important city with a prestigious temple to the goddess Ishtar, but it was not the capital of Assyria. The city reached its peak during the Neo-Assyrian Empire. Jonah would have visited Nineveh around 780 BC (2 Kgs 14:25), given that he ministered during the reign of Jeroboam II (*ca.* 793–753 BC) of the Kingdom of Israel, the exceedingly evil king whose wife was named Jezebel. Sennacherib (705–681 BC) rebuilt Nineveh as his capital and constructed a new city wall, complete with 15 major gates. The remains of this wall that have survived allow for a measurement of its circumference today, which calculates to almost 13 km, making for an occupational area with the potential for more than 7 km². Sennacherib's principal palace, which he dubbed "*the* palace without rival," was pillaged and burned in 612 BC, when Nineveh fell to a coalition of the Medes and Babylonians.

REHOBOTH CITY AS THE SECOND CITY IN
NIMROD'S KINGDOM IN ASSYRIA

The second Assyrian city of Nimrod's kingdom listed in Gen 10:11 is Rehoboth City (Hebrew: *rehovot 'ir*), another toponym with interpretive difficulties. There is no such site by this name known to be located in ancient Assyria, or referred to in the cuneiform record. Since the Hebrew direct object marker in front of the word can be translated "with," some have suggested that a literal translation of, "with open places of the city," would solve the dilemma. These public places would refer to various districts throughout the city that would have been built up within Nineveh. While this option is not impossible, its most serious detriment is that the words *reḥovot 'ir* appear in a sequence of toponyms, all of which are introduced by the direct object marker (*'et-*).

Therefore, given that this term almost certainly should be taken as one of these numerous cities within Assyria, strictly for the sake of grammatical consistency, the best option is to consider Rehoboth City as a site that simply has not been discovered by archaeologists as of yet or preserved in the literary record in a way that resembles the biblical word *reḥovot*. The latter option would come as no surprise, as the Egyptian conquest lists of Thutmose III and Sheshonq (i.e., biblical Shishak) contain many names of cities in Canaan and Israel that are completely unknown to scholars of today.

KALHU AS THE THIRD CITY IN NIMROD'S KINGDOM IN ASSYRIA

The third Assyrian site in Gen 10:11 is Kalhu (Hebrew: *kalaḥ*), which usually appears as "Calah" in English translations, a spelling that is merely a literal transliteration of the Hebrew writing of the toponym. The site of *kalaḥ* is identified confidently with the prominent Assyrian city of Kalhu. The earliest evidence of occupation at Kalhu is from the Jemdet Nasr Period, which is equivalent to the start of the Early Bronze Age (hereinafter EBA) in the Levant. Conventional dating for this period is *ca.* 3000 BC, based on [14]C (i.e., radiocarbon) dating. However, there is reason to date the physical evidence and the period as being more recent than this. Of greatest importance is that the Jemdet Nasr Period predates both the Early Dynastic Period and the Akkadian Period, meaning that the city was inhabited before Sargon of Akkad ever lived.

Some material cultural remains from the Old Assyrian Period of the 18th century BC were found at Kalhu, including the tomb of a chieftain located in the southeastern corner of the acropolis. Kalhu was a provincial capital during the Middle Assyrian Period, but its relative obscurity soon ended.

In the Neo-Assyrian Period, the capital of Ashur had become too small for Assyria's enormous administrative apparatus, so Ashurnasirpal II (883–859 BC) chose Kalhu as the new capital of the empire. Kalhu remained the capital until Sargon II (722–705 BC) selected Khorsabad (a.k.a. Dur-Sharrukin) to succeed it in 717 BC, where he built a large palace and temples, constructed massive city walls, and dug a canal to irrigate the region and provide water for the new capital's inhabitants.

In Gen 10:12, the text adds the parenthetical remark that *kalaḥ* is "the great city." The excavation of the site, the cuneiform record, and the historical annals from surrounding nations conspire to dispute the notion that Kalhu was a great city either at the time of Nimrod or in Moses's day. Therefore, the probability is greatest that this parenthetical statement was inserted by a later scribe who, while transmitting the text long after Moses lived, added this statement under the inspiration of God.

If this indeed was the case, the scribe most likely lived between the 9th and 7th centuries BC. Scribal updating of the Hebrew Bible—a practice unknown to the composition of the Greek New Testament—is not a problematic concept, given that in a landmark article that Michael Grisanti published in 2001, he demonstrated the occasional use of this practice by Hebrew scribes. Grisanti dubbed this as "textual updating," and he identified numerous examples that validate his claim.

Here are several examples: (1) While some scholars inexplicably have suggested that Moses prophetically wrote of his own death, burial, and final tribute in Deut 34:1–12, almost certainly this addition to the Pentateuch was composed by a later biblical writer or scribe, who simply updated the end of Deuteronomy anonymously. (2) The city of Dan received its name during the period of Canaan's settlement (after 1400 BC), which clearly began after Moses's death (in 1406 BC). However, the toponym appears in Gen 14:14, which undoubtedly falls within a biblical book that Moses composed. (3) The text in Gen 11:28 and 11:31 refers to Abram's place of origin as "Ur of the Chaldees," while the Chaldeans did not inhabit southern Mesopotamia until *ca.* 900 BC or become contenders for the Babylonian throne until the middle of the 9th century BC. This means that Moses never would have known of Ur as a Chaldean city. Grisanti's article can be consulted for even more incontrovertible scribal updates that are present in the Hebrew Bible.

RESEN AS THE FOURTH CITY IN NIMROD'S
KINGDOM IN ASSYRIA

The final city added to the list of Assyrian sites that were built up by Nimrod, which is recorded in Gen 10:12, is Resen (Hebrew: *resen*). Yigal Levin aptly noted that this city is totally unknown. Karel van der Toorn suggested that Rehoboth City and Resen should refer to other great Neo-Assyrian centers, such as Khorsabad. The flaw with this idea is that Nimrod long predated the Neo-Assyrian Empire, the time when Khorsabad flourished and became the Assyrian capital city. Khorsabad actually was built entirely during the decade that ended in 706 BC. Moreover, the only south-to-north movement (in Mesopotamia) of an empire-builder—which Genesis 10 portrays as the direction of Nimrod's expansionism—must be dated to the 3rd millennium BC, as the second and first millennia BC featured no such candidates until the kings of the Neo-Babylonian Empire. For this reason, van der Toorn's proposal to connect Khorsabad to Rehoboth City or Resen probably is invalid.

The Septuagint reads "Dase(n)" here, which may be explained by a scribal error of sight when the translator viewed his Hebrew exemplar (i.e., the manuscript that serves as a source when a scribe copies or translates its text onto a blank document), due to the similarity between the letters *dalet* and *reš* in the pre-exilic Hebrew script. Van der Toorn suggested that if Resen is a corruption of Desen, the possibility exists that the toponym refers to Khorsabad, which became Sargon II's capital in *ca.* 717 BC. Van der Toorn attempted to bolster this possibility by stating that Dur-Sharrukin rests halfway between Nineveh and Kalhu, but evidently the map he used was misleading, because Nineveh lies between Dur-Sharukin (to the north) and Kalhu (to the south). In the end, Van der Toorn wisely noted that the potential association of Dasen with Dur-Sharrukin is hardly more than a strained guess, one that likely is incorrect.

At present, the best option for Resen, or Dase(n) if the reading in the Septuagint is correct, is to declare that its position currently remains unknown. Wherever the former city of Resen is located, it must lie "between Nineveh and Kalhu" (Gen 10:12). Both Nineveh and Kalhu are situated along the Tigris River, on its eastern bank, meaning that the river acted as a natural boundary against enemies attacking from Mesopotamia or the Euphrates region. Nineveh sits upstream from Kalhu by 40 km, as the crow flies. The only notable Assyrian site between these two important cities is Alu Ashu-raya, which is located several kilometers downstream from Nineveh, but there is no justifiable reason to connect this city to biblical Resen. The difficulty with pinpointing the location of Rehoboth City and Resen should not be evaluated as alarming. After all, Nimrod lived extremely early in Assyria's history, a time that Assyriologists by no means understand comprehensively.

SECTION III

NIMROD IN HISTORY AND ARCHAEOLOGY

CHAPTER 5

CONNECTING THE HISTORICAL DOTS

NIMROD'S IDENTITY AS SARGON OF AKKAD

HAVING COMPLETED A DETAILED STUDY OF GEN 10:7–12 and an evaluation of the views for the identification of Nimrod that are most prevalent among scholars, the next task at hand is to connect Nimrod with the proper historical figure, and to demonstrate why this identification is secure. Nimrod is none other than Sargon the Great, the king of Šumer and Akkad, who is history's first empire-builder. The identification of Nimrod with either Sargon or Naram-Sin has been brought up in the past, generally only in passing. Thanks to the advances in archaeology, epigraphy, and other forms of ANE historical studies, a conclusive case now can be made for equating Nimrod with Sargon. The following discussion will serve to support the veracity of this claim. After concluding the task, reasons will be given as to why Sargon is preferred over his grandson, Naram-Sin, for the dubious distinction of being the proper historical figure who equates to biblical Nimrod.

SIMILARITY IN GEOGRAPHICAL AND GENEALOGICAL ORIGINS

BOTH IMPERIALISTS HAVE ORIGINS CONNECTED TO KISH/CUSH
According to Akkadian historical sources, Sargon's geographical origin is the city of Kish. The biblical text in Gen 10:8a indicates that Nimrod's genealogical origin is Noah's grandson named Cush. As anyone familiar with Genesis 10 knows, many of the nations of the ancient world were named after various descendants of Noah, so the possibility exists that Mesopotamian Kish (i.e, the city) is named after biblical Cush (i.e., the person), meaning that Nimrod and Sargon descended from the same man. Biblical Cush easily could have been rendered into English as *Kush*, and the vari-

ance of vowels between ancient languages is almost always purely incidental. This especially is the case with languages such as Hebrew, which did not record vowels in written form until many centuries after the beginning of its consonants-only alphabet originated in the 19th century BC.

The association of biblical Cush with the Šumerian city-state of Kish is not a new one. As early as 1914, Cornelius van Gelderen suggested that Cush is the "Babylonian city of Kish." In 1922, however, Emil Kraeling concluded that van Gelderen and others had failed in their attempt to connect Cush with Kish. The main argument lodged against this association is that the descendants of Cush were located in Africa and Arabia, from all that they understood about the Bible. Yet Livingston renewed support for van Gelderen's view in 2001, suggesting that Šumerian Kish "took its name from the man known in the Bible as Cush."

How, then, does one deal with the contention that biblical Cush allegedly is traced geographically to Africa, if Cush is to be connected with Šumerian Kish? The answer is that numerous descendants of Cush, from various regions, had the opportunity to name their town or their territory after the same progenitor. Cush is the grandson of Noah, and thus many peoples would have descended from Cush's progeny. There is no reason to restrict the use of his namesake to only one line that descended from him, because several lines may have honored him by calling their cities or territories "Cush/Kish." This is similar to how numerous descendants of Shem, who were scattered from one another geographically throughout the ANE, were called Semitic peoples and spoke various Semitic languages, the commonality of which betrays a common origin.

Moreover, this geographical positioning of Nimrod's Cush at Šumerian Kish makes much better sense of the location of the second river that deviated from the one that emanated from the Garden of Eden, which flowed around the entire land of Cush/Kush (Gen 2:13). How could the third and fourth resultant rivers be the Tigris and the Euphrates (Gen 2:14), which are known to border Mesopotamia, while the second river was in distant Nubia (or "Ethiopia," per KJV) of Africa, even with a supercontinent? The location of the river flowing around the land of Cush is reasonable only if this reference to Cush refers to a site in Mesopotamia. The possibility certainly exists that Mesopotamian Kishites eventually migrated to Africa, sometime after their native homeland had been established, and a handful of them chose to venture westward in Abram-like fashion.

Perhaps not coincidentally, Sargon of Akkad's origin traces back to the city of Šumerian Kish. His name actually is *Sharrum-kin*, which in later times was pronounced *Sharken*, and is preserved in the Bible as Sargon (Isa 20:1). However, this lone biblical reference to a king named Sargon alludes to Sargon II, a later king who ruled over the Neo-Assyrian Empire during the lifetimes of Isaiah and Hezekiah. In Akkadian, *Sharrum-kin* means, "the true/legitimate king," which strongly hints at his being a usurper (i.e., an illegitimate claimant of the throne who seized it by force), since he went to the trouble of announcing his legitimacy with his regnal name. The *Šumerian King List* states, "[As for] Sharrum-kin, his [father] was a date-grower. [Sargon was the] cupbearer of Ur-Zababa."

According to an ancient text known as the *Sargon Legend*, Ur-Zababa, the king of Kish, awoke from a dream and appointed Sargon as cupbearer (a.k.a. vizier, a high office). The claim was made that Sargon revolted against his master and seized the throne from him, at Kish. Not long afterward, Sargon expanded his control to other areas, which will be demonstrated shortly. Šumerian Kish was occupied first during the Jemdet Nasr Period, the Mesopotamian archaeological era immediately after the Late Uruk Period ended and immediately before the Early Dynastic Period began. According to the later *Šumerian King List*, Kish was the first city on which "kingship was lowered from heaven" after the worldwide flood.

Kish eventually came to dominate the landscape of Šumer, and by the Early Dynastic III Period, Mesopotamian rulers adopted the title, "king of Kish," which functioned as a claim to supremacy over Šumer. This title underscores the importance of understanding how Kish was the sole superpower of its day within the urban landscape in southern Mesopotamia. The trading network that preceded the Akkadian Empire originally ran from Uruk to Ebla, but the primary network subsequently shifted to the route from Kish to Ebla. Kish thus had become the leading figure in the jockeying for power in Šumer just prior to the rise of Sargon the Great. Kish survived into the Akkadian Period and beyond, so Sargon undoubtedly maintained control of this city from which he launched his kingdom.

Levin proposed that the decisive factor for linking Nimrod with Sargon is the identification of biblical Cush with the city-state of Kish. While this factor is both valid and vital, it is not nearly as compelling as the other arguments that can be made for equating these two empire-builders. The genealogical basis for Nimrod's being Sargon is established quite strongly with this link to Kish. Since the Akkadian language was so diverse from Šumerian, more resembling a Semitic language, the linguistic evidence supports this connection, especially since Semites such as Abram's forefathers originally had settled at nearby Ur, another contemporary Šumerian city of note.

SIMILARITY IN MILITARY ACTIVITIES AND IMPERIALISTIC VENTURES

BOTH IMPERIALISTS BROUGHT AKKAD INTO PROMINENCE

Both Sargon and Nimrod were credited with bringing Akkad into prominence. Given that Akkad has not been discovered, there are limitations as to what can be said about the ancient city that became the capital of the Akkadian Empire. Literary sources imply that Akkad was located in the vicinity of Babylon and Kish. The *Šumerian King List* states that Sargon was the "king of Akkad, who built Akkad, became king, and reigned 55 years." However, copies of the list vary between 40 and 54–56 in the recording of his regnal years, so it is difficult to know which preserved number is accurate. Critics who have disputed the *Šumerian King List* and Sargon's role at Akkad, such as Marc van de Mieroop, point to an inscription of Enshakushanna, king of Uruk, who claims to have conquered Akkad.

As the king of Uruk, Enshakushanna would have preceded Sargon's opponent—Lugal-zage-si, initially king of Umma, but later crowned king of Uruk—which may indicate that Akkad existed before Sargon came onto the scene. Akkad thus seems to have predated Sargon. This notion must be nuanced, however, as some additional background information is needed. As king of Uruk, Lugal-zage-si did claim to unify Šumer as a singular kingdom under his hegemony, but an Old Babylonian inscription describes how Sargon conquered Uruk in battle and captured Lugal-zage-si, whom he presented as a trophy to Enlil (i.e., the Šumerian storm god and king of the gods) at Nippur. This victory gave Sargon a clear path to control all of Šumer.

Sargon first restored Kish to its former greatness and returned its population to the city, which Lugal-zage-si had overrun or destroyed. Sargon also inherited Lugal-zage-si's possessions, with an impressive list of cities that includes Uruk (his capital), Ur, Umma, Lagash, and 50 other towns, as a Sargonic inscription from Nippur reads that Sargon defeated Lugal-zage-si "together with [his] 50 governors," making Sargon the *de facto* master over all of southern Mesopotamia. He even installed his daughter as *entu*-priestess of An (i.e., the sky god) at Uruk and *entu*-priestess of Nanna (i.e., the moon god and patron deity) at Ur. Sargon brought about a new day in Mesopotamian political organization, implementing a great number of social, religious, and artistic innovations, which created what must be regarded as a cultural bonanza.

One problem with reconstructing Sargon's biography is the dating of his conquest of the cities of southern Mesopotamia. While some have considered that a number of factors favor a date that is late in his reign, the order of events from the life of Sargon that were recorded in the Old Babylonian inscriptions clearly favors the view that Sargon's defeat of Lugal-zage-si and Uruk, followed by the conquest and demolition of the walls of many Šumerian cities, represents the initial phase in a series of events that led to his sovereignty over Mesopotamia and numerous lands beyond. Special attention is given to the rebuilding and resettling of Kish, suggesting that the city suffered a devastating defeat at an earlier date.

Yet Sargon clearly was intent on preventing rebellion. He consolidated his dominion over Šumer by deposing most of the rulers who had opposed him, then installing loyal governors in their places. The most logical time to suppose that Sargon built Akkad, which the *Šumerian King List* attributes to his handiwork, and established it as his capital city is soon after he conquered the cities of Šumer. With no overlord such as Lugal-zage-si to inhibit him from expanding northward, and with Kish probably existing in a dilapidated state, Sargon could exploit the situation by creating his idyllic city from which to rule Babylonia. He undoubtedly chose a site in northern Šumer with the intent of preparing for conquests to the north.

While the location of Akkad is unknown, virtually all scholars who theorize about its location consider it to be in the area known as the capital district, likely in proximity to Babylon and Kish. Not only did Sargon provide some kind of privileges and exemptions for Kish, but he continued to use the city as his capital while Akkad was under construction. What critics such as van de Mieroop fail to note is that Sargon never claimed to have built Akkad on virgin soil, nor does he say that he built his city from nothing. Ebla's archive reveals the political situation in Mesopotamia and northern Syria just prior to Sargon's dynasty and Akkad's rise. Kish is the toponym mentioned most often in the archive, making Ebla contemporary with the First Dynasty of Kish. Conversely, the archive makes no mention whatsoever of Akkad.

While the evidence from Ebla's archive *could* imply that Akkad was not in existence, it clearly suggests at the least that Akkad was an insignificant player in the politics of Šumer and the rest of the Fertile Crescent just prior to the rise of the Akkadian Empire. This scenario clearly is viable, and it was proven already that the Hebrew verb *banah* can mean, "build up."

Therefore, a plausible and evidence-honoring case can be made that Sargon built up a pre-existing Akkad after he had subdued all of southern Mesopotamia, having founded his new capital at a previously insignificant site that would provide him with a strategic launching point from which to extend his empire into the heartland of Assyria, whose lucrative trading network lie vulnerable, and to the northwest, where the untold wealth of Mari and Ebla awaited. The biography of Nimrod fits this course of events perfectly, even if cryptically and incompletely.

The kingdoms of Nimrod and Sargon both began in Šumer and expanded from there, most notably into Assyria. The first city listed as part of Nimrod's kingdom is Eridu, the southernmost Šumerian site and first city built in Šumer, which Moses soon would implement into the narrative and implicate in his story of Babel and its tower (Genesis 11). The second city listed as part of Nimrod's kingdom is Uruk, Mesopotamia's center of power when Sargon rose to the throne in Kish, and the city that he first had to defeat if he desired to rule over all of Šumer. The third city listed as part of Nimrod's kingdom is Akkad, which Sargon is credited as having built up and developed into his capital, "from which land" he could campaign to the north and widen the borders of his domain.

BOTH IMPERIALISTS INITIATED BUILDING
PROJECTS IN ASSYRIA

Both Sargon and Nimrod were involved in massive, initial building projects in Assyria. In the north, Sargon campaigned against Simurrum, a Hurrian region, which claim is supported by the evidence of a date formula from Nippur. This is the first recorded southern Mesopotamian penetration into Assyria militarily. Despite the lack of Sargon's own inscriptions that attest to northerly campaigns along the Tigris River, Georges Roux justifiably considered them just as certain as Sargon's better attested campaigns, due to the large number of Akkadian cuneiform tablets that have been excavated in the region. The extension of Sargon's rule to Ashur and Nineveh is attested by the honorific inscriptions on the monuments of native governors.

At Ashur, a head was found that distinctly dates to the reign of Man-Ishtushu, the second son of Sargon who ruled after him. Lorenzo Nigro even referred to the argumentation for this dating as being convincing. Since Man-Ishtushu's reign was less than impressive, both to ancient and modern historians, this head that signifies his control at Ashur almost certainly means that Ashur was seized under the rule of his father, Sargon. Inscriptional evidence confirms that Man-Ishtushu controlled both Ashur and Nineveh, where he renovated the Ishtar temple, as confirmed by a later Assyrian king, Shamshi-Adad I (*ca.* 1808–1776 BC), who found statues of Man-Ishtushu at both sites during the course of restoring the temples there.

The famous bronze head from Nineveh known as the Sargon Mask is clearly Akkadian, as well, although a dispute exists over which king it represents. Initial conclusions were that the head is that of Sargon, but many have suggested that it should be attributed to his grandson, Naram-Sin, based on the brilliant technique of craftsmanship and elaborate style. Yet the view of an earlier dating does fit the already-advanced metalworking in Mesopotamia of Sargon's day, so the mask certainly could represent his head. Regardless of whom the bronze head from Nineveh represents, all of the inscriptional and artifactual evidence from Ashur, Nineveh, and Nippur combines to paint a vivid picture of how Sargon of Akkad had established himself at the chief sites in Assyria, before either of his two sons or his illustrious grandson took the throne after him.

The presence of Sargon in Assyria is all the more plausible due to his involvement along the upper courses of the Euphrates and as far as north-western Syria, where he defeated the Amorites. He remains a strong candidate for the conqueror of Mari, and he overtook what was left of Ebla after its destruction at the hands of an invader. On his way to Anatolia, Sargon led his army up the Euphrates, which can be deduced from one of his inscriptions: "Sargon the king prostrated himself in prayer before Dagan in Tuttul. (Dagan) gave him the Upper Region: Mari, Yarmuti (and) Ebla, as far as the forest of cedars and the mountain of silver." His prayer was offered at the confluence of the Euphrates and Khabur Rivers, where Dagan was considered the "father of the gods" and Tuttul served as Mari's port of operations for its involvement in the Khabur River basin.

A Hittite king of the 17th century BC even recalled that Sargon crossed the upper Euphrates River over to the western side of the river in order to receive the submission of the city of Hahhum. Despite the inscriptional evidence related to northern Mesopotamia, and northern Syria to a greater extent, some critics still have doubted that Sargon was involved in Assyria. William Stiebing Jr. became convinced that Sargon never campaigned in northeastern Mesopotamia, citing a lack of material support for this claim. In addition to the aforementioned direct inscriptional evidence, there is pre-Sargonic circumstantial evidence from the archive at Ebla to oppose Stiebing's doubt.

Apart from Adab, no other southern Babylonian city was named in Ebla's archive beyond the illustrious Kish. Piotr Steinkeller stated that the obvious inference must be that during the Early Dynastic III Period, all of the commercial exchange between northern and southern Mesopotamia was conducted via Kish. This reality presupposes Kish's mastery over the cities and towns of northern Babylonia. Therefore, when Sargon defeated Lugal-zage-si, he inherited the mastery over the Assyrian lands of northern Mesopotamia and beyond. If inscriptional and circumstantial evidence is not enough to persuade critics that Sargon controlled northern Mesopotamia and Assyria, then perhaps evidence from archaeological excavations can finish the task.

Such archaeological evidence was excavated at the sites of Tell Mozan, Tell Leilan, and Tell Brak, all of which form a triangle in relatively close proximity and are situated immediately opposite the northern centers of Assyrian power, just on the other (i.e., western) side of the Tigris River. During the Tell Leilan IIID phase—which ended in *ca.* 2400 BC, corresponding to the transition from Early Dynastic II to Early Dynastic IIIA in southern Babylonia and the rise of the Third Dynasty of Kish—settlement patterns on the Khabur plains and the adjacent Assyrian steppe were altered radically with the sudden emergence of indigenous state-level society. This transition is seen in the large, planned city at Tell Leilan, whose population increased by more than sixfold during this time.

As Harvey Weiss et al. pointed out in their landmark article of 1993 on northern Mesopotamian civilization of this era, the Leilan IIA phase (*ca.* 2400–2300 BC) featured the construction of a 2-m-wide defensive wall around Leilan's acropolis and other vital areas, as well as the cessation of fine craft-incising on the ceramics and the initial appearance of mass-produced pottery. The military power of the Subarian countryside united against the threat from the First Dynasty of Lagash, which was dominant in Šumer at the outset of this phase, but the native inhabitants were unable to resist the might of Lugal-zage-si and Uruk when he gained supremacy in Šumer during the middle of the century.

The Leilan IIB phase (*ca.* 2300–2200 BC) began with a united Mesopotamia under Sargon and his empire. Akkadian rule brought imperialized, irrigation-based agriculture to central and southern Mesopotamia, which in turn altered life in northern Mesopotamia, as this technological advancement was reproduced in and around Assyria. The Akkadians established Tell Brak as an imperial distribution center, from where they controlled Tell Leilan and Tell Mozan. As Harvey Weiss et al. have demonstrated, numerous changes were instituted at Tell Brak due to Akkadian influence.

(1) Population redistribution removed second-level centers and sustained imperialized production. (2) The stacked kiln wasters (i.e., tin-glazed earthenware vessels that collapse when the clay is being fired in a kiln, thus failing to become functional pottery) that attest to (1.5-liter) vessel-production imply the distribution of standardized Akkadian worker-rations of barley and oil. (3) A city wall of 8 m in thickness was constructed for the

first time around the entire site. (4) Civic water courses were stabilized by canalization (i.e., drainage and sewage canals dug during construction of an ancient city), which cleared out water with drainage channels, reflecting Akkadian expertise in canal management that was developed in southern Mesopotamia.

The material culture even revealed a greater level of Akkadian influence than Hurrian influence. A brick palatial building attributed to Naram-Sin was excavated at Tell Brak. In *ca.* 2200 BC, corresponding to the reign of Naram-Sin, the Akkadian-dominated occupation of phase IIB at Tell Leilan and Tell Brak ended suddenly, and the sites were abandoned. The subsequent remnant occupation at Tell Brak utilized only half of the area that was occupied formerly. Similar abandonments occurred at almost all excavated sites of this period across the Khabur plains and the Assyrian plains, including Chagar Bazar, Arbit, Germayir, Tell B'deri, Kashkashuk, Abu Hgeira, Melebiya, Tell Taya, and even Tepe Gawra. The extant epigraphical documentation from southern Mesopotamia suggests that only remnant occupations remained at Urkesh and Nineveh.

With all of the inscriptional and archaeological attestation to Sargon and the earlier part of the Akkadian Empire evident throughout the north (e.g., Assyria, the Khabur triangle, and eastern Syria), Sargon undoubtedly is the first Akkadian king to have subdued these territories and configured them to serve the empire. This picture fits well with the biblical description of the exploits of Nimrod, who built up the principal cities of Assyria, including Nineveh, Rehoboth City, Kalhu, and Resen (Gen 10:11–12), even if two of these sites cannot be identified at present. All of these Assyrian sites were located immediately to the east of the Khabur triangle, where Akkadian material culture is attested during Sargon's lifetime. Therefore, Sargon's Assyrian conquests, civic improvements, and overall exploitation of northern Mesopotamian sites make him the ideal candidate for biblical Nimrod, whom Moses credited with building (up) numerous cities in Assyria.

BOTH IMPERIALISTS EXPERIENCED A LASTING INFLUENCE IN ASSYRIA

Both Sargon and Nimrod had a lasting influence that related to the land of Assyria. Toward the end of Sargon's reign, he introduced eponymic dating within the empire. Eponymic dating is a system for keeping track of successive years by designating each year with a title related to a memorable event from that particular year that best summarizes the year. As an example from the later Third Dynasty of Ur, one cuneiform tablet dates to "the month of Shulgi's festival, the year that the giant-sized boat was built." The most significant national event for Ur that year was the construction of an enormous boat, which probably sailed in the Persian Gulf. As a result, king Shulgi determined that the year would be named after this boat's construction.

If the eponymic dating system were applied to the United States, 2001 would be named after the terrorist attacks on September 11 of that year, and 2020 would be named after the outbreak of the COVID 19 pandemic. The eponymic system of dating replaced the older systems, such as dating by the names of local officials, which was used at Shuruppak, and dating according to the numbered regnal years of the king, which was used at Urukagina and Lagash. Eponymic dating was used subsequently in Assyria throughout its long history. In fact, the accurate dating of events within the first millennium BC for many ancient peoples is owed directly to the careful eponymic dating system that the Assyrians used and mastered.

For Assyriologist William Hallo, the greatest benefit of eponymic dating is that it provides an invaluable record of the principal events and accomplishments of the various Mesopotamian dynasties for over 500 years. This administrative innovation that was preserved indefinitely in Assyria demonstrates the profound and lasting influence that Sargon of Akkad, the great Akkadian ruler, had on Assyria. Nimrod similarly had a lasting influence on the Assyrians, at least as his exploits relate to the land of Assyria, which would be expected from the man who built up their principal cities. Probably between 710 and 700 BC, the prophet Micah uttered a prophetic message about what would happen when the Assyrians invade the Promised Land.

In this prophecy, he used synonymous parallelism to declare that "they will pasture the land of Assyria with the sword, and the land of Nimrod at its entrance points" (Mic 5:6). Here, Micah—writing about 1600 years after Nimrod's lifetime—equates the land of Nimrod with the land of Assyria. This exceedingly extensive gap in time between Nimrod's day and Micah's day demonstrates an enduring legacy among chronologically distant biblical authors that the first empire builder left behind regarding his exploits in Assyria. Therefore, the reigns of Sargon of Akkad and Nimrod both display a lasting effect regarding their impact on Assyria's early history.

BOTH IMPERIALISTS WERE LEGENDARY FOR
MILITARY EXPLOITS AND BRUTALITY

Both Sargon and Nimrod were legendary for their military exploits and brutality. While this characteristic is not exclusive to Sargon, without it the case would be weakened. His accession to the throne and subsequent submission of Mesopotamia and surrounding lands to Akkadian sovereignty were accompanied by a calculated propagandistic campaign, the first such enterprise to extend itself to these limits. At the level of official art, royal relief became a functional medium for conveying ideological messages designed to invoke fear into the hearts of his enemies. Two stelae and an obelisk will serve to testify to the strict links between ideological purposes and visual media during the founding phase of the Akkadian Empire.

Sargon's Stele of Ishtar, currently housed in the Louvre (i.e., a museum in Paris, France), displays a standing royal figure with a cloak over the left shoulder and whose left hand holds a net that contains seven living prisoners entangled within it. With the right hand, the royal figure strikes the head of the largest of the prisoners with the head of a mace, which is swinging at this captive within the net. The figure has been interpreted convincingly as Ishtar, the Akkadian dynastic deity who was worshiped as the goddess of war. Nigro has argued that the scene powerfully illustrates the victory that epitomizes the blessing of Ishtar in battle and the cruelty that the Akkadians practiced against the enemies that they faced and defeated.

A second stele of the Akkadian Empire, the highly celebrated Sargonic Victory Stele from Telloh, which likely dates to Sargon the Great's reign and exists only in fragmentary form, is summarized best by its publisher, Benjamin Foster: "Considering the nature of the relief and the inscription together, one may next inquire what this stele was intended to commemorate. The pictorial representations clearly suggest a successful military campaign with slaughtering and enslavement of captives." Oddly enough, the fragmented text makes no mention of military operations, but only lists tracts of land situated in the region of Lagash, with no personal names associated with them.

A third ideological and propagandistic tool from the reign of Sargon, also located in the Louvre, is the oldest obelisk-like monument of ancient Mesopotamian art, known as the Stele of Sargon. On the upper register of Side C of the obelisk, Sargon depicts a series of encounters on the battlefield. The imagery is marked at regular intervals by the repetition of Akkadian soldiers, with their muscle-chiseled legs visible through their kilts. The geometric patterns portray the determined advancement of the Akkadian army through continuous movement.

Nigro has argued that their enemies' postures, reflecting their confrontation with these imposing Akkadian soldiers, create a sequence of increasing drama. The first enemy soldier on the left has been struck in the flank by a spear that he is trying to extract, with his final ounce of strength. The second vanquished enemy is suspended by his arms. The third enemy is kneeling with his head pushed down against the ground, as an Akkadian soldier is binding him with neck-stocks. Another register of Side C depicts a considerable number of vultures, along with a wild dog, which together are feasting on a mass of human carcasses.

These stelae, which are merely a minor representation of a much larger corpus of evidence, depict the sheer brutality of the Akkadian army and the extent to which they went to inflict tortuous pain on their defeated and captured enemies. The stelae also demonstrate the ferocity with which the Akkadian soldiers carried out the political goals of their monarch, as well as the execution of the royal blueprint to dehumanize those enemies who were unfortunate enough to survive the battle. Just as with Sargon of Akkad, Nimrod carried out a campaign of world domination, at least that of the world he knew in and around Mesopotamia. He overpowered and subjugated all of the principal city-states of Šumer, and then he advanced to the north and overran Assyria by overtaking the notable city-states in the Assyrian heartland.

The biblical description of how Nimrod carried out this plan is explicitly clear: he became a powerful slaughterer in the sight of He-who-is (Gen 10:9), viciously killing the defenders and residents of the cities that he overtook throughout Mesopotamia and Assyria. He butchered men just as a man offering an animal sacrifice would take his blade and slaughter the creature, without conscience or regret. This is certain, because the qualification that these deeds were accomplished in the sight of He-who-is connotes mankind's sinful rebellion against his creator, in the spirit of Ps 66:7, which states, "He [God] rules by his mighty strength forever. His eyes watch over the nations. Do not allow the rebellious to exalt themselves." For this reason, the meaning of Nimrod's name is apropos, and his biography matches perfectly with Sargon the Great, the king of Šumer and Akkad, who ruthlessly built his empire on the blood and bodies of all those whom he slaughtered, all of which was performed in calloused defiance of He-who-is.

SUPERIORITY OF SARGON'S CANDIDACY OVER NARAM-SIN'S

Sargon's candidacy for being equated to Nimrod is superior to that of Naram-Sin's. Nonetheless, for a number of scholars, Naram-Sin is either just as worthy of being the ideal candidate for Nimrod as Sargon is, or a better one. As Yigal Levin stated, "The identification of Nimrod with either Sargon or Naram-Sin has been brought up in the past," such as Cornelius van Gelderen's suggestion in 1914 that Naram-Sin is to be equated with Nimrod. Moreover, not only does Naram-Sin come from the correct era and dynasty, which automatically makes this Akkadian king a legitimate candidate, but his exploits seemingly outshine those of his grandfather.

For example, votive and building inscriptions of Naram-Sin were found locally at Nippur, Adab, Ur, Marada, Girsu, Tutub, and abroad at Susa and Nineveh. Such inscriptions attributed to the grandson of Sargon, found at Nineveh, among other Assyrian cities, match well with Nimrod's foundation of this great Assyrian city. Naram-Sin's borders probably were even more expansive than those of Sargon, and he even adopted a new title, "king of the four quarters." Most scholars interpret this to mean that he claimed sovereignty over each of the four directions on the compass, and thus was the self-proclaimed king of the world. Naram-Sin even boasted of being divine, thus introducing the concept of divine kingship to the world.

Yet despite Naram-Sin's impressive résumé, his candidacy for being equated with Nimrod is hindered by numerous factors: (1) Naram-Sin claimed that he had performed a feat never before achieved in history:

the conquest of Ebla and Armanum. The one matter that he conveniently omitted is the claim of his grandfather, Sargon, who boasted that he accomplished a similar feat: the conquest of Mari, Jarmuti, and Ebla. Plus, Ebla was destroyed even prior to Sargon's invasion of the city, which will be discussed in Chapter 6. Therefore, Naram-Sin was not the first to conquer impressive cities such as Ebla.

(2) Naram-Sin was not the innovator that his grandfather was. The biblical narrator portrays Nimrod as a trendsetter, one who established his kingdom in Šumer, then later expanded it into Assyrian lands. Naram-Sin, however, began his reign with northern and southern Mesopotamia already in his possession. This directly opposes the details in the biblical text, which clearly limits the starting point of Nimrod's kingdom to southern Mesopotamia and outlines its expanding progression. Sargon clearly is the Akkadian king whose biography mirrors that of Nimrod as far as the origin, initial territory, and expansional direction of his empire.

(3) Gen 10:11 notes that Nimrod went out into Assyria and built up important cities there. The archaeological record for these northern territories, however, proves that a Sargonid king prior to Naram-Sin built up those cities. The stratigraphy reveals several phases of occupation during the Akkadian Period, but the buildings of Naram-Sin that were constructed in several of the northern cities, such as the palace at Tell Brak, are dated firmly to the occupation of those sites during the final phase of the Akkadian Period. For these three reasons, Naram-Sin must be rejected as a viable candidate for biblical Nimrod. Without any reasonable doubt, Sargon of Akkad rises far above any other candidate as the historical figure referred to in the Bible as Nimrod, the later descendant of Ham and Cush who built an empire in and beyond southern Mesopotamia.

CHAPTER 6

FILLING IN SOME OF THE BLANKS

NIMROD AND THE DESTRUCTION OF EBLA AND MARI

THE LAST CHAPTER SHOULD HAVE SUCCEEDED IN persuading the reader beyond a reasonable doubt—which criterion is sufficient for convicting someone of a crime in a court of law, at least in the United States—that biblical Nimrod is none other than Sargon of Akkad, the world's first empire builder. As a result, from this point forward, Nimrod's name will be used interchangeably with Sargon's name when referring to any accomplishments that history has attributed to Sargon of Akkad. The case also was made that this enigmatic man gained sovereignty over Mesopotamia and Assyria.

However, Nimrod's influence was felt far beyond these two lands, as it was mentioned already that he claimed to have conquered Mari, Jarmuti, and Ebla. While the possibility certainly exists that he overtook every city that he claimed to have defeated, sometimes enough historical information exists to dispute the claims of ancient rulers, especially those of kings who may not have been as successful in their military operations as their written annals claim that they were. This chapter focuses on Nimrod's expansionism beyond the lands described in the Bible as being part of his kingdom, notably to the northwest of his capital at Akkad.

CITIES OF MARI AND EBLA

DESCRIPTION OF MARI AND ITS PLACE IN
SYRIA OF THE EARLY BRONZE AGE

The ancient city of Mari consists of an upper and lower tell (i.e., a defensible mound or hill that consists of the dirt-covered remains of an ancient city or settlement), which are delineated by two concentric ramparts (i.e., a defensive wall, usually with parapets and a walkway atop the wall). The current size of the site is over 100 hectares, but in antiquity it may have encompassed an even greater area, up to at least 250 hectares. Mari was an extremely important city below the confluence of the Euphrates and Khabur Rivers, located almost halfway between Ebla (to the west-northwest) and Babylon (to the southeast). Despite the prosperity and power that the cities of the Khabur and Balikh plains possessed, the main center of economic and political power in eastern Syria during the EBA III undoubtedly was centered at Mari.

Without question, the key to Mari's success was its ability to control what was shipped from Anatolia and the upper region of the Euphrates River downstream to central and southern Mesopotamia. The Euphrates River provided the fastest and most effective means by which goods and commodities were conveyed to the residents downriver from Mari.

Andre Parrot first excavated at Mari, overseeing excavations for a remarkable 40 years (1933–1974). Jean-Claude Margueron served as the director of excavations at the site from 1979 to 2004, and he was followed by Pascal Butterlin, who overtook the project in 2005. Deep soundings have ascertained that the site was founded early in the 3rd millennium BC. Margueron proposed that Mari was established as a large-scale, urban settlement of over 250 hectares, reasoning that the city could not have survived without protection from flooding or access to water from the Euphrates.

DESCRIPTION OF EBLA AND ITS PLACE IN SYRIA OF THE EARLY BRONZE AGE

The western Syrian city of Ebla and its kingdom is known widely to have been one of the great regional powers in Syria during the EBA. As Michael Astour noted, Ebla dominated the region during the late 3rd millennium BC. The vast majority of the extant information from antiquity that sheds light on this great center comes from the thousands of inscribed clay tablets that were found in the archival room of Ebla's Royal Palace G, which was located on the city's main mound.

The palace and its archival room experienced a massive conflagration (i.e., destruction due to burning in an intense fire) near the end of the EBA III. Ebla's tablets span a period of about 50 years, encompassing the reigns of three successive kings, and they reveal that Ebla had gained control over several smaller kingdoms through military action and political alliance. The cities that were under Ebla's control include Carchemish, Emar, Gasur, Ebal, Ra'aq, and Burman. In the west, Ebla's dominion reached the Amanus Mountain Range, as attested by a divine designation that clearly refers to these mountains. However, just how far north along the Amanus chain the Eblaite territory actually stretched is impossible to establish, mainly because of the extreme lack of toponymic material from that area in later sources. In the east, the limits of Ebla's influence included at least Harran and Tuttul.

The relationship of these cities to Ebla has been understood by many to be client kingdoms that were granted a high degree of local autonomy, yet still loyal to their overlord. Their obligations to Ebla's king certainly included payment of a fixed tribute in the form of various goods: metals, livestock, cloth, crafts, wool, and textiles. Unfortunately, there is slim archaeological evidence testifying to Ebla's supremacy over the upper Euphrates region. The 24th century BC, corresponding to Phase 4 in the Euphrates sequence, does not witness any radical reorganization or recon-figuration of settlements. Sites previously occupied in Phase 3 continued to be inhabited during Phase 4, and there is no appreciable increase or dimin-ishment in the sizes of the sites during this period. However, the archive definitely does imply a subservient relationship.

RIVALRY OF MARI AND EBLA

The first matter to discuss regarding Nimrod's imperialistic expansion beyond Mesopotamia and Assyria is whether he destroyed Ebla and/or Mari, which were two extremely powerful and influential cities to the west of the Euphrates. During much of the EBA in the Levant, and especially during the EBA III (2350–2100 BC), the unrivaled powers in Syria and the northwestern Levant were Mari and Ebla. This can be stated confidently, because all of the other city-states of the region were obliged to submit to the hegemony of one of these two great centers of power, on occasion switching their allegiance to one side or the other for the sake of political or practical gain.

These two dominant city-states, located on opposite sides of the Fertile Crescent, had prominent dynasties whose influence infringed not only on their own immediate vicinities but on much more distant territories throughout the region. They both were involved heavily in interregional trade during the third millennium BC, which greatly increased their profiles and growth in size and population. Naturally, their mutual desire for economic monopolization and regional control brought them into direct conflict with one another, leading to a series of wars and skirmishes that normally were fought in the very outlying areas that they wished to suppress, and which they intended to administrate.

These thoroughly ambitious rivals eventually met similarly unhappy fates in the form of a certain curtailing of their power and regional dominance, and ultimately their destruction, to one extent or another. The palace and central area of Ebla was sacked and burned in an intense fire that crippled the city. Conversely, Mari was devastated by a city-wide destruction and conflagration that left her metropolis as a total loss. Excavations at Mari have revealed that the pre-Nimrodic palace, the temple precinct, and probably the entire city were destroyed in the fire, with evidence of preliminary vandalism. Directly under the destruction stratum at Mari lay tablets in a script similar to that of Ebla's texts, but displaying some traits that reflect more recent composition than those at Ebla.

The obvious question is how these bitter rivals met their unfortunate ends. The greater focus in this chapter is on Mari in particular, although the fates of both cities were intricately bound, and thus the fate of both cities must be addressed. Regarding the primary task of determining whether Nimrod was behind the destruction of either city, numerous alleged culprits have been suggested by scholars. An opinion that was popular at one time is that Naram-Sin of Akkad, Nimrod's grandson, destroyed both Ebla and Mari during campaigns that he launched to the west. However, this view has been proven to be faulty, so few if any still advocate for Naram-Sin as the destroyer of these two regional powers.

Two views remain popular among most scholars for the destroyer of Mari. First, some consider that the city of Ebla, the principal trading rival of Mari, whose power to the west of the Euphrates was unrivalled during the EBA III, was the perpetrator. Second, many believe that Sargon the Great (a.k.a. Nimrod), the ruler of Akkad and founder of the Akkadian dynasty, was responsible for the destruction of both Mari and Ebla. Giovanni Pettinato noted that an ancient text even incriminates Sargon as the conqueror of Mari and Ebla: "Sargon the king prostrated himself in prayer before Dagan in Tuttul. (Dagan) gave him the Upper Region: Mari, Yarmuti, (and) Ebla, as far as the forest of cedars and the mountain of silver." Nimrod supposedly captured these cities in order to secure and protect the commercial route from Anatolia to Mesopotamia against the threat of ambushes by local kings along the way.

Peter Akkermans and Glenn Schwartz added that an analysis of the cuneiform tablets and material culture at Ebla indicates a contemporaneity of the last decades of Palace G—the room where Ebla's textual archive was discovered—with the early Akkadian Period in central Mesopotamia and late in the Early Dynastic III Period in southern Mesopotamia. Therefore, they concluded that Sargon likely is the destroyer of Ebla's Palace G, whose demise should be placed in the latter part of the 24th century BC. Lisa Cooper of the University of British Columbia became convinced that Ebla's palace was destroyed either by Sargon or his grandson, Naram-Sin. Of important note before putting these claims to the test, however, the Sargonic inscription does not state that Sargon destroyed these cities, just that Dagan gave all of them into his hand.

MARI IN THE EARLY BRONZE AGE

MARI'S PLACE IN SYRIA OF THE EARLY BRONZE AGE

The trading network that preceded the Akkadian Empire originally ran from Uruk—and subsequently Kish—to Ebla, with Mari located along that route. In fact, Ebla's archive reveals an important trading network through Mari known as the Kish-Mari-Ebla axis, which delivered commodities into (e.g., timber, dates, olives, pottery, porcelain, grains, etc.) and out of (e.g., lapis lazuli, a deep blue semi-precious stone greatly valued in antiquity) southern Mesopotamia. A hoard of finely-worked, precious items was found in a jar at Mari, including beautifully carved figurines of stone, gold, and lapis lazuli beads.

Some of these items display southern Mesopotamian manufacturing, such as a long lapis lazuli bead with an inscription of Mesanepada, a king from the Šumerian city of Ur. Thanks to an expansionary policy, the

Kingdom of Mari seemingly gained considerable territory, as its kings campaigned successfully in upper Mesopotamia, where Mari seized parts of the Khabur plain and conquered towns and cities up the Euphrates River all of the way into Anatolia. The cities taken in Mari's military campaigns include Emar, Ebal, Gasur, Burman, and Carchemish.

At this time, Ebla was obliged to pay tribute to Mari, but under Ebla's king, Irkab-Damu, Mari's great rival located to the west of the Mediterranean reasserted itself and reversed the balance of power. As a result, Ebla subjugated many of the cities and towns that recently had fallen into Mari's hands. More will be said about the conflict between Ebla and Mari. The archaeological record confirms that the Euphrates River basin long served as a principal avenue of trading and cultural exchange. This basin obtained its greatest importance much earlier, during the Late Uruk Period, when settlements with an unmistakably southern Mesopotamian material culture appeared along the banks of the Euphrates River as far north as Anatolia.

The majority of these settlements of the Uruk Expansion were inhabited by southern Mesopotamian colonists and merchants, who situated themselves in this distant region and acquired raw materials such as silver and copper from the mines of the Taurus Mountains. The continued importance of the river into the Early Dynastic Period of Mesopotamian archaeological periodization is deduced from textual sources such as those from Ebla. This city's foreign relations and commerce were facilitated by the Euphrates River, which led downstream to the important centers of power in southern Mesopotamia such as Kish, Uruk, and Ur, providing the means by which precious goods such as lapis lazuli were conveyed to Ebla and beyond.

PURPOSE FOR MARI'S HAVING BEEN FOUNDED

One important question is how to account for the power and influence of Mari, a city built along the desert in a valley devastated by the floods of the Euphrates, making any agricultural endeavors extremely risky. Why was Mari even built? This is the question that went unanswered for Parrot. Moreover, it plagued Margueron, his successor, for the first 25 years of his directorship at the site. In order to answer this question, Margueron spent countless hours examining the living quarters, basements, terraces, traces of streets, and the surrounding areas, including the former riverbed of the

Euphrates and other waterways. He realized that these were not always spectacular discoveries, rarely being understood immediately as important, but quite significant for the overall understanding of the site and its role in the geographical, historical, and economic context of the region.

After all of Margueron's research, pondering, and careful consideration of the data, he finally came to understand why Mari was built at the outset of the Levantine Bronze Age. The revelation about Mari, spread over a dozen years but remaining unpublished until somewhat later, was the existence of a major center of metallurgy, whose origin dates back to about 2625 BC or slightly after. Vestiges of the metallurgy were visible throughout the city.

The existence of this lucrative industry, which allowed Mari to produce arms and tools, justified everything that the excavators had uncovered. Amélie Kuhrt confirmed this claim when she observed that the evidence for military equipment at Mari, at least by the Early Dynastic III Period in Mesopotamia, if not sooner, is virtually identical to the military equipment excavated in southern Mesopotamia.

This metallurgical industry had to be exceedingly lucrative, as the cites of the alluvial plain in southern Mesopotamia that demanded building supplies were up to 400 hectares in size, while the cities of northern Syria were rarely over five hectares, which is a minute fraction of the size of the cities in Šumer. Several discoveries were crucial to the identification of this industry. A major navigable canal was discovered, which followed the Euphrates for 120 km and allowed the transportation of copper and wood from the Taurus Mountains to support Mari's metallurgical activities.

An irrigation channel that also was discovered at Mari allowed agricultural production in an area that otherwise did not receive sufficient rainfall to grow crops, given that Mari was located outside of the dry-farming line that left most of Mesopotamia unable to be farmed without the use of irrigation. A third canal protected the city from flooding and allowed large boats to enter Mari, which undoubtedly hauled copper that was transported southeastward from Anatolia. Plus, Mari was protected by a levy bank and double ramparts.

MARI'S DESTRUCTION AND SUBSEQUENT REBUILDING

The destruction that Mari suffered was total. There is no evidence of any subsequent rebuilding soon after this except at the palace, which could indicate that there was an occupational hiatus in the city's history. The reconstruction that transpired in the palatial district was accompanied by pottery that dates to the Akkadian Period. After Mari's destruction in the 23rd century BC, the Akkadians rebuilt the palatial district and appointed a military governor (Akkadian: *shakkanakku*) to run the city's affairs in the interest of Akkad.

For this reason, some scholars have theorized that the culprit must have been Naram-Sin, and not Sargon, since it could be viewed as impossible for such Akkadian pottery to be there so quickly already if Sargon had destroyed the city. However, this argument is unsound, as the destruction of Mari and its reoccupation under early Akkadian intervention are not necessarily mutually exclusive. After all, numerous Levantine cities of the middle of the 2nd millennium BC allegedly were "destroyed" by Thutmose III, the pharaoh who chased Moses out of Egypt, but almost immediately afterward were recorded in royal annals or on toponym lists as populated and thriving cities.

MARI AS THE DESTROYER OF EBLA

MARI'S UPPER HAND IN THE CONFLICT WITH EBLA

One other possibility that must be explored, in addition to the potential destruction of Mari by an Akkadian king, is whether Ebla was the destroyer of Mari. Now that a better picture has been painted of Mari's role in the ancient world during the EBA, attention turns to the case for whether Mari is the destroyer of Ebla of this era. Through Ebla's regional expansion, the city came in contact with other major political powers, including Mari. Ebla's archive reveals a commercial relationship that existed between these two ancient powers. For example, Ikun-išar, the only ruler of Mari consistently referred to in the archive as "lord" (Šumerian: *en*), delivered goods to Ebla. At the same time, these competing giants came into conflict with one another.

One reason for this conflict with Mari is that Ebla—with its close geographical proximity to Anatolia—had immediate access to valuable copper and (minor) tin deposits from the Taurus Mountains, the very materials that Mari required in its possession to fuel its vital bronze-based manufacturing industry, because Ebla controlled the trading routes from Anatolia. Another reason for this conflict is their mutual interest in dominating the northern Euphrates valley and the wealthy region of the Khabur triangle, which led to a series of wars between them for political and economic control of this territory. The series of battles that ensued between Ebla and Mari, which is documented in Ebla's archive, was extensive and complex.

At the outset, Mari held the supremacy under the reign of Nizi while conducting its policy of expansionism. A letter from Mari's next king, the renowned Enna-Dagan Letter, was aimed at intimidating Ebla with its threatening tone. The letter recounted the series of victories that were won by Mari and made clear Enna-Dagan's plan to follow the foreign policy of Iblul-Il, the predecessor of Nizi, which was a program of political hegemony and domination. Included in this program was the requirement of tribute in staggering and unparalleled amounts for so early in history. Iblul-Il had exacted 547 kg of silver and 42 kg of gold. Nizi received 72 kg of silver and 8 kg of gold. Enna-Dagan extracted 72 kg of silver and 4 kg of gold. The Eblaite administration preferred to call these gifts, a term that they probably employed for ideological reasons.

EBLA'S EQUAL FOOTING IN THE CONFLICT WITH MARI

The brief reigns of Nizi and Enna-Dagan, two kings of Mari, marked the beginning of the city's decline in the 3rd millennium BC. A few months before the death of Ebla's king, Irkab-damu, he appointed a man named Ibrium with the task of strengthening Ebla. Irkab-damu had brought Emar into Ebla's sphere of influence, which was a sign of Ebla's inching into Mari's territory. Mari retained its control over Tuttul on the Balikh River, near the confluence of the Euphrates, and the border between Ebla's and Mari's spheres of influence ran between Emar and Tuttul. For roughly 30 years, the two states exchanged messengers and ceremonial gifts on equal footing. One of Ebla's tablets records a military defeat suffered by Mari, at whose hands there is no mention, which news undoubtedly was received with great satisfaction at Ebla.

All signs indicate that Mari's leadership was weakened, but neither Mari nor Ebla seem to have been capable of conducting an offensive operation against the other at this point. The two cities then entered into a treaty, which was sealed by representatives who swore respective oaths in the temples of the patron deities of both cities. In the following year, the peace treaty notwithstanding, Ebla apparently supported a rebellion of Tuttul against Mari, even donating a gift to the person who delivered the news that Mari had been defeated by Tuttul. A few years later, Ebla managed to expand its northern borders, defeating the mighty Nagar, the city that controlled the northern Khabur plain, which represents a major expansion.

Published pre-Sargonic tablets from Tell Beydar indicate that the Khabur triangle formed a major political entity that comprised several cities and was ruled by the king of Nagar, plausibly identified with Tell Brak, the largest mound of the area, and the administrative center of the Akkadian Empire in this region during the reign of Naram-Sin. No pre-Sargonic tablets were found at Tell Brak, but the excavators identified two destruction levels there that preceded the construction of Naram-Sin's palace.

Mari had to confront Nagar in order to prevent this city's influence from extending over the entire area of the southern Khabur region as far as the Euphrates. Therefore, it was in Mari's best interest to maintain good relations with Ebla. Mari actually had to concede to the inevitable: allowing Ebla to have access to the Euphrates River, even though Mari maintained control over Tuttul and the southern Balikh valley, as the great city of Ebla scrambled to consolidate its holdings and influence in northern Syria.

MARI'S REASSERTION OF SUPERIORITY
IN THE CONFLICT WITH EBLA

The next important player that entered into the events recorded in Ebla's archive is Kish, which creates a bit of a problem. Kish, the city appearing in the texts from Ebla most frequently, is thought by some to represent the Kish of southern Mesopotamia, whose dynasties were among the most formidable before the rise of Akkad, yet by others to signify a northern Kish, usually associated with Kashkashok, a small site that is located practically at the tip of the inverted Khabur triangle. Probably the best view to hold is that some references to Kish may indicate Kashkashok or a city named Kish that was located elsewhere to the north, while others refer to the powerful Kish of the upper portion of southern Mesopotamia, a point that needs to be proven.

Piotr Michalowski was driven to posit that a northern Kish is an otherwise unknown city written KISH that lay somewhere in the Khabur region, rather than to assume the existence of an unattested Nagar that lay in Akkad and had extensive contacts with Syria in the middle of the 3rd millennium BC. He was followed by Francesco Pomponio, who also posited a Kish in the eastern part of the Khabur triangle, to the north of Nagar. Pomponio's reasons for this are threefold: (1) the association of Kish with Nagar in the archive from Ebla, (2) too great of a distance between Ebla and Kish of southern Mesopotamia, and (3) a similarity between the personal names of Kishites and Eblaites in the archive.

Michalowski provided several other reasons for adhering to a local Kish in the Eblaite texts: (1) The children of a king (Šumerian: *lugal*) of Kish were provided with rations and gifts that are similar to those that were given to persons from small towns in the immediate vicinity of Ebla. (2) In many instances, the Kish of the tablets from Ebla is paired with Nagar. A well-known ancient site by the name of Nagar indeed is attested in the Khabur region. However, to date there is no known site of Nagar located in central or southern Mesopotamia.

When looking for a suitable site in the Khabur region, Michalowski found that according to the Old-Babylonian Emar-itinerary, there was a place in the Khabur region that was named Kishkish. This seems to be the same thought that Doug Frayne had when he suggested that the Kish of the administrative texts from Ebla can be equated safely with modern Kashkashok. All of this provides strong argumentation for the view that a local Kish may be the intended site for some of the references to Kish in Ebla's archive. However, the question remains as to whether all of the references to Kish in the archive can be connected to this northern site.

A case can be made for the identification of Ebla's Kish with the Kingdom of Kish that is attested in southern Mesopotamia. Michalowski was pessimistic when he suggested that the Kish that was located in Akkad may not be attested in the administrative texts from Ebla. At the same time, he conceded that in other texts, Kish and Mari in fact are closely related, in the sense that a traveler from Ebla went to both places on the same journey. This is far from the only viable argument. Michael Astour observed that Kish is associated more frequently with Mari in the archive than it is with Nagar.

Plus, what is so important about Kishkish that in the minds of Eblaite scribes this site demands a level of attention that is equal to that of the great Mari? Besides, most of Ebla's transactions with Kish were conducted through intermediaries from Mari. Even more convincing is that from TM.75.G.2268, which records an agreement with Mari, Eblaite merchants could travel to Mari—and from Mari to Kish—using deep-water boats (Akkadian: *má-gur*). This alone is enough reason to ascertain that the Kish of the archive, or at least one of the Kishes referenced there, was situated on the Euphrates, downstream from Mari. Taking an upstream journey on the Euphrates and then sailing up the Khabur River from there to Kishkish would be unthinkable. If anything, the traveler from Ebla would go to Kishkish first, then downstream to Mari.

Finally, Ebla gifted one mina of silver to Teshna of Mari, the bearer of the news that Kish had been defeated. Considering that Mari, Kishkish, and Ebla form a virtual isosceles triangle, it would seem odd if the news of Kishkish's defeat would go to Mari first, then from there to Ebla. The road from Kishkish to Ebla would be traveled nearly as quickly as that from Kishkish to Mari. Moreover, Ebla is upstream from Mari. In contrast, Mari is located virtually on a line between Kish (of southern Mesopotamia) and Ebla. All travel from southern or central Mesopotamia, and thus news as well, would go through Mari first. This is not even to mention the question of what difference the battles of insignificant little Kishkish would make to mighty Mari or powerful Ebla. Nagar was the main player in the Khabur region anyway, not Kishkish.

As Astour correctly noted, the texts from Ebla deal with the independent Kingdoms of Mari, Kish, and Nagar. Therefore, being that strong arguments exist for the northern Kish view and for the southern Kish view, the discussion of the relationship between Ebla and Mari in the days of the archive from Ebla will continue under the assumption that the context of each individual reference must determine whether one or the other location is to be favored, because the archive apparently refers to two different Kishes.

About the time that Mari was experiencing difficulties maintaining control in the Khabur region, Kish came under attack. Given that the military fortunes of tiny Kishkish would have been of little consequence to Ebla's scribes, the likelihood is quite strong that southern Kish is in focus here, which is the view of Alfonso Archi and Giovanna Biga. Six years later, Šumerian Kish was defeated once again, probably by Enshakushanna of Uruk. This time, Mari would have participated in the battle. Another two campaigns were necessary before a definitive victory over Kish could be claimed. The following year, the third overall, Kish was defeated completely in a decisive campaign. With these crucial losses in battle, the formerly mighty dynasty of Kish was stripped of its power in southern Mesopotamia.

EBLA'S REGAINING OF EQUAL FOOTING
IN THE CONFLICT WITH MARI

As the campaign against Kish had been raging, Kish's formidable adversary at Mari succeeded in conquering some towns, and Mari even intensified its commercial relations with Ebla. Two men from Mari, acting as agents for a commercial group from Tuttul, arrived at Ebla bearing news that the towns of Kish had been conquered, and they received six shekels of silver for their efforts. Six years later, Ebla and Mari renewed their alliance, as Ebla was experiencing difficulties, including the death of its minister, Ibrium, after 18 years of faithful service to the king. This is a time when Mari was slightly ahead in the fluctuating balance of power.

This imbalance in Mari's favor is observable in the form of a substantially more valuable "gift" that Mari's king sent to Ebla than the one Ebla's king sent to Mari. However, the swing in this direction did not seem to last too long. A text from the same year mentions clothing required for a military expedition against Mari, possibly signaling a site under Mari's control rather than Mari, itself. Another document speaks of gold that was sent from Ebla to Kablul, a city that had been under Ebla's authority for at least 20 years. There is no doubt about Ebla's military action that year against the interests of Mari, and the *mu-Du* text reveals that this expedition ended with an outcome that was favorable to Ebla.

When Ibbi-zikir followed in his father's footsteps as Ebla's minister, diplomatic relations between Mari and Ebla intensified, and the exchange of gifts increased, especially on the part of Mari. In the first 10 years of Ibbi-zikir's ministry, he consolidated Ebla's power over northern Syria, and he led numerous military campaigns in the region. Mari attempted to fulfill its part, following a similar strategy in the area of the middle Euphrates, and its greatest victory apparently was the one over Haddu, an ancient city that possessed a kingdom in northern Syria and is identified with modern Malhat ed-Deru.

An uninterrupted series of victories made Ebla's king confident in his own power. After 25 years of sworn peace, which was maintained through the regular exchange of envoys and ceremonial gifts, the rivalry with Mari actually had not been eliminated, so obviously the treaty was not entirely binding in the minds of either side. Two routes linked northern Syria with the eastern regions and the great centers of Babylonia: the northern route was controlled by Ebla as far as the region of Nagar, while the southern route ran along the Euphrates down to Babylonia, which required passage through Mari. On account of how the trading routes for these two great powers intersected, permanent peace between them hardly could have lasted.

EBLA'S MAJOR VICTORY IN BATTLE DURING THE CONFLICT WITH MARI

As for Mari, the earlier exploits of Iblul-Il demonstrate that the city considered it vital to extend its dominion over the entire region of the middle Euphrates. If Mari did not attempt to subjugate Ebla, it was merely because Mari deemed itself incapable of winning a definitive victory over Nagar, which had to be prevented from interfering in the Euphrates valley. Mari also had to deal with the threat to the south that Kish posed, although that problem finally was alleviated, temporarily if not permanently. Being that the pendulum now was about to swing forcefully in the direction of Ebla, no other political event is represented so richly or frequently in the archive as the campaign against Mari that transpired during the last years of Ebla's king, Išar-damu.

This event was preceded by careful diplomatic preparations while the army was being equipped. An announcement was made about the departure of Ibbi-zikir, who led Ebla's troops on a journey to Mari in the 13th year of his ministry, which is a clear violation of the treaty between Ebla and Mari. The texts from Mari's archive, although worded tersely, provide a clear picture of the diplomatic activity that continued throughout the war. During the march on Tuttul, Ibbi-zikir met with the brother of Kish and his party, along with Ennani-il from Haddu. Several kings joined them along the way, and when they had ventured 190 km from Tuttul, the army reached Terqa, which was located only 50 km upstream from Mari.

The decisive battle was fought near Terqa, as Mari's army marched up the river valley to meet the Eblaite entourage there. No details of the battle were recorded, as the only mention of Ebla's victory is from the news of Mari's defeat that was brought to Ebla by messenger. Ibbi-zikir and his counselors apparently were not confident about laying siege to Mari. Yet there is no doubt that Ebla won a decisive victory at the battle. After Ibbi-zikir's victorious return, celebrations took place at Ebla. Then, in order to consolidate this success, Ebla quickly formed alliances with the ruling houses of Nagar and Šumerian Kish, whom they had aided by weakening their feared rival on the Euphrates. Ebla, by renewing pacts with longstanding allies, reaped the fruits of her past diplomatic contacts.

The plan for Ebla to consolidate its newfound prestige in the Levant by means of a dynastic marriage between Keshdut, the daughter of Išar-damu, and the son of the king of Kish took shape during diplomatic negotiations that were conducted in the aftermath of the war against Mari. Once again, southern Kish must be in view, as a dynastic marriage with the king of Kish-kish makes absolutely no sense after Ebla's victory over the great city of Mari. Kish obviously had risen back to prominence after the earlier defeat it had suffered. By forging an alliance with Nagar and Kish, Ebla created a political orb—even if only for a brief period of time—that incorporated both northern Syria, the middle Euphrates, and northern Babylonia.

EBLA'S DESTRUCTION AFTER RISING TO
PREEMINENCE IN THE CONFLICT WITH MARI

Ebla's alliance represents a peak in her history, as the city's good fortunes would not last long enough to be enjoyed. Three years after this event, the palace at Ebla and the attached buildings all were destroyed and burned in an intense fire. Ebla's ambition to be a regional power thus was put to an unceremonious end, once and for all. The question that this begs, which is completely related to the identity of Mari's destroyer, is who was responsible for destroying Ebla, and how extensive was that destruction. Ebla's Royal Palace G, where the archive was stored, was a total loss. The palace was abandoned, and a retaining wall of mudbrick was built at the edge of the court of audiences, in order to prevent the palace-debris from sliding down the slope.

Is it justified to equate the fire of Palace G with a catastrophe of the city as a whole? There is no continuity in settlement on the acropolis, where the royal palace had stood, at least in the western and southern sectors, which were excavated. A new palace, discovered in 1993 and roughly contemporary with the Third Dynasty of Ur (2111–2004 BC), eventually was built in Area D on the acropolis, in the northern part of the lower city and directly north of the burned palace of the Early Dynastic Period. As for the city of Ebla overall, Michael Astour has contended that not only was there no break in cultural development, but there was no reduction of size in the residential area. Traces of post-destruction occupation were found in various places in the lower city, including its periphery.

Astour became convinced that Palace G is the only part of the city that was burned down. He even considered that a natural disaster, arson, or an accident could have caused Palace G's demise. He further theorized that there is no reason to infer that an enemy was responsible for the fire. In fact, since there are no signs that the city was sacked before being burned, he believed that the evidence speaks against an attack by a foreign enemy. He asked why plunderers would leave behind 22 kg of unworked lapis lazuli that was found a few yards from the doomed palace. Excavations also uncovered lesser quantities of carnelian, rock crystal, obsidian, and remnants of gold foil that were overlays for wooden furniture. He considered it unlikely that such furnishings, which were fit for a king, would have been left in the palace by invaders prior to torching it.

Paolo Matthiae agreed with Astour that there is no evidence of interruption in the continuity of occupation at Ebla after the destruction of Palace G. He said that the transition from Mardikh IIB1 to IIB2 is marked by the destruction of the palace but not by any actual break in cultural development. The chronological limits of the period have been approximated based on its plentiful ceramic material, both *in situ* (from the acropolis and lower city) and in the soil reused for the core of the great earthen rampart of the following period. The phase immediately after Palace G's destruction corresponds to the pottery of the Amuq J sequence (i.e., an archaeological phase for the Amuq Plain of western Syria), which is an internal development and refinement of the ceramic ware of the Amuq I sequence that was characteristic for the Mardikh IIB1 period.

An important synchronism between the palaces of Ebla and Mari emerged during the excavations of 2000 and 2001, under the direction of Jean-Claude Margueron. In Palace P-1, the second and last level of the pre-Sargonic palace, which dates to *ca.* 2291–2200 BC by [14]C (i.e., radiocarbon) analysis, seal impressions were found bearing the name of Išgi-Mari. Mari's Palace P-1 was in use already during the last 30–35 years of Palace G, the period corresponding to the administrations of Ibrium and Ibbi-zikir, who were contemporaries of two of Mari's kings: Iku(n)-išar and HI-da-ar.

One result of this discovery is the certainty that the destruction of Ebla's palace predated the fall of the city of Mari. Since HI-da-ar, Mari's king, is mentioned in the texts from Ebla's archive, he reigned both at the time of Ebla's fall, and for an unknown number of years afterward. He was succeeded by Išgi-Mari, who was in power when Mari was destroyed. Since Išgi-Mari is unknown in the texts from Ebla, the destruction of the palace at Ebla must have occurred prior to the destruction of Mari. This information is crucial to understanding the sequence of events related to the conflict between Ebla and Mari.

DATING EBLA'S DESTRUCTION

As for the dating of Palace G's destruction, Pettinato believed that *ca.* 2500 BC is the proper date. He suggested this date for a number of reasons. First, the only sure synchronism in Ebla's archive is the one between Ar-En-num, the third king of Ebla named in the corpus, and Iblul-Il, a king of Mari who clearly lived before the establishment of the Sargonic kingdom. Second, there is a total absence of references to the city of Akkad in the archive. Third, the city most frequently mentioned in the archive is Kish, followed by Adab.

On account of this, Pettinato became convinced that the period of the archive preceded the rise of Akkad and was contemporary with the First Dynasty of Kish (2600–2500 BC). Fourth, in the commercial texts, Kish and Adab occur side-by-side, bringing to mind the great king of Kish named Mesalim, who extended his domain over Adab, consequently linking Ebla's dynasty to Mesopotamia, where Mesalim was a leading figure. Fifth, the texts of the archive often speak of "the king of Kish" (Šumerian: *lugal-Kiš*) and a person with the unusual name "Mesalim" (Šumerian: *me-sà-li-ma*), which recalls the name of a known king of Kish.

There are numerous flaws in Pettinato's case, which Astour has pointed out. First, Pettinato's first and second arguments are explained with equal plausibility by a date immediately before the rise of Sargon, or any time between the First Dynasty of Kish and Sargon's accession onto the throne. Therefore, *ca.* 2350 (middle chronology) or 2300 BC (low chronology) would work fine. Second, Kish survived into the Sargonic period, so there is no reason to demand a date of 2500 BC for Kish's presence in Ebla's archive.

Third, the notion of Mesalim is no more than a reminiscence, as this name is not documented. Fourth, when Astour counted the reigns of the nine kings of Mari from the accession of Lamgi-Mari to the destruction of Palace G during the reign of Mari's king, HI-da-ar, he was forced to move down the terminal year of the destruction of Palace G after 2400 BC, even if one follows the middle chronology. Therefore, Pettinato cannot be correct in dating Ebla's destruction to the end of the First Dynasty of Kish in *ca.* 2500 BC.

Since Pettinato's theory does not coincide with the data, other options must be explored. Paleographers have attributed Ebla's archive to the end of the Early Dynastic IIIв Period (*ca.* 2400–2330 BC), according to Astour. However, Astour did not state the reasons for this choice. Instead, he quoted several scholars who weighed-in on the topic of the dating of the writing of the tablets. In fact, some of these scholars whom he quoted suggested that the period ends after Sargon ascended the throne, while others said that it ends prior to Sargon's accession. While the work of paleographers is valued, certainly the advent of Sargon marks a logical point for a change in material culture throughout much of the Fertile Crescent.

The conclusions of some of these paleographers seem to be in line with the effect on the dating of the archive that must be taken into account on the basis of an important archaeological find. The lid of a vase found in Room L.2913 at Ebla, from the same stratum as the archive, contains the cartouche of Pepi I (*ca.* 2334–2279 BC), the third king of Egypt's 6th Dynasty. While Egyptian dates are not completely secure for the 3rd millennium BC, the time period of Pepi I is attributable to the latter part of the 24th century BC with a reasonable amount of assurance.

Therefore, the timeframe for the fall of Ebla's Palace G occurs in the latter part of the 24th century or early in the 23rd century BC. If Sargon of Akkad indeed ascended the throne in *ca.* 2320, as the present author is convinced, then the destruction of Ebla's palatial district probably took place between 2334 and 2320 BC. In terms of relative dating, Ebla fell to Enšakušana of Uruk about 24 years after the fall of Kish, and at least 13 years before the fall of Mari. These numbers are borne out after making a historical reconstruction based on the data obtained from Ebla, Mari, and other Mesopotamian sources.

IDENTIFYING THE DESTROYER OF EBLA

For the vast majority of the time period covered in the tablets comprising Ebla's archive, Kish was the only Babylonian city of which Ebla received regular news from the messengers of Mari, as mentioned already. Therefore, Kish was the political hub of central—and perhaps even northern—Babylonia. Ebla considered its alliance with Kish to be so vital that after their victory over Mari, they sealed it with a political marriage between the princess of Ebla and the king of Kish. The capture of Adab, which falls 11 years after the demise of Kish, is attributed to Lugal-zage-si—the king of Umma, and then king of Uruk, who called himself "king of the land." Archi and Biga argued that at this time, Sargon had been ruling for at least 19 years.

Not only was Kish an important international player for Ebla, but for Mari, as well. Mari took part in the war against Kish, in years 10–12 of Ibrium's ministry at Ebla, which cannot be forgotten when considering the eventual fate of Mari. If Ebla was destroyed about 24 years after the fall of Kish and 13 years after the conquest of Adab by Lugal-zage-si, then to whom can the destruction of Ebla be attributed? The total sacking, destruction, and burning of the acropolis at Ebla, if accomplished by an external enemy, logically would have occurred at the hands of Mari. Nagar, the regional state to the east of the Euphrates, was never strong enough to confront Ebla. No powerful Babylonian or Šumerian dynasty would have been willing or able to attack Ebla before first eliminating Mari from the scene, so none of them seems to be a legitimate option.

The one plausible scenario is that Mari, unquestionably seething after their open-field loss in battle at the hands of Ebla, quickly recovered from its defeat. Despite Ebla's alliances with Nagar and Kish, Mari managed to consolidate its holdings, rebuild an army, and—a mere three years later—carry out a successful, full-scale assault on its bitter rival to the west. Therefore, given all of the historical considerations at the time of Ebla's destruction, Mari should be accepted as the city responsible for the destruction of Ebla and its Palace G.

At this time, HI-da-ar still must have been Mari's king, as the Eblaite sources make no mention of any dynastic succession. There currently is no way to determine how long his reign lasted. What the newer sources from Mari show is that he was succeeded by Išgi-Mari. The only other option for Palace G's demise is Astour's notion of a natural disaster, arson, or an accident as the cause, rather than an enemy. However, this purely conjectural option does not fit the evidence nearly as well, so the probability of its validity is not at all high.

POSSIBILITY OF EBLA AS THE DESTROYER OF MARI

The final question to answer is whether or not Ebla could have been the party responsible for the decimation of Mari. Undoubtedly, Ebla was crippled from the destruction that the city suffered. Scholars disagree as to whether Ebla was occupied immediately after the defeat. All agree that the palace was abandoned, and that the rebuilding of the lower city was not imitated on the acropolis. However, some scholars are adamant that Ebla's loss was not categorical, and that it was rebuilt soon after its defeat, if only to a limited extent. Either way, it is difficult to imagine that the Ebla that remained or was rebuilt would have been anywhere close to powerful enough to destroy the mighty city of Mari completely, especially when Ebla refused to attempt this feat at the earlier time of its pinnacle, fresh after resoundingly defeating Mari's army outside of Terqa.

NIMROD AS THE DESTROYER OF MARI

With the strong unlikelihood of Ebla's being the culprit responsible for the utter destruction of Mari, Sargon of Akkad (a.k.a. Nimrod) remains as the most plausible candidate. Sargon was the king of Akkad, a city that the *Šumerian King List* reports as being built (up) by him, and he ruled for an amazing 55 years or so, from *ca.* 2320–2265 BC (middle chronology) or 2270–2215 BC (shorter chronology). One problem that makes an evaluation of Sargon's candidacy as the destroyer of Mari a difficult task is the lack of a royal archive preserved from his reign. The archive either has yet to be discovered, or it did not survive in antiquity.

Mario Liverani perceptively pointed out that no palace or archive belonging to Sargon or his distinguished grandson, Naram-Sin, has been discovered, and that their temples and burial places have not been located. An effective and large-scale improvement of what is known about Sargon and his capital of Akkad could come only after excavation. Unfortunately, the location of Sargon's capital has yet even to be discovered. Until Akkad is identified positively and explored systematically, whether an archive exists there or not, more questions will be asked about the Akkadian monarchs than answers can be offered.

Only finding the city of Akkad or Sargon's archive would solve the question completely as to his candidacy as the destroyer of Mari. However, one form of hard evidence implicating Sargon as the destroyer of Mari is the year-name he assigned in his eponymic dating list to "the year in which Mari was destroyed," all but certainly implying that this is a personal boast about his own accomplishment.

One circumstantial piece of evidence linking Sargon to Mari's demise, which comes from extant sources, is that after Mari's rebuilding—whenever that process took place, exactly—the city was administered by Akkadian governors whom Sargon's successors had appointed, suggesting to some scholars that Sargon destroyed the city. Mari remained abandoned for one or two generations, but then it was rebuilt and restored to prominence.

One of the common criticisms that has led some scholars to dismiss the possibility of Sargon's being the destroyer of Mari is that the Eblaite texts—which are contemporary with the city of Mari that was destroyed at the end of the EBA III—make no mention of Akkad whatsoever, but instead refer to the Kingdom of Kish, and quite frequently.

This could lead to the belief that Akkad was not in existence when Ebla was destroyed, thus meaning that Sargon was not in power. However, this objection dissipates once it is accepted that the destruction of Ebla's palace, with the period's one textual archive, predated the fall of Mari. With a minimum of 13 years between the two destructions, and no known maximum number of years for this gap, Akkad need not appear in the Eblaite archive for Sargon to have destroyed Mari.

NIMROD'S EXPANSION TO THE EAST, NORTH, AND NORTHWEST

Sargon soon campaigned far beyond the traditional borders of Šumer and Akkad. His first conquests may have been in the west, since the Amorites felt his presence as early as Year 3 or 11. Another option is that Sargon first campaigned to the east, in Elam and Barakhshi (a.k.a. Markhashi), which he totally subdued. From there he ventured to Dilmun, a region in antiquity that remains unidentified but is thought to include the island of Bahrain, which would have been accessible only by boat, and possibly eastern Saudi Arabia along the shores of the Persian Gulf. According to a later epic called *King of Battle*, Sargon eventually penetrated deeply into Anatolia, in order to protect the rights of Akkadian traders by securing the commercial route from Anatolia to Mesopotamia against the ambushes of local kings.

A Hittite king of the 17th century BC even recalled that Sargon crossed the upper Euphrates to receive the submission of Hahhum. To the north, Sargon campaigned against Simurrum, which is known from a date formula from Nippur. This is the first recorded southern Mesopotamian penetration into Assyria, which presumably came about later in Sargon's reign and as such fits well with Nimrod's biography. On Sargon's way to Anatolia, he led his army up the Euphrates River, which is deduced from the previously cited Sargonic inscription: "Sargon the king prostrated himself in prayer before Dagan in Tuttul. (Dagan) gave him the Upper Region: Mari, Yarmuti (and) Ebla, as far as the forest of cedars and the mountain of silver."

His prayer took place in Tuttul, at the confluence of the Euphrates and Khabur Rivers, which city was formerly Mari's port of operations for its involvement in the Khabur basin. Given that Mari and Ebla represent not merely cities but territorial regions, Yarmuti also must be a territorial region. Michael Astour conjectured that Yarmuti is none other than the Khabur triangle, a densely settled and wealthy region that was an attractive prospect for tribute and loot, for which reason it became the heartland of the Empire of Mitanni in the middle of the 2nd millennium BC. This makes sense geographically, because Yarmuti would fall between Mari and Ebla, as per the order in the inscription. The cedar forest probably implies the Amanus Mountains, where copper was mined, and the mountain of silver is likely the Taurus Mountains, the location of silver mines.

SECTION IV

NIMROD IN IMITATION AND LEGACY

CHAPTER 7

FIRST TO PLAY FOLLOW THE LEADER

NARAM-SIN OF THE AKKADIAN EMPIRE

IMPACT OF NIMROD'S EMPIRE BUILDING

NIMROD'S CONQUEST OF A LARGE PORTION OF the ancient Near East—which includes Mesopotamia, Assyria, and parts of Elam, Anatolia, and Saudi Arabia, to name several important parts of the empire—left a lasting imprint on the peoples of the ancient world. He was legendary in and around Mesopotamia for many centuries after his death, which is reflected by the great number of times that his name (i.e., as Sargon) appears in later inscriptions. Even Moses was impressed enough by Nimrod's exploits that he wrote about this powerful king roughly 900 years after he accomplished these feats. However, Nimrod was far from the last empire builder in ancient history, and this fact obviously was not lost on Moses when he composed Genesis.

A number of subsequent empires arose in and around the Fertile Crescent, four of which were named and discussed on multiple occasions by Daniel the prophet. The lives and exploits of some of these empire builders after Nimrod are worth investigating, even if just to understand why Moses was so concerned about this pattern of empire building that he wanted to address the blueprint for his fellow Israelites to understand how this is an evil practice to avoid. Moses understood clearly that kings would arise over Israel, and he undoubtedly included Nimrod's story in Genesis 10 for the expressed purpose of deterring future Israelite kings from following in the footsteps of this ruthless conqueror.

This chapter and the next one include a description of the empire building of the following kings: (1) Naram-Sin of the Akkadian Empire, the grandson of Nimrod who expanded the empire that his grandfather had built; (2) Ur-Nammu of the Third Dynasty of Ur, who forged a minor empire in Mesopotamia with Šumer at its core; (3) Hammurabi of the Old Babylonian Empire, who joined Ur-Nammu as the two famous authors of law codes used to establish order and preserve justice in the empire; (4) Thutmose III of Egypt, the greatest conqueror of any Egyptian kingdom or dynasty; (5) Esarhaddon of the Neo-Assyrian Empire, who enjoyed the most expansive empire throughout all of Assyrian history; (6) Nebuchadnezzar II of the Neo-Babylonian Empire, the empire builder who interacted with Daniel; (7) Darius I of the Medo-Persian Empire, who inherited and expanded the empire that conquered the Judahite Kingdom of David's progeny; and (8) Alexander III of the Greco-Macedonian Empire, the southern European king who conquered more nations and enveloped more territory into his domain than any of his fellow empire builders before him.

AKKADIAN EMPIRE BETWEEN NIMROD AND NARAM-SIN

The death of Sargon of Akkad was not the end for the empire that he built in and around Mesopotamia. Two of Sargon's sons, Rimush and Man-Ish-tushu, succeeded him as Akkadian kings, reigning for 22 or 24 years combined. They apparently continued in the footsteps of their famous father, consolidating the empire that he had built. Rimush, Sargon's first successor but second son, according to the *Šumerian King List*, suppressed numerous insurrections by unruly governors over the Šumerian cities. Upon Rimush's accession to the throne, the Šumerian cities of Adab, Zabala, Umma, Kidin-gira, Ur, and Lagash all rebelled. The rebellion—a desperate, all-out effort to shake off the Akkadian yoke once and for all—ultimately failed. In Rimush's third year, he campaigned outside of Mesopotamia, subduing Elam and Parahšum.

The second son to rule, Man-Ishtushu, was the older of the two brothers and was credited by the later Assyrian king, Shamshi-Adad, as the man who built the Ishtar temple at Nineveh. According to Hallo, Man-Ishtushu's rule over distant Ashur and Susa is attested by the honorary inscriptions on the monuments of native governors, a tribute to Mesopotamian imperialism that would continue on all of Babylonia's frontiers for the next millennium.

Walther Sallaberger and Aage Westenholz noted that Man-Ishtushu apparently continued the tactics of his predecessors, at least regarding foreign policy, as he traveled to Cilicia, on which trip he reportedly overtook Armanum and Ebla, felled cedars of Lebanon, and reached the source of the Tigris and Euphrates Rivers.

Other than these few events, the memory of the two ruling sons of Sargon is preserved only in the omen literature, a genre that essentially began with Sargon and became a characteristic vehicle of Mesopotamian historiography. Hallo pointed out that according to these omens, both brothers were killed by their own courtiers, in one case with the king's own cylinder seal, which has long spikes on which these seals were mounted before being attached to a chain that was worn around the neck. The reigns of Sargon's two sons were eclipsed by that of his grandson, whose rule deserves its own chapter in this book even if simply because he was the first illustrious emperor after Sargon, and because he was Sargon's own blood relative.

ILLUSTRIOUS REIGN OF NARAM-SIN

Man-Ishtushu's assassination paved the way both for the accession of his son, Naram-Sin (*ca.* 2241–2185 BC), and the most brilliant period that the Sargonic empire—and perhaps any Mesopotamian empire—ever would enjoy. The new king experienced an almost unparalleled reign of 55 years. Although not every copy of the *Šumerian King List* preserves the number 55 for Naram Sin's regnal length, there is no convincing reason to doubt that the correct number is between 54 and 56 years, as it would be difficult to accommodate in any shorter span of time all of the achievements and innovations that are attributed to his reign.

PERSONAL ACCOMPLISHMENTS AND EXALTATIONS

Among the accomplishments of Naram-Sin, the most conspicuous one just may be the transformation of the royal titulary (i.e., the royal titles that are given to a king). Hallo noted that until this time, Mesopotamian kings were content to specify the political or cultic relationship between the ruler and his geographical domain—such as, "lord/high priest of Šumer," "king of the nation," "lord/high priest of the territory of Uruk," or "king of the territory of Ur." On what appear to be the earliest inscriptions of Naram-Sin's reign, he was acclaimed with the modest title, "king of Akkad."

According to Sallaberger and Westenholz, about halfway through Naram-Sin's reign, he introduced the title, "the mighty one, king of the four corners" (of the world), a title that was used by every future king who proudly aspired to universal dominion over all of Mesopotamia. Not content with earthly honors, Naram-Sin also allowed himself to receive the title, "god of Akkad," which later led to a cult of the living ruler and his deceased predecessors and for all practical purposes was indistinguishable from the cult of the mythical gods who long had been worshipped in Mesopotamia. As was true for the cult of the gods, the one established for Naram-Sin centered around a statue of the king.

DOMESTIC AND ADMINISTRATIVE REFORMS

In the domestic realm, Naram-Sin perpetuated and institutionalized the reforms with which Sargon only began to experiment. As with Sargon's daughter Enheduanna, Naram-Sin's daughter, Enmenanna, became high priestess of the moon-god at Ur. Regarding the policies of Sargon, Naram-Sin found high clerical or civil positions for his numerous progeny, including Shar-kali-sharri, who succeeded his father and ruled after him for a lengthy 24 years. Of their combined 80 regnal years, the classical period of Sargonic rule, almost half of these years are known by name, thanks to the eponymic dating system. Without this system, it would be difficult to reconstruct the history of much of this period in Akkad and throughout Babylonia.

The increased need for—and attestation of—year-names under Naram-Sin and Shar-kali-sharri is an indicator of the prosperity and economic growth of their time. During their reigns, legal and administrative documents appear not only at Lagash and Ur, from where such texts are known to predate Sargonic times, but also—for the first time—at sites such as Adab, Nippur, Susa, Gasur (later Nuzi), and the Diyala Valley. The language in these documents is as often Akkadian as Šumerian, and such royal patronage of the once-despised tongue may have inspired the beginnings of Akkadian *belles-lettres* (i.e., artistically fine literature).

Another sign of Akkadian prosperity is the amount of artwork that dates to this period. Nearly all surviving Sargonic artwork can be attributed to Naram-Sin's reign. The visual arts enjoyed a vibrant new era, mirroring in visual form the confidence that world domination must have inspired in the political sphere. Stone carvings, reliefs, and sculptures all display individualized facial features of their subjects. The forceful modeling of rippling muscles, along with the confident rendering of background land-scapes, while owing something to early dynastic precedent, set the Sargonic style apart from that of all other periods. The bronze head of an unidentified Sargonic king—now thought by many scholars to be Naram-Sin—found at Nineveh, the Victory Stele of Naram-Sin, and the nearly life-sized bronze statue of Naram-Sin from Bassetki are representative of this innovation.

FOREIGN RELATIONS AND IMPERIAL EXPANSIONISM

As for foreign affairs, Naram-Sin proved to be a worthy Sargonic king, as he dominated a great portion of the ANE. From Purushkhanda in the northwest to Magan in the southeast, a consistent pattern of military, dip-lomatic, and commercial activity is attested. For Hallo, the most graphic evidence consists of pictorial representations of the great conqueror, such as his Victory Stele found near Diyar Bakr, which commemorates a triumph over the Lullubi, a mountainous people whose king, Anu-banini, flaunted his power with an Old-Akkadian rock relief from Saripul. Naram-Sin added all of upper Mesopotamia—ancient Subartu, which includes the trans-Ti-gris and Al-Jazira—to the empire, in a sustained effort of conquest over many years.

Equally explicit evidence of Naram-Sin's activities is furnished by his votive and building inscriptions found both locally (at Nippur, Adab, Ur, Marada, Girsu, and Tutub) and abroad (at Susa, Nineveh, Tell Brak, Bass-etki, and Mari). Moreover, at Tell Brak, the remains of the king's fortress, or palace, provide testimony that more than a momentary occupation of the area was intended. Inscriptions and date formulae furnish contemporary evidence for other conquests abroad (e.g., Magan, Simurrum, Mardaman, Arman, and Ebla) and for building operations close to home (e.g., Nippur and Zabalam). Dated economic texts also furnish direct evidence of eco-nomic activity at sites such as Tutub, Adab, and Nippur.

REVOLT AGAINST AND DEMISE OF NARAM-SIN

Naram-Sin referred to a time "when the four corners all at once rose against him, and he had to fight nine campaigns in one year." Sallaberger and Westenholz noted that later tradition attributes Naram-Sin with battles against both Babylonians and hordes of barbarians. This tradition may be conflating the rebellion he experienced with the later fall of Akkad, because the great revolt against Naram-Sin was purely a Mesopotamian affair. While fragments of the revolt have survived, nothing is stated about its motivating forces. Later tradition implicates Kish as the chief fomenter of the rebellion, as this city was described as being ungrateful for the devastation they experienced at the hands of Sargon and Naram-Sin.

Hallo believed that the death of Naram-Sin is difficult to explain with any certainty, but later tradition about him is as abundant as that about Sargon, only less unanimous. The lost ending of the Cutha Legend presumably recalled the empire's ultimate deliverance from the rampaging hordes of Anubanini. In another fragmentary text, Naram-Sin similarly extricated himself from the Kish-led rebellion that included most of his native Akkadian and Šumerian subjects.

However, an equally persistent tradition, recorded in the Šumerian version against Nippur and its god, Enlil, and in the Akkadian version against Babylon and Marduk (i.e., the chief god in the Babylonian pantheon), depicts Naram-Sin as the model of the hapless ruler who came to grief at the end of his reign, and whose downfall was facilitated by his own sacrilege.

CHAPTER 8

OTHERS WHO PLAYED FOLLOW THE LEADER

NIMROD'S LEGACY ECHOED THROUGHOUT ANTIQUITY

THIRD DYNASTY OF UR UNDER UR-NAMMU

COLLAPSE OF AKKADIAN DYNASTY LEADS TO POWER STRUGGLE IN MESOPOTAMIA

With the collapse of the Akkadian Empire under Shu-Durul (*ca.* 2136–2121 BC), the Sargonic kingdom was divided into petty states such as Lagash, Umma (now under Gutian rule), Uruk (its Fourth Dynasty), and a greatly-reduced city of Akkad. The brief era that followed is known variously as the Late Akkadian, Post-Akkadian, or Gutian Period. By far, the most important of these city-states was Lagash, whose surviving tradition through inscriptional evidence refers to a triumph over the city of Anshan (in Elam, to the east of the Persian Gulf) and Elam as a whole.

Plus, the king of Lagash, Gudea, seemingly extended his domain as far as Adab and Uruk (both in Šumer). Yet Hallo noted that outside of mentioning the few military conquests that occurred, the inscriptions of the period are devoted mostly to economic and religious pursuits: irrigation, trade, temple-building and dedications, and the installation of the king's chosen personnel.

Therefore, in this comparatively peaceful interlude after the end of the Akkadian Empire, commerce and trade thrived, and both literature and sculpture-making flourished. According to Postgate, Uruk defeated the Gutians decisively before the end of the 22nd century BC, which later was celebrated as a dramatic example of divine retribution. Utu-hegal, the conqueror of the Gutians, who ruled at Uruk for only 7½ years, enjoyed some level of prestige in Šumer, having settled a boundary dispute between Lagash and Ur in favor of Lagash, and having restored Uruk's sovereignty over Ur, which he administered through a governor named Ur-Nammu. Yet this governor was destined for greater things, including the founding of Ur's Third Dynasty, which became the world's next empire after the Akkadian Empire that Nimrod had established, and the initiating of a Neo-Šumerian Renaissance.

UR-NAMMU'S IMPLEMENTING OF DOMESTIC CONSTRUCTION PROJECTS

In and around the city of Ur, Ur-Nammu devoted his energy to the reconstruction of the wharves for overseas trading, and to the implementation of a substantial program of irrigation works, thus assuring the city's economic self-sufficiency that it needed to match its new religious prestige. Next, he proceeded to rebuild the temples of the national Šumerian deities—Enlil and Ninlil—in Nippur, already the traditional religious and cultic center of Šumer and Akkad for much of the 3rd millennium BC. This won him the allegiance of the priesthood at Nippur, and in about Year 4 he was honored with the title, "king of Šumer and Akkad."

This prestigious title secured Ur-Nammu's connection to Nimrod, and he won religious legitimization throughout southern Mesopotamia for his political aspirations by rebuilding the ancient sanctuaries, which he accomplished at Ur, Nippur, and throughout the cities of Šumer and Akkad. His building and votive inscriptions reflect his construction of temples to the principal deities of Eridu (Enki), Uruk (Inanna), Larsa (Utu), Kish (Ninhursag), and probably Umma (Shara), as well as some additional deities at Ur (Nin-egal, Nin-gubla), itself. Perhaps his most notable building projects are Ur's magnificent ziggurat and a defensive wall to keep out the Amorites, the latter of which is commemorated by a year-name in Ur's eponymic dating list.

UR-NAMMU'S ENACTING OF THE OLDEST PRESERVED LAW CODE IN WORLD HISTORY

Perhaps Ur-Nammu's most enduring venture is his promulgation of the oldest surviving law code known to history. This code, while it did not survive in complete form, represents a conscious effort to collect actual legal precedents, perhaps serving as a guide for future generations. These precepts were phrased within the format of conditional statements (e.g., "If a man . . ."), a form that became normative for ANE precedent law not only in Šumer, but also in Akkad and among the Hittites in Anatolia.

It is questionable whether Ur-Nammu's law codes were intended as binding in court, although their active role is well-attested during the reigns of his successors. Hallo noted that although no evidence exists to confirm that the courts within the Third Dynasty of Ur appealed to written law as the basis for their decisions, Ur-Nammu's law codes marked him as the "shepherd" of his people who was genuinely interested in justice for all of them, so in this respect his innovations provided a model for many subsequent kings and kingdoms.

UR-NAMMU'S AMASSING OF AN EMPIRE IN SOUTHERN MESOPOTAMIA

The return to centralized rule in Mesopotamia is portrayed in the sources as having begun with the expulsion of the Gutians. At a time no later than Utu-hegal's death, Ur-Nammu asserted the independence of Ur from Uruk by claiming certain royal rights, eventually refortifying the city, establishing an eponymic dating system at Ur, and assuming the title, "king of Ur." After that, he forced into submission the autonomous and local rulers who had depended on the Gutians. According to Postgate and Van de Mieroop, the exact course of Ur-Nammu's acquisition of his empire is not known, but by the end of the reign he had established control over most of Šumer and Akkad.

Hallo argued that Ur-Nammu secured the loyalty of the inhabitants of Ur by initiating a massive building program in honor of Nanna, the Šumerian moon-god, and Ningal, the consort of Nanna, who together comprised the two patron deities of the city. At enormous expense, Ur-Nammu built up the great terrace at Ur and erected a giant ziggurat (i.e., monumental stepped-tower) on top of it, a practice that was imitated wherever Šumerian models influenced religious architecture. To this day, the ruins at Ur preserve the essence of Ur-Nammu's architectural plans, although the actual structures often were repaired or rebuilt after his lifetime.

UR-NAMMU'S ACQUISITION OF VASSAL STATES
THROUGH FOREIGN EXPANSION

According to Hallo, Ur-Nammu resorted to arms when he fought, defeated, and killed Nammahani, the last independent ruler of Lagash, a battle that redrew the boundary between Lagash and Ur, but this time in Ur's favor. Ur-Nammu demonstrated great foresight in victory, as Lagash was left with only a measure of sovereignty over its reduced territory.

Moreover, Nammahani's old viceroy was appointed to govern Lagash as a loyal servant of Ur-Nammu, and Ur's king even built a new canal for its inhabitants. Lagash, as with other ancient Mesopotamian city-states, was transformed into a province within the new empire. In return for pledging allegiance and contributing taxes and labor toward the interests of Ur, these vassal states were confirmed in their old territorial claims, which is recorded in detailed stelae that were erected at Nippur.

FAILURE OF UR-NAMMU'S SUCCESSORS
TO EXPAND THE EMPIRE

Ur-Nammu apparently met his death in battle, in this case against the Gutians, which is a rare fate for ancient Mesopotamian kings. The successors of Ur-Nammu onto the throne during the Third Dynasty of Ur failed to expand the kingdom that he had built in Mesopotamia. The first to follow him onto the throne was his son, Shulgi (ca. 2094–2046 BC), who reigned for 48 years. From the testimony of the date formulae, the first half of his long reign was devoted to the same peaceful pursuits that had occupied Ur-Nammu, notably the building, furnishing, and staffing of temples and royal palaces. Yet beginning with Year 24, no less than 15 year-names record military triumphs, all on the eastern side of the Tigris River.

Hallo pointed out that Shulgi's primary target was the Kingdom of Simurrum, which was located mainly in the Zagros Mountains and was the object of at least nine campaigns. According to the omen literature, the capture of their ruler, Tappan-darah, was the principal event of Shulgi's reign. In Year 35, Shulgi secured his rear against the Amorite threat from the west by constructing a defensive wall—a predecessor of the later Amorite wall—at the narrow waist of the Mesopotamian valley, where the Tigris and Euphrates flow closest to each other. For Postgate, a common purpose ran through these measures: to blunt the external threats that toppled the Akkadian Empire, and to turn the tide decisively in Šumer's favor.

Among the more than 50 royal princes and princesses known by name who were born to Shulgi were Amar-Sin and Shu-Sin. Both of them succeeded Shulgi onto the throne of Ur, with Amar-Sin as the first to rule. Hallo noted that although the *Šumerian King List* calls Shu-Sin the son of Amar-Sin, a contemporary seal inscription and a later copy of a love song between Shu-Sin and his wife, Kubatum, identify him as the son of Shulgi, which may be the more reliable source. Each brother ruled for nine years, having been bestowed with the honor of deification at the time of their accession, and they each essentially pursued Shulgi's policies.

All nine year-names for Amar-Sin's reign (*ca.* 2046–2037 BC) are connected to military campaigns that he conducted. His campaigns in the east, although only briefly noted in the date formulae, are described in detail on Old Babylonian copies of stelae erected at Nippur and Ur. In Year 5 of Shu-Sin's reign (*ca.* 2037–2028 BC), he defended himself against the increasing pressure of Amorite nomads with a major enlargement of Shulgi's wall.

Shu-Sin's famous Amorite wall extended for 275 km in length, which was intended to deter the Amorites from advancing into Ur's domain. According to Hallo and Postgate, though, the empire built by the kings of the Third Dynasty of Ur survived Shu-Sin's reign only briefly, as the combined threat of the Amorites from the northwest and the Elamites from the southeast proved to be the undoing of his son, Ibbi-Sin (*ca.* 2028–2004 BC).

ABRAM'S RESIDENCE AT UR DURING
THE THIRD DYNASTY OF UR

The birthplace of the biblical patriarch Abram and the location of his formative years is left unstated in Genesis, although Moses does indicate that the land of his brother's (i.e., Haran's) birth is Ur (Gen 11:28). Sometime during Abram's adulthood, he was residing at Ur, because he and his family are said to have departed from Ur in order to enter the land of Canaan

(Gen 11:31; 15:7). The text clearly implies that the family traveled through Harran, because Abram's father, Terah, died while they were residing there (Gen 11:32).

While Abram's birth is known to have occurred in 2166 BC, what remains uncertain is the amount of time that he resided in his birthplace of Ur. He left Haran for Canaan in 2091 BC at the age of 75, but Moses was silent about how old he was when he departed Ur for Haran. According to Dead Sea Scroll manuscript 4Q252, Abram departed from Ur when he was 70 years old, equating to 2096 BC. If this record is correct, Abram resided in the most powerful city in the ancient world for the first 15 years of Ur-Nammu's reign, meaning that God sent him out of Ur when it was the ancient world's preeminent city. The equivalent is being born in Rome during the Roman Empire, in Paris during the French Empire, or in London during the British Empire. God removed Abram from this great city for a greater purpose elsewhere.

The two chief seats of the worship of the Semitic moon-god, Sin (Akkadian: *Sîn*, Šumerian: *NANNA*), were Ur and Harran, and perhaps this commonality is not a coincidence. One of Abram's brothers, Haran (Gen 11:26), shares the same name as the site of biblical Haran, which usually is associated with Harran, a village of Şanlıurfa in the Urfa region of southeastern Turkey. Terah's son, Haran, died while still at Ur (Gen 11:28), meaning that he did not accompany his family for the rest of their long trek along the Fertile Crescent.

Suggesting that Terah or a member of his family named the site after his deceased son might be problematic, because Abram and Terah were born after the earliest reference to Harran in an ancient writing. The site is mentioned on a tablet from the Ebla archive found in Palace G (= Mardikh IIB1 = Amuq I in western Syria, per Stephen Batiuk and Timothy Harrison), which can be dated to roughly 2330 BC, due to the presence of an artifact within the archive that mentions the Egyptian king, Pepi I (*ca.* 2334–2279 BC). The archive at Ebla preceded Abram's and Terah's births by over a century.

However, given that the only two Mesopotamian sites with the moon-god as the patron deity are Ur and Harran, it remains quite plausible that Abram's family took the worship of Nanna with them from Ur and implemented or elevated his cult at Harran. The biblical text explicitly states that Abram's family served other gods (Josh 24:2), so their worship of the moon-god (Nanna) and his consort (Ningal) would coincide with the Bible perfectly. While Christians often choose to sanitize the lives of cherished figures of biblical history, the fact remains that Abram's family members undoubtedly were no less flawed than the believers of today.

OLD BABYLONIAN EMPIRE UNDER HAMMURABI

PRELUDE TO THE REIGN OF HAMMURABI

During the Old Babylonian Empire (*ca.* 1894–1595 BC), Babylonia was ruled by a series of Amorite kings. The Amorites long had been a thorn in the flesh for the Mesopotamian city-states that rose to power between the Tigris and Euphrates Rivers, not only in the 2nd millennium BC, but also in the 3rd millennium BC. During the earlier Akkadian Empire, water levels had dropped for the two dominant rivers that defined Mesopotamia, causing the Amorites, who were nomadic herders by trade, to migrate their animals into the irrigated lands between the two rivers. This insurgence provoked the Akkadian kings to repel the Amorite advance, leading to the construction of Shulgi's defensive wall and Shu-Sin's full-blown Amorite wall.

The Amorites nonetheless rose to power early in the 19th century BC, forming a coalition of cities around the northern part of the Fertile Crescent. Demarcating these cities in a clockwise direction from the Levant to Mesopotamia, the coalition consisted of at least Hazor, Qatna, Alalakh, Mari, and Babylon. Knowledge about this Amorite league derives from a cuneiform archive at Mari that was collected under Zimri-Lim, Mari's Amorite king at the time. This amazing textual archive contains over 25,000 tablets and dates to a period of about 70 years, which equates to *ca.* 1827–1757 BC.

Babylon became the key player among the powerful Amorite city-states, and Hammurabi's father, Sin-muballit, even felt emboldened enough to join a coalition of Šumerian cities that includes Isin and Uruk, which was designed to check the power of Larsa's king Rim-Sin on Babylon's southern flank. Sin-muballit spent the last 20 years or so of his reign strengthening the walls of cities within his kingdom, undoubtedly awaiting an attack from Larsa. According to Jack Sasson, by the time that Hammurabi took the throne from his father, Babylon's territory had expanded to an area of 160 x 60 km in size.

HAMMURABI'S RISE TO KING OF ŠUMER AND AKKAD

Hammurabi ascended to the throne of Babylon as its sixth Amorite king and experienced a lengthy reign of 43 years (*ca.* 1792–1750 BC). Much of what is known about him comes from the year-names in his eponymic dating formulae. Hammurabi launched military excursions between his Years 6 and 10. In Year 6, he confiscated the cities of Isin and Uruk, which had been under Larsa's control. In Year 7, he attacked the country in which Larsa was located, which is called Emutbal.

This was not a direct attack on Larsa, but a weakening of this bitter enemy by eliminating those who could be loyal to Larsa if a war between these two powers were to break out. In Year 9, Hammurabi invaded Malgium, although he did not conquer this Elamite vassal state. In Year 11, he allegedly conquered Rapiqum, which was located in close proximity to Mari. He later told a diplomat from Mari that Shamshi-Adad I of Ekallatum had conquered Rapiqum, then afterward invited Hammurabi to share in its control.

Hammurabi spent Years 12 through 28 consolidating his kingdom by engaging in cultic construction and other religious activities, irrigation works, and enhancing fortifications. In Sasson's estimation, the decade that followed these years served to alter the political landscape of Mesopotamia radically. During Hammurabi's Year 29, intrigue among the powers in and around Mesopotamia led to war and attrition. Elam attempted to create such a strong conflict between Hammurabi and Larsa's Rim-Sin that they would engage in war against one another. When Hammurabi and Rim-Sin caught wind of this scheme, they combined forces instead of attacking each other.

Their alliance was joined by Amorite forces from the north, including Yamhad and Mari, and this coalition defeated Eshnunna, Shubartu, and Elam. These victories essentially provided Hammurabi with *de facto* control of southern Mesopotamia. However, Hammurabi was angered that Larsa's army hardly participated in the campaign, and he allegedly heard from a divine oracle that Larsa should be punished for their insolence. In Hammurabi's Year 30, he conquered Larsa and annexed it into what was now the Old Babylonian Empire. He thus assumed the illustrious Sargonic title, "king of Šumer and Akkad."

Yet this was not the end of Hammurabi's conquering and expansionism. In Year 31, he again defeated Eshnunna and its allies, and in Year 32 Babylon even defeated Mari. During Year 34, Babylon's armies reached from one edge of Assyrian territory to the other edge, causing Sasson to declare that Hammurabi became the dominant power between Elam (to the east) and the Euphrates (to the west). All of the great and small powers of Mesopotamia—including Larsa, Isin, Kish, Uruk, Ur, Mari, Eshnunna, Shubartu, Malgium, Rapiqum, and others—were subjugated and incorporated into Babylonia's new Amorite empire.

HAMMURABI'S EMPIRE FELL SHORT
OF NIMROD'S VAST DOMAIN

As with the Third Dynasty of Ur three centuries before it, Hammurabi's impressive Amorite empire of the 18th century BC fell short of the vast domain that Nimrod enjoyed. Shulgi's empire mimicked Nimrod's by stretching into Elam to the east, but Hammurabi's did not. More importantly, neither Shulgi's nor Hammurabi's empire extended into Anatolia to the northwest or deep into Assyrian lands to the north. Therefore, for well over 500 years after Nimrod's conquest of a large part of the ANE, no conquering empire-builder enjoyed the same vast amount of territory as he did. This makes Moses's choice of Nimrod as the model evil-empire-builder all the more understandable, as the Sargonic legend never was surpassed in the ancient world between the lifetimes of Nimrod and Moses.

EGYPTIAN EMPIRE UNDER THUTMOSE III

BACKGROUND TO THE REIGN OF THUTMOSE III

Two pharaohs typically come to mind when most people think about the great Egyptian rulers of the New Kingdom (1560–1069 BC): Tut and Ramesses II. King Tut, whose abbreviated name is short for Tut-ankh-amun (1347–1338 BC), which means, "the living image of Amun" (i.e., the Egyptian god of the wind), is known primarily from Howard Carter's discovery of his undisturbed tomb in 1922. The tomb contained an astounding number of grave goods, with over 5,000 objects, including a sarcophagus made of solid gold, elaborate furniture, thrones, archery bows, and much more.

The truth is that Tut-ankh-amun was an insignificant pharaoh who, as the third from the last king of the 18th Dynasty, ruled during a time of weakness and decline in Egypt. This comparative level of limited strength throughout the 14th century BC is known from the Amarna Letters (*ca.* 1378/7–1346/5 BC), which often document the futile pleas by the petty rulers of Canaan for the Egyptian king's help against attackers who most frequently are called the *Habiru* (= Hebrews). According to EA (i.e., Amarna Letter) 109: "Previously, at the *mere* sight of an Egyptian, the kings of Canaan fled bef[ore him, but] now the sons of Abdi-Ashirta make men from Egypt prowl about [like do]gs."

Ramesses II (1290–1223 BC) is known best from the portrayals of him as the exodus pharaoh in Cecil B. DeMille's *The Ten Commandments* (1956) and Disney's *The Prince of Egypt* (1998) in their blockbuster films about the Israelite exodus from Egypt. Yet the biblical, historical, and archaeological evidence overwhelmingly conspire to date the exodus to 1446 BC, which is roughly two centuries earlier.

The evidence also implicates Amenhotep II as the exodus pharaoh, who alone among all of Egypt's kings of the 18th and 19th Dynasties meets every measurable biographical requirement of the exodus pharaoh, as demonstrated in *Origins of the Hebrews*. Possibly as a result of the public attention Ramesses II has received as the mistakenly-dubbed exodus pharaoh, he is referred to popularly as Egypt's greatest and most illustrious king.

Once again, popular opinion proves misleading, as he definitely is unworthy of this moniker, at least when it comes to power, wealth, and imperialistic conquest. Ramesses II admittedly was prolific at building cities, temples, and monuments to his own glory, but his international ventures were limited in number of campaigns, expansiveness, and lasting holdings. His most notable Asiatic campaign was his second, whose climax came against the Hittites at the Battle of Kadesh, and most scholars are unified in evaluating the engagement as a draw. After this failure restricted Ramesses II's control in the Levant to Canaan, his third Asiatic campaign was a bit more successful, as his army marched to Syrian Damascus.

In Ramesses II's final Asiatic campaigns of Years 8 and 9, he led his army to Tunip, which he captured. While he did claim to acquire towns in Retjenu (i.e., the Egyptian word for the Levant), these successes were short lived, and several of his battles against the more important city-states of Syria ended indecisively at best. The true sign of his limited strength is that he signed a peace treaty with the Hittites in Year 21, a concession that a powerful Egyptian king never would have made. The proof is in the pudding, as this treaty signaled the end of Ramesses II's Asiatic campaigning, and the end of his failed attempt to restore Egypt to the past glory that the nation enjoyed during the days of Thutmose III and early in the reign of Amenhotep II.

THUTMOSE III AS THE KING WHO SOUGHT TO KILL MOSES

Egypt's one true empire-builder is Thutmose III (1504–1450 BC). When Egyptologist Donald Redford wrote in reference to EA 109, which was cited above, he associated the reign of Thutmose III with the time when the kings of Canaan fled from the presence of Egyptians in Canaan. In fact, this is the pharaoh who "sought to kill Moses" (Exod 2:15a) in *ca.* 1486 BC after Moses struck down an Egyptian from a belief that God was using this event to grant the Hebrews deliverance from their enslavement in Egypt (Acts 7:23–24). Thutmose III's extraordinary reign extended into Year 54, as he outlived numerous sons who were in line to succeed him. Not coincidentally, the pharaoh who chased Moses out of Egypt must have ruled for over 40 years.

Moses fled from an unnamed pharaoh who sought to execute him for killing an Egyptian (Exod 2:15), departing from Egypt when he "was fulfilling 40 years of age" (Acts 7:23). Only "after 40 years had passed" did God appear to him at the burning bush (Acts 7:30), which immediately follows the statement that "in *the course of* those many days, the king of Egypt died" (Exod 2:23). Moses died when he was 120 years of age (Deut 34:7). Therefore, according to Moses's biography, the pharaoh who preceded the exodus pharaoh must have ruled beyond 40 years, a criterion not met by the modest reign of Seti I (*ca.* 1305–1290 BC), who was Ramesses II's predecessor and the first king of the 19th Dynasty.

The exodus pharaoh thus necessarily *followed* an exceedingly lengthy reign, not *boasted of* an extremely long reign, as was the case with Ramesses II. Inexplicably, proponents of the view that the exodus occurred in the 13th century BC have ignored or circumvented this crucial biographical requirement. For example, James Hoffmeier attempted to escape from this problem by arguing that Exod 2:23 does not specify a period of 40 years. Yet Hoffmeier apparently ignored or overlooked how Acts 7:30 *does* specify what Moses left unstated, as the passage in this equally-inspired New Testament book authored by Luke clearly infers that Moses did not return to Egypt until at least 40 years after he was chased out the country by the deceased king.

THUTMOSE III AS EGYPT'S GREAT EMPIRE-BUILDER

For good reasons, many historians have referred to Thutmose III as the Napoleon of Egypt, and not just because they both were about 5'6" tall while alive. Young Thutmose inherited the throne from his father, Thutmose II, on Month 1, Season 3, Day 4 (Pakhons 4, *ca.* April 29) of *ca.* 1504 BC. Thutmose III was the rightful heir to the throne, but he soon shared the kingship with Hatshepsut, his stepmother and aunt, as the lesser of two co-rulers, since he was only about two years old when his father died.

As the adult coregent, Hatshepsut served as the *de facto* ruler, initially dating her reign from the year of her coronation. Between the second and seventh year in her role as coregent, she began backdating her reign to coincide with her young coregent's regnal years, a practice she continued for the balance of her reign until she abdicated the throne in Year 22. Thutmose III then became sole ruler after her abdication, which continued until his death in Year 54.

Hatshepsut was a prolific builder who consolidated the kingdom extremely well within Egypt, and when Thutmose III took over as sole regent, he established a sound administrative structure and carried out extensive building programs. His construction efforts included extending the structures at Karnak, building numerous monuments and buildings (e.g., at Abydos, Aswan, Heliopolis, Memphis, Thebes, Kom Ombo, Armant, el-Tod, Medamud, Esna, Dendera, and numerous sites in the Nile River Delta), adding decorations on Hatshepsut's temple at Speos Artemidos, and constructing or improving forts and temples in Nubia (e.g., Sai, Faras, Dakka, Argo, Kubban, Semna, and Gebel Barkal).

Within only weeks after Hatshepsut's abdication, Thutmose III launched a campaign into western Asia to counter a rebellious coalition led by the king of Kadesh, who believed that Hatshepsut's abdication was a sign of Egyptian weakness and rallied his vassals at Megiddo. The young king scarcely could concede control of Canaan to the expansionistic plans of this Syrian king, and the amassing of such a large force so close to the Egyptian frontier clearly required a preemptive strike by Thutmose III. His first Asiatic campaign thus began late in Year 22 (*ca.* 1483 BC), when the king departed from Memphis. According to Hoffmeier's and Pritchard's translations of the Armant Stele, which was discovered in the temple of Montu Armant near ancient Thebes, "[Year 22, Month 4, Season 2, Day 20(?) . . . (he) proceeded] from Memphis, in order to slay the lands of feeble Retjenu on the first occasion of victory."

The Egyptians besieged Megiddo for seven months during Thutmose III's first Asiatic campaign, and when the city fell in December of *ca.* 1483 BC, all of the Canaanite leaders—with the exception of the king of Kadesh, who had fled—surrendered. *The Annals of Thutmose III*, which were inscribed on the walls of his Karnak temple at Thebes, record Megiddo's fall with the often-cited phrase, "He who captures Megiddo captures a thousand cities." The reason for this saying is that Megiddo guarded the Great Trunk Road, the international highway through Canaan that was known in New Testament times as the *Via Maris*, which controlled the main trading route and the flow of traffic between Africa and Asia.

Once these petty kings were in Egyptian hands, they were required to take this vow: "The peoples of the Levant will not rebel again on any other occasion," and, "We will never again act evilly against *Men-kheper-re* ("The established one of the manifestation of Re," i.e., Thutmose III's throne name)—who lives forever, our good lord—in our lifetime." At Megiddo, Thutmose III captured a vast amount of booty from his enemies: 3,400 prisoners of war, 892 chariots, 502 bows, 200 coats of mail, 2,041 horses, and 24,816 other animals. Judging from this list, the Battle of Megiddo—which certainly showcased his brilliance as a tactician—involved the largest number of forces that ever participated in Thutmose III's Asiatic campaigns.

In subsequent Asiatic campaigns, Thutmose III penetrated further and further northward into the Levant. Early in Year 33 (*ca.* 1472 BC), he launched his 8th and most glorious campaign: a direct attack against territory under the control of Mitanni, which rivaled Egypt for the status of the top superpower within the ANE. As Redford detailed, the ingenious pharaoh transported materials and supplies to Byblos by ship, where he built prefabricated assault-crafts out of Lebanese cedar trees. These assault-crafts then were disassembled and transported in carts at the rear of the convoy, as the entire expeditionary force proceeded inland on a northeasterly march, crossing the Lebanese Mountains into the Orontes Valley.

The Egyptian army passed unopposed through Kadesh and Tunip, but when they neared Aleppo, Mitanni resisted. Three sharp engagements ensued, all of which the Egyptians won, allowing Thutmose III to proceed to the bank of the Euphrates River at Carchemish. The Mitannian army crossed over to the eastern bank of the river, confiscating or destroying all river-crafts in the vicinity. The Egyptians, in a move that came as a complete surprise to the fleeing Hurrian forces, then reassembled their prefabricated assault-crafts, crossed the river on them, pursued the bewildered Mitannians on foot, then routed the enemy downstream and eastward toward the Balikh River, while the local nobility took refuge in caves. Thutmose III showed no mercy to the local inhabitants, as his army burned down all of the towns that they encountered along the Euphrates.

Thutmose III's records boast of this victory. According to Hoffmeier's translation of the Armant Stele, "He ferried across the Euphrates River and trampled the cities on both sides, they being destroyed forever with fire." On the Gebel Barkal Stele of Thutmose III that Hoffmeier also translated, which was erected 14 years later in the temple that he built at Gebel Barkal near the Fourth Cataract, the king boasted, "There was no one to save them throughout the land of Mitanni (Egyptian: *Naharin*), because its lord had fled out of fear. I destroyed his cities and his villages and set them on fire, and my majesty turned them into mounds of ruin, never to be resettled."

After Thutmose III crossed the Euphrates at Carchemish and penetrated into Mitannian territory, he erected a boundary stele on the riverbank alongside that of his grandfather, Thutmose I. The Armant Stele records the event: "On the [eastern] side (of the Euphrates River), he erected a victory stele." This act was a sure sign that he intended for the conquest to be permanent, a conclusion that is confirmed by how the king's charioteer was rewarded with 150 *stat* of land in territory that belonged to Mitanni, clearly for his service in the military operation. In addition to the Egyptian victories and acquisitions, they received tribute, which is specified in great detail, from Mitanni's vassal-states of Assyria and Babylon, and eventually from Cyprus. This point in time unequivocally represents the most far-reaching imperialistic expansion in Egypt's history.

Thutmose III ultimately embarked on an astounding 17 Asiatic campaigns. As William Hallo and William Simpson pointed out, some of them increased Egyptian holdings (1st and 5th–8th), while others were merely punitive (9th, 10th, 14th, and 17th) or tours of inspection (2nd, 3rd, 4th, and 13th). During the three successive years that followed the first campaign, the Egyptian army conducted these inspections in the Levant in order to reaffirm the royal claim to the new territory and to collect tribute. Six of these campaigns were directed against Kadesh. Scholars universally agree that in all of them, Egypt's ultimate enemy and true arch rival was the middle-Euphrates state of Mitanni, the other dominant ANE superpower of the day. However, with the campaign of Year 33 that brought Egyptian success all of the way to and along the Euphrates River, Thutmose III proved that Egypt was the greater of the ancient world's two superpowers of the day.

To be fair, calling Thutmose III's domain an empire is generous, despite the fact that his campaigns established Egypt as the leading superpower during the first half of the 15th century BC. While he essentially held onto his conquests as far as the Euphrates River during the balance of his reign and passed them along to his son—Amenhotep II (*ca.* 1453–1416 BC), who in *Origins of the Hebrews* was proven to be the exodus pharaoh—the loss of the Egyptian army and all of Egypt's firstborns at the time of the 10th plague on Egypt described in the Bible so thoroughly decimated Egypt's male population that their short-lived empire evaporated much faster than it was built. God humbled the Egyptians greatly by ending their run as a superpower, and they never again threatened to be the most powerful nation in the ANE world.

NEO-ASSYRIAN EMPIRE UNDER ESARHADDON

RISE OF THE NEO-ASSYRIAN EMPIRE

An Assyrian king named Ashurnasirpal II (*ca.* 884–859 BC) followed his father, Tukulti-Ninurta II (*ca.* 890–884 BC), in taking strong military action that reestablished the Assyrian Empire. Yet this soon-to-be mighty Neo-Assyrian Empire (*ca.* 911–609 BC) that Ashurnasirpal II began would eclipse the grandeur and geo-political territories acquired during either the Old Assyrian Empire (*ca.* 2004–1364 BC) or the Middle Assyrian Empire (*ca.* 1364–912 BC) before it. In fact, this great empire exceeded all of the empires that preceded it.

Many powerful Neo-Assyrian kings sat on the throne during the course of the empire. The policies of Ashurnasirpal II continued during the long and active reign of his son, Shalmaneser III (*ca.* 859–824 BC), who campaigned 31 years to extend Assyrian rule to Cilicia, the Levant, and the Persian Gulf. Šuppiluliuma II (859–857 BC) of the Kingdom of Patina, a Neo-Hittite rump state in Syria that was centered at Tell Tayinat of the Amuq Plain, was a member of the northern coalition that attacked Shalmaneser III during his campaign to the west in 858 BC, near Litibu of Sam'al.

The Assyrians claimed that they defeated this coalition, acquired chariots and teams of horses from them, and later erected a statue by the source of the Saluara River (near Mt. Amanus, in the Hatay region of Turkey), but this was only the first battle of a war that did not provide the Assyrian king with lasting success. Later in the war, Shalmaneser III invaded the land of Patina by crossing the Orontes River and approaching Alimuš, "a fortified city of Šuppiluliuma (II) of Patina." The Assyrian scribes claimed that the army conquered Alimuš, carried off booty, captured the great cities of the Patinean, and received tribute from the coastal kings.

Shalmaneser III's first three Levantine campaigns were directed at Carchemish, which he captured in *ca.* 857 BC. He also incorporated Beth-Eden, whose capital (Til-Barsip) was captured in *ca.* 856 BC and renamed as "Shalmaneserburg." A king named "Ahab the Israelite" (Akkadian: *A-ha-ab-bu Sir-'i-la-a-a*), the evil king of Israel's Northern Kingdom who followed Omri on the throne (1 Kgs 16:28), supplied 10,000 men and 2,000 chariots, according to the first reference to Israel in the Assyrian annals. The clash was so fierce that although neither Hamath nor Damascus was taken, the Assyrians did not return for three years (1 Kgs 22:1).

When the Aramean king of Damascus named Hadadezer was assassinated in 842 BC, Shalmaneser III marched against his successor, Hazael (1 Kgs 19:15), "the son of a nobody" (i.e., a usurper who gained the throne apart from royal succession), whose army was routed at Mt. Hermon. While claiming the defeat of Hazael, the Assyrians failed to capture either him or Damascus, where he had taken refuge. However, they did ravage the surrounding countryside, plunder the rich Hauran plain, and march to the Mediterranean coast at Carmel, where tribute was received from Tyre, Sidon, and "Jehu, son of Omri" (i.e., the reigning Israelite king [1 Kgs 19:16–17]). Despite Hazael's familial attribution of Jehu and that this line of kings came to be known in Assyrian inscriptions as the house of Omri, Jehu did not descend from Omri. In fact, he actually exterminated the house of Omri (2 Kgs 10:10–17).

Jehu's offering of tribute to Hazael is not recorded in the Bible, but perhaps it was induced by Israel's need for support against Hazael's raids into their territory (2 Kgs 10:32). If this was Jehu's plan, it proved to be unsuccessful. The submission of the Israelite king is depicted on the Black Obelisk, as either Jehu or his ambassador is portrayed as kneeling before Shalmaneser III while porters present "silver, gold, golden bowls, vases, cups, buckets," and other objects as tribute. After another attempt to take Damascus in *ca.* 838 BC, Shalmaneser III ceased campaigning in western Asia, a sign of the growing power of the Syrian city-states. The end of Shalmaneser III's reign was consumed by domestic revolution.

In *ca.* 806 BC, the young Assyrian king named Adadnirari III (*ca.* 811–783 BC) undertook an expedition to Arpad of northern Syria, near the Mediterranean Sea. He launched another one during the following year, when he took Hazazu and broke up the powerful coalition that was developing between Damascus and states as far away as Malatya, also in northern Syria. In *ca.* 804 BC, Adadnirari III struck Tyre and Sidon, which were coastal cities further to the southwest.

A Judahite king named Joash (a.k.a. Jehoash [2 Kgs 12:1]), anxious to annul the burdensome treaty that Hazael had imposed on him, apparently took this opportunity—as Jehu did before him—to obtain Assyrian help.

The archaeological evidence related to this request is a royal stele uncovered at Tell ar-Rimah in Iraq, in which Adadnirari III listed tribute from "Joash of Samaria" (Akkadian: *Yu'asu Samerinā*) before that from Tyre and Sidon. When the Assyrian king entered Damascus and took spoils from Ben-hadad, thus weakening the Syrian power base, Israel most likely was allowed to strengthen trade relations with Damascus and recover lost territory (2 Kgs 13:25).

Adadnirari III received the submission of all the Chaldean chiefs of southern Mesopotamia, but as Donald Wiseman noted, the king's early death led to disturbed conditions. His eldest son, Shalmaneser IV (*ca.* 783–773 BC), seemingly had limited authority, as he contended with his general, Shamshi-ilu, who claimed credit for Assyrian success against the Urartians. A second son, Ashur-dân III (*ca.* 771–754 BC), campaigned unsuccessfully in Syria, with the event's being marked by the ominous sign of a solar eclipse on 15 June 763 BC, a significant event because it provides an absolute date for Assyrian chronology. At home in Assyria, a plague occurred, along with a revolt in the cities of Ashur, Gozan, and Arapha. Ashur-nirari V (*ca.* 755–745 BC), the third son of Adadnirari III, probably was killed in a revolt within the palace, but these years of ineffectual rule ended when his younger brother, Tiglath-pileser, took the throne.

Tiglath-pileser III (*ca.* 745–727 BC) took immediate and vigorous action to strengthen Assyria's central authority by dividing imperial territory into provinces, requiring of them the same direct allegiance to the king as he required of the heartland's districts. By reestablishing control over outlying regions, he intended to bring conquered territories into a close-knit empire. Tiglath-pileser III first marched to the Karun River, reminding Nabonassar of Babylon and the Chaldean chiefs of his superior military power, then offered sacrifices in their principal shrines. However, the growing might of the new Syro-Urartian coalition under Mati'-ilu of Arpad demanded his attention. His troops defeated Sardur III of Urartu at Samsat on the Euphrates, and Arpad was besieged for three years, until finally it was incorporated as an Assyrian provincial capital in *ca.* 741 BC.

Tiglath-pileser III next campaigned against a coalition of peoples who gathered in southern Syria, whose revolt was instigated by Azriyau of Jaudi/Yaudi (Akkadian: *Azriyau Yaudi*). As Galil pointed out, this Azriyau has been identified variously as Azariah of Judah (2 Kgs 14:21), a king of the same name who ruled at Ya'diya (a.k.a. Sam'al, modern Zincirli), and the king of Hamath. If he was the Judahite king, which is the most likely identification, this demonstrates that the Kingdom of Judah (Hebrew: *Yəhudah*) had grown strong before Azariah's death (2 Kgs 15:7). Judahites are listed among the prisoners who were settled at Ullabu, which is near Bitlis.

This victory opened the way for Assyrian arms to reach Phoenicia and for northern Syria to be annexed into the Neo-Assyrian Empire in *ca.* 738 BC. As Timothy Harrison noted, this Assyrian victory incorporated the Kingdom of Kunulua/Unqi at Tell Tayinat into the Assyrian province of Kullani. During the siege of Arpad, Rezin of Damascus and Menahem of Samaria paid tribute to Tiglath-pileser III. The 1,000 Israelite talents were calculated by the number of males of military age at the current Assyrian value of a slave (i.e., 50 shekels), by which Tiglath-pileser III confirmed Menahem's power (2 Kgs 15:19–20).

Tiglath-pileser III intervened in the Levant again in *ca.* 734 BC, when Hiram of Tyre was allied with Rezin of Damascus. According to Wiseman, the cities of Tyre, Sidon, and neighboring Mahalib (i.e., the Ahlab of Judg 1:31) were required to pay tribute. The latter, with Kashpuna, was included in a new province of Simirra, and the whole area west of Damascus to Samaria, including Gilead, was overrun. Hanunu of Gaza fled to Egypt as the Assyrians advanced to Wadi el-Arish (i.e., the Hebrew Bible's "brook/wadi of Egypt") and set up a golden image of the Neo-Assyrian king there and in Gaza.

Idi-bi'li was appointed as the local governor and oversaw the Egyptian frontier. When the king of Ashkelon was killed, his successor—along with Sanipu of Amman, Qauš-Malaka of Edom, Salamanu of Moab, and Ahaz of Judah—sent tribute. These developments may have caused Ahaz to appeal for Assyrian aid against Rezin of Damascus and Pekah of Israel, but Ahaz received little help despite his acceptance of vassal status (2 Kgs 16:7). Judah was invaded, and Jerusalem was besieged (2 Kgs 16:5; 2 Chr 28:19–20). Two years later, after Pekah's assassination, Tiglath-pileser III captured Damascus (*ca.* 732 BC), annexed part of Israel (2 Kgs 15:29), and—according to his annals—installed Hoshea as king over Israel (2 Kgs 15:30).

Meanwhile in Babylonia, disturbances followed the death of Nabonassar in *ca.* 734 BC. An Aramean chief claimed the throne, and Tiglath-pileser III tried feverishly to persuade the Babylonians to rise up against this pretender to the throne, offering promises of tax exemption. When this attempt failed, the Assyrian army marched against the Aramean usurper, routed his army, and laid waste to his tribal lands. Tiglath-pileser III assumed power in Babylon in *ca.* 729 BC, participating in their renowned New Year's Day festival under his local name of Pul (2 Kgs 15:19; 1 Chr 5:26).

Tiglath-pileser III died peacefully in his old age, but the reign of his son, Shalmaneser V (*ca.* 727–722 BC), is obscure, since his annals did not survive. Wiseman pointed out that knowledge of Shalmaneser V's reign must be reconstructed from a broken Assyrian eponymic dating list and references in the *Babylonian Chronicles*, the former of which states that he besieged Samaria for three years (2 Kgs 18:9) in response to king Hoshea's failure to pay tribute (2 Kgs 17:3–6). One of the *Babylonian Chronicles* describes how Shalmaneser V "broke [the resistance of] the city of Samaria." Whether or not the king personally accompanied his army to the site, this matches the biblical evidence well. According to Rodger Young's calculations, Samaria fell in 723 BC on the Nisan calendar (i.e., after March/April of 723 BC), which would put Shalmaneser V on the throne when the city was captured.

There is no mention in 2 Kgs 17:6 of the name of the attacker to whom Samaria fell, and although this seems to have been Shalmaneser V, some have credited the conquest to his successor, Sargon II (*ca.* 722–705 BC), who later claimed to have conquered Samaria in his accession year. The problem with Sargon II's candidacy is that (1) Albert Olmstead, Hayim Tadmor, and Edwin Thiele reasoned that Shalmaneser V captured Samaria, because Samaria fell before Tishri 1 of 723 BC, and Sargon II's accession did not occur until December 722 BC or January 721 BC; (2) Wiseman noted that in Sargon II's early annals from Aššur, Nineveh, and Kalhu, he never claimed to be the conqueror of Samaria; and (3) Tadmor has shown that Sargon II was busy quelling a revolt in Babylon in 722 or 721 BC. Therefore, Shalmaneser V remains a far better choice for Samaria's conqueror.

As Wiseman noted, Sargon II had to counter the increasing interference of Egypt in Levantine affairs, and that of Elam in Babylonian affairs.

Both were the result of Assyrian expansion that had cut them off from trade with their neighbors. Whenever there were dissidents among these people, they would turn to outside powers for help. Yet Sargon II first had to settle disturbances among his own citizens, who had reacted against his father's burdensome demands for labor and taxes for military operations. In Babylonia, the Chaldean leader Marduk-apla-iddina II (a.k.a. Merodach-Baladan [in the Bible]) of the Bīt-Yakin tribe took advantage of the change in Assyrian leadership by proclaiming himself king, with help from Humbanigaš I of Elam.

In *ca.* 720 BC, Sargon II's forces clashed with the rebels at Der and claimed victory, although the *Babylonian Chronicles* describe the encounter as an Elamite and Chaldean victory. Either way, Marduk-apla-iddina II remained in control of the main Babylonian cities for the next 10 years. About this time, Ilu-bi'di of Hamath, the only remaining independent Syrian prince, attempted to meet the Assyrians in another battle, at Qarqar. Despite Egyptian help sponsored by the exiled Hanunu of Gaza, Ilu-bi'di was unsuccessful, and Hamath was reduced to provincial status. The Hebrew prophet Isaiah saw the lessons to be drawn from these conflicts (Isa 10:5–7), one being that Assyria's purpose was to destroy and cut off many nations.

Gaza, aided by an Egyptian named Sib'e (perhaps the So of 2 Kgs 17:4), was involved in this uprising. In a battle on the Egyptian border near Raphia, they were defeated. Hanunu was captured along with 9,053 prisoners, and Sib'e fled. The Elamites probably were responsible for inciting a revolt by the peoples in the Zagros Mountains. In *ca.* 713 BC, Sargon II raided the region of Hamadân and Kermanshah and took booty from the Medes. Further north, a revival of Urartian opposition was reported to Sargon II by his local officials.

Ursa (a.k.a. Rusas I), the king of Urartu, continually harassed the Assyrian garrisons until Sargon II's 8th campaign in *ca.* 714 BC, a major offensive designed to capture Musasir and defeat the Manneans (i.e., the Minni of Jer 51:27). The expedition is detailed in both *The Annals* of Sargon II and a letter to the Assyrian god, which perhaps was read at a victory parade at Ashur. From *ca.* 717 to 712 BC, Sargon II kept pressuring Carchemish (now an Assyrian provincial city), Cilicia, and all the Neo-Hittite states along the Taurus Mountains (i.e., Melid, Kummuh, and Tabal) that were influenced by

Ursa and Mida of Phrygia but then turned to him for help against the westward thrust of the Cimmerians (i.e., the Gomer of Ezek 38:6).

In *ca.* 711 BC, the Egyptian pharaoh *pi'ru*—probably Shebitku (*ca.* 714–705 BC), the second of the Cushite dynasts who ruled from Napata, in Nubia—instigated an uprising at Ashdod, a city that formerly was part of the Philistine pentapolis. Once again, the Assyrians won, and "the rulers of Philistia, Judah, Edom, and Moab brought tribute and gifts for the god, Ashur." Even the Egyptian king sent tribute. As Wiseman noted, although Judah is named, this does not imply that Sargon II attacked or entered their lands. Isaiah (20:1–6) interpreted the defeat of Ashdod by the Assyrians as such: for Judah to look to Egypt for help was certainly in vain, as pharaoh simply handed over to the Assyrians Yamani of Ashdod, who had fled to him for refuge.

In *ca.* 710 BC, Sargon II moved against Babylonia and Marduk-ap-la-iddina II, his arch enemy. The Assyrians marched down the eastern bank of the Tigris, forcing the Chaldean tribes to retreat southward. In their wake, the cities—tired of 10 years of rule under Chaldean tribesmen—opened their gates and welcomed these Assyrian deliverers. According to Wiseman, Sargon II celebrated the New Year's Day festival as "vice-regent of Babylon," showing that this act, in itself, was no mark of kingship. Marduk-apla-iddina II's homeland of Bīt-Yakin, the largest and most powerful of the Chaldean tribes, was overrun after two years of intense struggle. Yet after Sargon II's withdrawal, the Babylonian king was left in charge again.

Sargon II lived at Kalhu until *ca.* 706 BC, when he moved to Dur-Sharrukin (a.k.a. Khorsabad, the "Fortress of Sargon," located about 24 km northeast of Nineveh) and made it his capital. The Assyrian king's labor force had spent 11 years working to complete the construction of this city, but he was unable to enjoy it for long, because he was killed while at war in Tabal during the very next year. When Sennacherib was the crowned prince, he served Sargon II as a military advisor on the northern frontier. He essentially enjoyed calm there and to the east, which—except for uprisings in the Zagros, Cilicia, and Tabal—enabled him to concentrate on other fields. He experienced more serious troubles in Babylonia and the Levant.

Sennacherib's (705–681 BC) restoration of Nineveh was interrupted by trouble in Babylonia, where Marduk-apla-iddina II, faithful to Sargon II since *ca.* 710 BC, made another bid for independence. He had the support of the Arameans, Elamites, and Arabs. Marduk-apla-iddina II, following the disappearance of the little-known Marduk-zakir-Sumi II, had been holding the throne with the title, "king of Babylon," until Sennacherib defeated him and his allies near Kish in *ca.* 703 BC. Sennacherib plundered Babylon, deported 208,000 prisoners to Nineveh, and installed Bel-ibni as king. The Assyrians then ventured into the marshes of southern Mesopotamia to pursue Marduk-apla-iddina II, who meanwhile reappeared in Bīt-Yakin. This time, Marduk-apla-iddina II fled to Elam, which eventually led to a maritime expedition in *ca.* 693 BC to capture him, as ships were built at Nineveh, carried overland from Opis on the Tigris, and manned by Phoenicians.

The expedition was too late, though, as the old Chaldean king had died in exile by then (*ca.* 694 BC). The Elamites invaded Babylonia, captured Sippar, and removed the pro-Assyrian Ashur-nadin-sumi from the throne in Babylon. The struggle continued for seven years, until the Babylonians, using Elamite auxiliaries, met the Assyrian army at Halule. Although the Chaldeans and their allies were defeated, Assyrian casualties were heavy. Angered by this setback, Sennacherib besieged the Chaldeans in their sacred city of Babylon for nine months before he destroyed it completely in *ca.* 689 BC. The statue of the god Marduk was carried off to Assyria, and Sennacherib procured the prestigious title, "king of Šumer and Akkad," which Nimrod is the first to have assumed. For the time being, Babylonian resistance was brought to a halt.

Rebellion broke out in the Levant, as well. In *ca.* 701 BC, Sennacherib marched to the Phoenician coast and reimposed control over Little Sidon, Zarephath, Mahalib, Ušu, and Acco, taxing them in the process. Sidon's king Luli fled, so Sennacherib overtook the city and replaced him with a nobleman named Ethba'al. Tyre was bypassed, but after Ashkelon, Dagon, and Joppa were sacked, the rulers of Arvad, Byblos, Ashdod, Ammon, Moab, and Edom submitted and paid tribute. Sennacherib defeated the Egyptian army at Eltekeh, after Egypt—Hezekiah's ally—intervened, and then he slaughtered Ekron's elders. Resisting the vicious Assyrian imperialist usually came at a steep price, but Hezekiah of Judah refused to capitulate.

According to the Sennacherib Prism, the Assyrians ravaged Judah, capturing 46 walled cities and the villages around them, taking 200,150 captives, and virtually isolating Hezekiah "like a caged bird in Jerusalem" (cf., 2 Kgs 18:13). Wiseman suggested that the Judean capital may have been left under blockade while the Assyrians protected their flank against a possible Egyptian conquest of Lachish, but Sennacherib probably besieged and conquered Lachish before even approaching Jerusalem. Since Hezekiah sent word to Sennacherib while the latter was at Lachish (2 Kgs 18:14), it is difficult to believe that the invading king would have left an ongoing siege of the capital city where his rival king was confined.

From Lachish, Sennacherib sent word back to Hezekiah and demanded the release of Padi, the pro-Assyrian ruler of Ekron, and Hezekiah was forced to pay a considerable tribute (2 Kgs 18:13–16; Assyrian Taylor Prism of *ca.* 691 BC). Confirmation of its receipt is found in the words of Sennacherib, who said that "on Hezekiah, its king, I laid my yoke." Padi was freed, and Hezekiah was "besieged in his capital city of Jerusalem like a bird in a cage," as recorded on the Sennacherib Prism. The Assyrians soon raised the siege (2 Kgs 19:32–34), although two different reasons were given.

The Bible attributes this halt to the slaughter of "the Angel of He-who-is" (2 Kgs 19:35), while Herodotus (2.141) attributes it to a plague of mice that devoured the Assyrian bow-strings and shield-straps, which is usually interpreted as describing a plague. The *Assyrian Annals* are noticeably silent about the cause of the Assyrian withdrawal, although Wiseman noted that scholars often attribute it to news of troubles in Babylonia.

Sennacherib's death was interpreted by the Babylonians as divine punishment for his actions against their capital. The *Babylonian Chronicles* state that he was murdered by one of his sons, while 2 Kgs 19:36–37 notes that he was killed by two of his sons in the temple of Nisroch (i.e., Ninurta, the god of war). Sennacherib died on 20 Tebitu (January) of 681 BC and was succeeded by his youngest son, Esarhaddon.

ESARHADDON AS NEO-ASSYRIA'S KING
WITH THE LARGEST EMPIRE

The imperialistic efforts of Sennacherib and his predecessors set the stage well for Esarhaddon (681–669 BC) to inherit an extremely expansive kingdom and extend it beyond the limits previously experienced by any king of the Neo-Assyrian Empire. Yet Sennacherib's death plunged Assyria into a dynastic crisis. Esarhaddon was the youngest son of Naqi'a, the king's favorite wife inside of his harem, so although he was his father's chosen heir, he was not the firstborn son. According to Erle Leichty, Esarhaddon was quite close to his mother and came to rely heavily on her judgment. Young Esarhaddon took refuge in Cilicia or Tubal to escape his brothers as they fought for the throne, but his supporters called for his return to Nineveh, where he was crowned king in *ca.* 681 BC.

In 680 BC, Esarhaddon announced that he would rebuild Babylon, the city that the gods allegedly had decreed should lie in ruins for 70 years, with construction evidently having begun in 678 BC. By Wiseman's calculations, the fulfillment of this supposed prophecy required a numerical modification of the prophesied wait, with the help of a hermeneutical leap since it was only 11 years. The Babylonian numerals for $60 + 10 = 70$ years thus were allegorized to become $10 + 1 = 11$ years, the exact time since its destruction under Sennacherib. The work was not completed until *ca.* 669 BC, but it won him the loyalty of the Babylonians. They proved this by repulsing an Elamite attack in *ca.* 675 BC, helping Assyria against the son of Merodach-Baladan, who attempted to recapture Ur, and by repelling the Bīt-Dak-kuri tribe, which seized land near Babylon. The Bīt-Dak-kuri chief was replaced by a pro-Assyrian agent.

Esarhaddon experienced resistance in Anatolia from *ca.* 679 to 669 BC. As Wiseman noted, the major pressures against Assyria proper came from the nomadic Scythians, who pushed through Tubal and Cilicia toward Šupria, which is located to the southwest of Lake Van. Esarhaddon warred successfully against the army of the Cimmerian king, Teušpa, whom he claimed to have killed personally in battle. An Assyrian princess may have been given in marriage to the Scythian king, Bartatua, whose father had died in battle after attacking Esarhaddon. Yet by the end of Esarhaddon's reign, Assyria would lose Cilicia and Tubal.

Assyria's conquered people in the Levant also resisted Esarhaddon's rule, notably from 679 to 677 BC. The border garrison near Egypt at Arzani was reinforced in 679 BC, and three years later Esarhaddon quelled the Arabs in a series of raids. Phoenicia was suppressed by firm resistance from

Sidonian rebels. Abdi-Milkuti, the Sidonian king, was executed in 677 BC, while his city was sacked and his land was given to Tyre. During the winter of 673 BC, Esarhaddon and his army invaded Egypt, with the intent of incorporating Egypt's land into the empire. This attempt failed miserably, as the Assyrians were routed in battle near Ashkelon by the Cushite pharaoh, Taharqa (690–664 BC).

Esarhaddon was forced to consolidate his troops after this defeat, and he did not venture into warfare with Egypt again until 671 BC. This time, he came with a larger army and probably less disregard for Egyptian military capability. He led his army in their first of three encounters against the Egyptians, which the Assyrians won. A bad omen evidently was prophesied about Esarhaddon's survival if he were to engage in future clashes with Egypt, so he did not lead his troops into battle for the next two encounters between the rival powers. The Assyrians nonetheless prevailed in both battles, allowing them to capture Memphis, the Egyptian capital at the time, and to loot the city's wealth. Esarhaddon followed standard Assyrian protocol by relocating a huge contingent of surviving Egyptians to the other side of the empire.

With the conquest of Egypt in 671 BC, the Neo-Assyrian Empire had reached its geopolitical zenith. In the northeast, Assyrian territory included Lake Van and bordered the Kingdom of Urartu. In the north, Assyria possessed the entire Euphrates River valley and beyond, all of the way to the mouth of the Iris (Turkish: Yeşilırmak) River and the border of Cimmeria. To the northwest, Esarhaddon's empire extended to Lake Tuz, located in Anatolia's hinterland and on the border with the Kingdom of Phrygia, and included the southern part of northern Anatolia's Halys River. To the west, the empire enveloped virtually the entire Levant and the island of Cyprus. To the southwest, Esarhaddon possessed all of Egypt and part of Nubia/Cush. The southern border included Sinai and extended eastward from there to the Persian Gulf. To the east, Assyria's control extended to their border with—by listing from south to north—Elam, Media, Mannaea, and Scythia.

Esarhaddon was a forceful and dynamic ruler, and his ingenuity is reflected in his ability to solve the problem of the rebellious Babylonians—which began with the rebuilding of the very city of Babylon that his father had burned to the ground—because none of his predecessors was able to institute a successful foreign policy that kept Babylonia from rebelling against imperial rule. As a military leader, he was popular and effective, eventually even extending the Assyrian Empire deep into northeastern Africa. Fascinatingly, Leichty said that Esarhaddon was no Caligula or Nero, but was more like Claudius (i.e., all being Roman emperors of the 1st century AD). While Esarhaddon may not have been as self-obsessed as Caligula or Nero, he certainly was no less vicious than either of them.

After all, the evidence clearly attests to Esarhaddon's brutality in the handling of foreign nations. He executed the Sidonian king and sacked his city simply for insisting on its independence. When he defeated Egypt, he did more than send off the survivors to the opposite end of his empire. The king recorded on his victory stele that he killed multitudes of pharaoh's men and struck him five times with the edge of his javelin, and that he captured, devastated, and burned Memphis down to the ground. Plus, Esarhaddon showed no mercy to his two brothers who were responsible for the murder of their father, Sennacherib.

Esarhaddon's brothers fled to the country of Urartu on the shore of Lake Van, then slipped away from there to the king of Shubria, who provided them with asylum in violation of his oath of loyalty to Assyria. Esarhaddon led an expedition to find his murderous brothers, which is recorded in his *Letter to the Gods*. The king of Shubria, Ik-Teshub, harbored the brothers in his capital, forcing Esarhaddon to besiege the city. When the Assyrians broke through and secured control of the capital city of Ubbumu, Ik-Teshub and Esarhaddon's brothers fled into the citadel, which required another siege.

The Assyrians eventually broke that siege also, then seized Shubria's king and Sennacherib's brothers, none of whom was spared or shown mercy. Esarhaddon cut off their hands, noses, and ears, gouged out their eyes, then returned their bodies to Assyria. Such is the brutality of the great empire-builder, Esarhaddon, who followed in the footsteps of his father—and Nimrod of long before—both by his indiscriminate brutalizing of people created in the image of God and by exalting himself with the title, "king of Šumer and Akkad." Assyria's most powerful king was no less vicious than any of the great empire builders of greater antiquity.

NEO-BABYLONIAN EMPIRE UNDER
NEBUCHADNEZZAR II

RISE OF THE NEO-BABYLONIAN EMPIRE

The second major empire of the first millennium BC is the Neo-Babylonian Empire (626–539 BC), which was founded by Nabopolassar (626–605 BC), although this empire lasted 215 years less than the Neo-Assyrian Empire. The gap in the Assyrian annals after 639 BC makes it difficult to trace Neo-Assyrian decline under the aging Ashurbanipal, the son of Esarhaddon who ruled after him as his chosen heir. After Ashurbanipal's death in 627 BC, the Babylonian tribes were brave enough to launch an attack against an Assyrian garrison in northern Babylonia in August of 626 BC.

The rebellion of suppressed people against the authority of their oppressor immediately after its leader's death occurred many times throughout the ANE. When the Assyrian army marched to relieve Nippur, which along with Babylon was seized by Nabopolassar, they were forced to retreat. The Babylonian army successfully defended Babylon against Assyrian attack, and Nabopolassar was proclaimed king of Babylon 1½ months later, which signals the founding of the Neo-Babylonian Empire.

Early in Nabopolassar's reign, the Assyrian military machine was still a threat to Babylonian independence, although Nabopolassar managed to hold power with only brief interludes. His son, Nebuchadnezzar, the crowned prince of Babylon, defeated the Assyrians in the middle Euphrates in *ca.* 616 BC, driving them back to the heart of Assyria proper. In *ca.* 614 BC, Media—a new force in ANE geopolitics that was located due east of Assyria's great cities—laid siege to Ashur, one of the four Assyrian capitals.

The Medes, who succeeded Elam in Iran, overtook Ashur under Cyaxares (625–585 BC) and began massacring its citizens. Nabopolassar arrived on the scene after the city had fallen, and near the ruins of Ashur he formed an alliance with the powerful Cyaxares. This treaty relegated northern Mesopotamia to the Medes and left Nabopolassar free to roam in central Mesopotamia and Syria. Nabopolassar was a major participant in the fall of the other Assyrian capitals, including Nineveh, which fulfilled the prophecies of Nahum (2:8–10; 3:5–7) and Zephaniah (2:13–15).

Assyria's last gasp effort at survival as an independent kingdom was a futile alliance with Egypt. In a sudden reversal of policy, the Egyptians realized that Babylonia was now its main threat. In *ca.* 609 BC, at Megiddo, the Judahite king Josiah (*ca.* 640–609 BC) attempted to block the path of Pharaoh Neco II (*ca.* 609–594 BC), who was advancing northward to assist the remnants of the Assyrian army near Carchemish, on the northwestern bend of the Euphrates. Although Josiah lost his life in this effort (2 Kgs 23:29; 2 Chr 35:20–24), his attempt to impair the Egyptian advancement contributed to the Babylonian victory.

Whether because of old age or ill health, Nabopolassar left the command of the army to his crowned prince, Nebuchadnezzar. The young general led the Neo-Babylonian forces to an impressive and decisive victory against the Egyptians at Carchemish in the spring of 605 BC. The Battle of Carchemish provides an important synchronism for Israelite history and chronology, as Jer 46:2 confirms the date for this event by stating that the battle occurred in Year 4 of Jehoiakim's reign (*ca.* 609–597 BC).

Two biblical passages actually refer to the Battle of Carchemish, and they seemingly present a contradiction in how they date the event. While Jer 46:2 indeed states that Nebuchadnezzar defeated the Egyptians at Carchemish in Year 4 of Jehoiakim, the text of Dan 1:1 reveals that Nebuchadnezzar besieged Jerusalem in Year 3 of Jehoiakim. Since the Battle of Carchemish chronologically preceded Nebuchadnezzar's deportation of the surviving Jews from Judah after the conquest of Jerusalem, there appears to be a historical contradiction between these two biblical passages.

Yet as Rodger Young pointed out, Daniel used accession-year reckoning—which the Babylonians also used, but their first day of the year differed from that of the Judahites. Accession reckoning does not count the king's accession year as the first year of his reign (Nisan calendar: Apr 2 – Apr 2). In contrast, Jeremiah used non-accession reckoning, which does count the king's accession year as the first year of his reign (Tishri calendar: Sept 10 – Sept 10). Daniel's "Year 3 of Jehoiakim" (accession reckoning) thus was the same as Jeremiah's "Year 4 of Jehoiakim" (non-accession reckoning), so they do not contradict one another in their dating of Nebuchadnezzar II's regnal years. With the pivotal Babylonian victory over the Assyrians at

Carchemish, the entire Levant was open to Nebuchadnezzar as he pursued the Egyptians southward.

NEBUCHADNEZZAR II AS NEO-BABYLONIA'S
KING WITH THE GREATEST DOMINION

On 15 August 605 BC, Nabopolassar died in Babylon, forcing Nebuchadnezzar to race across the desert in two weeks, beginning on 26 August, in order to claim the throne on 7 September 605 BC. Only rarely in antiquity did anyone attempt to travel straight through the Eastern Desert, but the crowned prince could not allow his absence to embolden any potential rival in the homeland to usurp the throne of his father's vast kingdom.

Nebuchadnezzar II (605–562 BC) was coronated after arriving home safely, instantly possessing most of the former territories of the Neo-Assyrian Empire. With the friendly Medes consolidating their power to the north and east, he was free to concentrate on the Euphrates valley and the Levant, as far as Egypt. He reestablished Babylonia as the leading power in the ANE, and his reign rivaled Hammurabi's in size and strength.

Nebuchadnezzar II's domestic building activities may have been unrivaled in antiquity for their splendor and lavishness. Bill T. Arnold noted that a number of royal palaces already existed when the king ascended the throne, but that did not stop him from building a magnificent new palace late in his reign. The ruins of this structure contain a museum in which he housed a large collection of antiquities, accentuating his interest in archaeology and history. Classical authors credit Nebuchadnezzar II with the building of the so-called hanging gardens of Babylon. These written sources describe elaborate roof gardens for his Median wife, who missed her luxurious homeland. The beautiful buildings and structures dating to this time, which includes as many as 50 temples, made Babylon one of the seven wonders of the ancient world.

Humanly speaking, Nebuchadnezzar II's famous pride (Dan 4:30) was understandable. He transformed Babylon into the greatest city of the ancient world. Its magnificent walls were entered by eight gates, each named after a god, and the modern ruins are spread over 2,000 acres to form the largest ancient site in Mesopotamia. The famed Ishtar Gate played an important religious role in the life of the city and is the best preserved among all of the gates. The surface of the entrance was covered with blue enameled bricks, which served as a background for alternating red-and-white dragons that are symbolic of Marduk, along with bulls, which are symbolic of Adad, the storm-god. The gate was approached by an impressive processional street, which was about 20 m wide in places and paved with white limestone and red breccia.

Bordering the street, walls as high as 20 m were found still standing, decorated with lions almost 2 m in length, symbolic of Ishtar, with red or yellow manes on a blue ceramic background. Along this street, the king would accompany the statue of Marduk in a grand procession each spring at the *akītu* festival, which celebrated the start of the new year. It is believed that the king and Babylon's inhabitants participated in the renewal of nature and the procuring of their destiny for the coming year. As Arnold described, such a ceremony in this extravagant setting must have inspired devotion and great awe among the people.

The scope of Nebuchadnezzar II's imperialistic aspirations is seen in his '13-year' (per Josephus, only) siege and apparent victory at Tyre, as prophesied by Ezekiel (26:7–14) and recorded by Josephus (*Against Apion* 1.1.21 §156), and his invasion of Egypt in *ca.* 570 BC. His empire surpassed Hammurabi's in geographical dimensions, yet in Nebuchadnezzar II's inscriptions he prided himself more in his domestic building activities than his foreign conquests. In fact, his military campaigns were motivated to a large degree by a desire to acquire booty to finance his ambitious rebuilding of Babylon and 12 other Babylonian cities.

Nebuchadnezzar II encountered Judahite resistance with his first and second invasions. During brief raids into Judah over the 17 months after he became king, he besieged Jerusalem, plundered the Temple articles, and captured Daniel and his friends (Dan 1:1–7). This first invasion of Jerusalem took place in 605 BC. Pockets of resistance to the powerful Babylonian king did occur, especially in the Levant. After a battle with the Egyptians in *ca.* 601 BC, in which both sides suffered great losses, Judah's king Jehoiakim suddenly switched allegiance from Babylonia to Egypt, believing that the Egyptians were more powerful.

In retaliation, Nebuchadnezzar II personally led an attack force of the Babylonian army against the Kingdom of Judah. Jehoiakim died before the siege of Jerusalem began, leaving his son, Jehoiachin (*ca.* 598–597 BC), on the throne. According to the *Babylonian Chronicles*, the invading army captured Jerusalem on 16 March 597 BC. The Babylonians captured Jehoiachin, deported him and other members of the royal family to Babylon, and replaced him with Jehoiachin's uncle, Zedekiah (2 Kgs 24:17). However, this major setback for the Judahites did not scare them into permanent submission to the invaders.

After Nebuchadnezzar II easily suppressed an insurrection attempt in Babylon (*ca.* 595 BC), Zedekiah led Judah to align itself with Egypt again. Nebuchadnezzar II's response was quick and fierce, a devastating third invasion. According to Rodger Young, the Neo-Babylonians laid siege to Jerusalem on 27 Jan 589 BC (2 Kgs 25:1; Jer 39:1; Ezek 24:1–2), and the city fell on 29 August 587 BC. Nebuchadnezzar II's general, Nebuzaradan, so thoroughly razed the city (2 Kgs 25:8–10) that the trauma of it left a lasting legacy in the Jewish psyche, as exemplified with the writing of Lamentations. Archaeological evidence suggests that the population of Judah fell from 250,000 in the 8th century BC to half of that after Jerusalem's destruction.

As Arnold noted, Judah apparently made a final attempt to attain independence in *ca.* 582/1 BC, but this was squelched easily by Nebuzaradan (Jer 52:30). Nebuchadnezzar II died in *ca.* 562 BC, after a lengthy rule of 43 years. Arnold is correct that this monarch's reign is one of the most amply documented periods of Babylonian history, yielding royal inscriptions, chronicles, private and administrative texts, legal materials, and letters. History has honored this dynasty as the apex of Babylonia's wealth and political power, but all of it would be lost in less than a quarter of a century, which clearly reflects the futility of building an empire.

MEDO-PERSIAN EMPIRE UNDER DARIUS I

RISE OF THE MEDO-PERSIAN EMPIRE

The Neo-Babylonian Empire's sudden demise led to the immediate elevation of the Medo-Persians to the status of exclusive world power within the ANE, especially due to the efforts of Cyrus II (*ca.* 559–530 BC). Edwin Yamauchi asserted that Cyrus II, who is known to historians as Cyrus the

Great, is considered by many to be the most outstanding figure in all of Achaemenid history. Cyrus II showed rare ability to blend diplomacy with military skill, tolerance, and wisdom. The Persians called him "father," while the Greeks respected him. God even referred to him as "my shepherd" (Isa 44:28) and "my anointed" (Isa 45:1).

For reasons presently unknown, king Nabonidus (*ca.* 556–539 BC) of the Neo-Babylonian Empire installed Belshazzar (*ca.* 553–539 BC) as his co-regent in Babylon three years after becoming king. The Nabonidus Chronicle states that the royal father "entrusted the 'camp' to his oldest (son, Belshazzar), the firstborn. . . . He let everything go, entrusted the kingship to him, and he himself started out on a long journey." As Clines noted, Belshazzar remained subordinate to Nabonidus, which is reflected in Dan 5:16. "But I personally have heard about you, that you are able to give interpretations and solve difficult problems. Now if you are able to read the inscription and make its interpretation known to me, you will be clothed with purple and wear a necklace of gold around your neck, and you will have authority as the third ruler in the kingdom."

Nabonidus held the first position in the empire, while Belshazzar enjoyed the second position, and Daniel received the third position. The demise of Media after Cyrus the Great defeated the Medes in 550 BC under their king, Astyages, put Persia into direct conflict with Babylonia. Nabonidus, however, concentrated on westward expansion. Roy Hayden noted that Nabonidus built a palace at Tema in the Arabian peninsula with his son Belshazzar in control at Babylon. In 547 BC, Cyrus II turned his attention first to the north and to the west. Assyria and Cilicia yielded, while Ashur and Harran were captured, and a decisive battle was fought with Croesus of Lydia. Although winter was approaching, Cyrus II pushed onward to Sardis, which he captured after a 14-day siege, after which Croesus was captured and subsequently became an advisor to Cyrus.

The Medes and Persians seem to have spent 546 to 540 BC consolidating their control over the eastern parts of his empire, while the subjugation of the Ionian Greek cities was accomplished by Harpagus, after a campaign that required three years to complete. The eastern frontiers were extended to include the Aryan tribes, Parthia, and the Bactrian tribes as far as Samarkand. Cyrus II—the leader of the Medo-Persian armies and king of Persia while still under the suzerainty of his uncle, Cyaxares II/Darius the Mede, king of Media—now was powerful enough to deal with the Neo-Babylonian Empire.

The idea that "Darius the Mede" of the book of Daniel was the same person as Cyaxares II, king of Media while Cyrus II was (under him) king of Persia, was the conviction of Josephus in the first century AD, Jerome in the late third and early fourth centuries, John Calvin in the 16th century, James Ussher in the 17th century, and virtually all of the conservative Bible commentators in the 18th and 19th centuries. The research of Steven Anderson brought to light this rich heritage of the identification of Darius the Mede of Daniel with the Cyaxares II of Xenophon's *Cyropaedia*, demonstrating the near certainty of the identification, as well.

To protect the Babylonian capital from the upcoming Persian onslaught, Nabonidus brought the images of most of the Babylonian gods into Babylon from the neighboring cities. According to Hayden and Yamauchi, this act alienated the priests, who were already discontented with the king due to his neglect of the worship of Marduk. Gubaru, also known as Gobryas, the governor of Gutium and formerly an outstanding general of Nebuchadnezzar II, was the most important Babylonian to defect to Cyrus II, as it was Gubaru who was instrumental in the Medo-Persian conquest of Babylon.

In order to attack Babylon, the Medo-Persians and their allies had to outflank the Median wall, which stretched 38.6 km from Sippar on the Euphrates to Opis on the Tigris. Cyrus II may have crossed the Tigris just south of Opis. According to the *Babylonian Chronicles*, he "did battle at Opis on the Tigris against the army of Akkad." By 10 October, the Persians captured Sippar "without a battle." Herodotus (1.191) indicated that the Persians then moved against the capital and gained entrance into Babylon by diverting the Euphrates River upstream so that the Medo-Persian soldiers could enter the city by utilizing the lower water level, which some scholars find difficult to accept.

Yet as Herodotus correctly described, and as the excavations of Robert Koldewey confirmed, Babylon not only was bisected by the Euphrates, but it also was penetrated by many canals. The height of the Euphrates would have been at its lowest level at this time of year, normally about 0.3 m deep. According to Yamauchi, more than one ancient text mentions a famine, which—if caused by a dry year—would mean that the river level was even shallower. The theory that the Persians penetrated the city's defenses by entering through a water channel thus seems more credible than the idea of Walther Hinz, who suggested that the Babylonians left the gates open and allowed Gubaru to enter, without even realizing that he had defected to the enemy.

According to Dan 5:1–4, Babylon fell when Belshazzar was using the vessels from the First Temple sacrilegiously to celebrate during a great festival for his nobles. Herodotus (1.191) relates that at this time "they were dancing and making merry at a festival." Xenophon (*Cyropaedia* 7.5.15) stated that the Medo-Persian army chose to attack during a certain festival when "all of Babylon was accustomed to drink and revel all night long." Both the *Babylonian Chronicles* and the Cyrus Cylinder claim that Gubaru and his troops entered Babylon "without a battle." This occurred on 13 October 539 BC, although Cyrus II did not enter the city until 29 October.

Belshazzar was killed, but Nabonidus was spared, as he was exiled to the province of Carmania, in the east, where, according to Berossus, "Darius the king took some of the province for himself." Berossus's Darius, who must have had authority over Cyrus in 539 BC, only can be Daniel's Darius the Mede. This ancient extra-biblical reference effectively refutes the critics who concluded that Darius the Mede is a fictitious character whom Daniel merely invented. At the same time, this extra-biblical corroboration supports the view that the book of Daniel was composed in the 6th century BC, due to its exact documentation of these events.

According to propagandistic Persian texts disseminated after the conquest of Babylon, the inhabitants greeted Cyrus II not as a conqueror, but as a liberator, and they spread green branches onto his path. The Cyrus Cylinder, another form of propaganda, claims that Cyrus II showed his concern for the starving people and restored their "dilapidated dwellings." Moreover, an inscribed fragment in the Yale Babylonian Collection was identified in 1970 by Paul R. Berger as part of the Cyrus Cylinder. This fragment notes that Cyrus restored the city's inner wall and moats, which may mean that they were damaged during the conquest of Babylon.

The Persians claimed that when Cyrus II entered Babylon in October of 539 BC, the people welcomed him as a liberator, which is highly disputable. Nonetheless, the conquest of Babylon ended the last native empire in ancient Mesopotamia, just as Arnold stated. For the first time in Babylonian history, foreigners would control the country without assimilating its culture, and the region became a mere province in a large empire whose center was located outside the boundaries of Mesopotamia. For the next millennium, Indo-Iranians and Indo-Europeans would dominate Babylonia.

Cyrus II instituted the enlightened policy of placating the gods of his subjected peoples, instead of carrying off their cultic statues and citizens, as was the practice of the Elamites, Hittites, Assyrians, and Babylonians before him. The generosity he showed by permitting the Jews to return to their homeland was not unique to them, but instead it was paralleled by his benevolence to the Babylonians and other peoples. From a biblical perspective, ultimately He-who-is "stirred up the heart of Cyrus" (Ezra 1:1), prompting him to return the exiles "without any payment or reward" (Isa 45:13). A Hebrew copy of Cyrus II's edict to the Jews is preserved in Ezra 1:2–4, and an Aramaic memorandum that refers to part of this edict is found in Ezra 6:3–5.

According to Ezra 6:8, Cyrus II not only permitted the Jews to return to their own homeland, but he even gave them *carte blanche* authorization to rebuild the Temple and funded the project with resources from the imperial treasury. Because the accounts in Haggai and Zechariah do not mention monetary support from the Persian treasury, some have questioned the promises made in Ezra 6:8. Yet extra-biblical evidence demonstrates that such imperial financing was a typical practice of Persian kings to help restore sanctuaries throughout their empire. As Yamauchi pointed out, Cyrus II repaired the Eanna temple at Uruk, the Enunmah temple at Ur, and numerous temples in Babylon. Regarding the utilization of this policy by future Medo-Persian kings, Cambyses provided funds for reconstructing the temple at Sais in Egypt, and Darius I ordered a complete rebuilding of the temple of Amun at Hibis, in the Khargah Oasis of Upper Egypt.

DARIUS I AS MEDO-PERSIA'S KING WITH
THE GREATEST DOMINION

Darius, the son of Hystaspes, the satrap of Bactria and Persis, was born in *ca.* 550 BC. As Yamauchi pointed out, he was not a member of Persia's royal family, but he belonged to a collateral Achaemenid line. Darius served under Cambyses II in Egypt as a spearbearer among the immortals, an elite force of 10,000 royal soldiers. Both his father and his grandfather, Arsames, still were alive at the time of his accession in 522 BC, at which time Darius was about 28 years old.

Darius I (522–486 BC) was an excellent administrator, and he spent much of his energy reorganizing the empire. Hayden noted that Darius I established 20 Persian satrapies, placing a military commander and a tax official, who answered directly to the king, in each satrapy. Inspectors, called "the ears of the king," made periodic and unannounced visits, which served to prevent the threat of internal rebellion or uprisings. A network of roads was created to facilitate travel and communication. The king built a new palace at Susa in 521 BC, and he founded an entirely new capital at Persepolis in 518 BC.

Darius I became legendary for his military exploits and foreign acquisitions. The extent of his campaigns in the East is unknown, but he claims to have expanded Medo-Persian rule over the Scythians. In addition, after suppressing the rebellious provinces in the region, he proceeded eastward, perhaps in 516/5 BC, in order to conquer the territory that became the satrapy of Hindush, along the Indus River in modern Pakistan. According to Yamauchi, this area provided the Persian coffers with untold treasures, consisting of some 360 talents of gold annually.

To the southwest, Darius I invaded Egypt and spent six months there, all in response to Egypt's rebellion against him. Herodotus reported that the satrap whom Cambyses II had appointed provoked Darius I by minting his own silver coins in imitation of the king's golden darics. Yamauchi added that a study of demotic documents of the time indicates that Egypt enjoyed stable religious and economic practices during this reign. During a visit in 497 to 496 BC, Darius I both had the temple of Amun built at Hibis and granted donations to the temple of Horus at Edfu.

Following in the footsteps of Egypt's Sesostris III (*ca.* 1878–1840 BC) long before him, Darius I built a canal between the Nile River and the Red Sea, an astounding accomplishment that would have required an enormous labor force. A number of Middle Kingdom inscriptions refer to a canal dug by the Egyptians between the Pelusiac branch of the Nile and the Red Sea, and satellite photos have revealed its location. The canal that Darius I built, though, extended some 80 km and was perhaps 45 m wide and 3 m deep. This ambitious project required about a dozen years to construct, but Aristotle wrote in his *Meteorology* treatise that neither Sesostris III's nor Darius I's version of the 'canal of the pharaohs' ever was completed. They both learned that the level of the seawater in the Red Sea was higher than that of the freshwater in the Nile River, so they could not allow the seawater to spoil the river water.

The Greek cities of Ionia, in Asia Minor, were subjugated to the Persians shortly after Cyrus II's conquest of Lydia in 547 BC. During the rule of Darius I, the Persians found it convenient to rule the Ionian cities through Greek tyrants. In 499 BC, however, a Greek tyrant named Aristagoras led a revolt against the Persians among the Ionian cities, which was supported by 20 Athenian ships. During the following year, the Ionian rebels and their allies managed to burn the lower city at Sardis. In the wake of this revolt, the island of Cyprus also revolted against the Persians.

In response, the Persians mobilized and crushed the revolt in a decisive battle that took place off of the island of Lade, near Miletus, in 494 BC. By diplomacy and military action, Darius I had reestablished control over the Greek cities of Ionia, and Miletus was punished severely for revolting. According to Yamauchi, the Persians may have regarded the Athenian participation as a breach of the earlier treaty of 507 BC, as well as a violation of the city's status as a so-called vassal, which may cast a different light on the wars between the Persians and the Greeks that resulted from the Ionian revolt.

For Hayden, the Grecian action may have been a convenient excuse for Darius I to initiate his hidden intent: the conquest of the Greek mainland. In 492 BC, Darius I sent an expedition led by his son-in-law, Mardonius, to punish the Greeks. Unfortunately for the Persians, much of their fleet capsized off of the peninsula of Mount Athos in the northern Aegean Sea. The expedition was not a total loss, though, as the Persians gained a foothold in Europe with the submission of Thrace and Macedonia. A second expedition was sent in 490 BC and was led by Darius I's nephew, this time directly across the Aegean.

The Persians then traveled to Eretria, which was betrayed to them after a one-week siege. News of the Persian invasion and the fall of Eretria quickly arrived at Sparta, 80 km away. The Spartans responded that they could not march until the moon was full, believed by most to be an observance of the Carneian Festival of Apollo, although Yamauchi noted that some associate the reluctance with a general lunar superstition. The Persians, meanwhile, chose to land at the Bay of Marathon, which set the stage for one of the most significant battles in human history.

The ten Athenian generals were divided evenly as to whether they should remain behind to defend Athens or take the offensive at Marathon. Callimachos, the military ruler (Greek: *polemarch*), broke the tie in favor of attacking. While Callimachos had nominal control in the battle, they all recognized that Miltiades was the decisive leader of the Grecian forces. Once the opposing armies had taken their positions, a delay of five or six days occurred before the battle began. In Yamauchi's mind, the Athenians may have been waiting for the promised reinforcements from Sparta, while the Persians may have been waiting for aid from pro-Persian sympathizers.

At the Battle of Marathon, the Athenians had a force of about 9,000 hoplites (i.e., heavily armed infantrymen who fought in a phalanx formation, usually eight men deep). The hoplites carried shields in their left hand and spears in their right. There also was a contingent of about 1,000 men from Plataea, a city to the northwest of Athens. The Persians, who may have had two or three times as many soldiers as the Athenians, were not heavily armored but relied mainly on their archers, whose range was 150 m or slightly more. In order to combat the Persian advantage, Miltiades devised the brilliant tactic of having the Greek soldiers charge the Persians at the pace of a full run.

The Athenians deliberately weakened their center and strengthened their flanks. The Persians thus broke through the center, but the Greeks countered by swinging their wings around and catching the Persians in a classic pincer movement. After this decisive moment in the battle, the Persians fled toward a large marsh to the north and scrambled onto their ships that were anchored in the bay. Herodotus recounted that 6,400 Persians died, while only 192 Athenian and Greek forces died.

Yamauchi noted that some scholars are suspicious of these figures, as lopsided casualties are typical for ancient battles recorded in classical, biblical, and ANE sources. However, the greatest number of casualties was inflicted when the Persians were being chased from the battlefield, after having been routed in battle. One puzzling aspect in Herodotus's account of the battle, for which he is criticized, is the lack of mention of the involvement of the Persian cavalry, after he had stressed their presence several times earlier.

Despite the pivotal Medo-Persian loss at Marathon that prevented the potential conquest of the Greek mainland, Darius I attained the height of the empire's dominion and glory. He ruled from the Indus and Jaxartes Rivers in the east to the Aegean Sea and Egypt in the west, and from the Persian Gulf in the south to the Caspian and Black Seas in the north. Throughout the next century-and-a-half (*ca.* 486–338 BC), his successors were concerned with consolidating the empire that he had acquired and organized.

The text in Ezra 4:1–5 documents the attempts of Gentile residents in Judea to frustrate the Judeans and prevent the construction of the Second Temple that the post-exilics began to build under the edict of Cyrus the Great. The people of the land succeeded to some degree, as they "discouraged the [Judean] people and frightened them from building" (Ezra 4:4). Ezra then noted that the local residents hired consultants to frustrate the plans of the Judeans "all the days of Cyrus, king of Persia, even until the reign of Darius (I), king of Persia" (Ezra 4:5). This implies that from the time the Jews returned after the edict of Cyrus I in 537 BC until Year 2 of Darius I (Haggai 1:15), on 21 Sept 520 BC, these Gentiles successfully prevented them from completing the Second Temple. This includes the entire intermediary reign of Cambyses II (530–522 BC).

Events during the reign of Darius I are discussed again in Ezra 4:24–6:15, including the beginning of the work to rebuild the Temple (Ezra 5:2). During this time, Haggai and Zechariah prophesied to the Jews in Judea, and particularly in Jerusalem (Ezra 5:1). Although the Judeans had to deal with an attempt by the governor of the "land beyond the River" to demand a halt to the work of building the Temple and the walls around Jerusalem (Ezra 5:8), the Temple's construction was completed in Year 6 of Darius I's reign (Ezra 6:15). As Yamauchi noted, the Second Temple was finished on

12 March 515 BC, just over 70 years after the destruction of the First Temple in 587 BC.

Darius I placed a curse on "any king or people who put their hand to alter [the decree], or to destroy this house of God that *is* in Jerusalem" (Ezra 6:12). The Hebrew verb used for the cursing is *magar*, which is a *hapax legomenon*, meaning that it appears only once in the entire Hebrew Bible, making it challenging to translate. The Greek verb that the Septuagint's translators used to render this word is *katastrepho*, the nominal form of which is transliterated into English as "catastrophe." The Greek word used here for, "inflict a catastrophe," seems to fit the context accurately, and the sense of the word in English represents its meaning fairly well, as any attack on the Second Temple would result in catastrophic consequences for the perpetrator.

The Second Temple was destroyed by the Romans in AD 70, under Titus, the son of emperor Vespasian. Titus became emperor in AD 79 but died in AD 81, a mere 2½ years after taking the throne. Not only was his reign short, but it was marred by disasters. Mt. Vesuvius erupted violently a mere four months after his accession, an event that buried Pompeii and Herculaneum and killed thousands of people. In spring of Titus's Year 1 (AD 80), Rome experienced another destructive fire, just about 14 years after the one that devasted the city during the reign of Nero in AD 64, which burned large parts of the city for three days.

According to Suetonius, a plague broke out in the wake of the fire. In addition, war broke out in Britannia, and Terentius Maximus led a rebellion. The brief reign of Titus thus seems to bear all of the markings of a fulfillment of Darius I's curse, namely that the king who destroys the Second Temple, which was built during the Medo-Persian Empire, would be subjected to catastrophe at the hands of the God of Israel. For all of Darius I's impressive accomplishments and acts of benevolence, historians have dubbed him, 'Darius the Great.' He was a complicated person: a voracious empire builder, an occasionally benevolent king, a brutal protector of his empire, and a powerful tool in the hand of the living God.

GRECO-MACEDONIAN EMPIRE UNDER ALEXANDER III

RISE OF THE GRECO-MACEDONIAN EMPIRE UNDER PHILIP II

For all of their glory and vast dominions, none of the great empires of the ancient world—including the Akkadian, Third Dynasty of Ur, Old Babylonian, Egyptian, Neo-Assyrian, Neo-Babylonian, and Medo-Persian empires—rivaled the Greco-Macedonian Empire under Alexander III in the amount of territory within its domain. This young king eclipsed all of the greatest empire-builders of prior history. Yet Alexander III's empire was led primarily by Macedonians, rather than Greeks, and his father, Philip II (359–336 BC), is the Macedonian king who was the mastermind of the carefully-crafted plan to conquer the East.

Since warfare was a normal part of Macedonian life, all of Macedon's national institutions were designed to promote military service and efficiency. According to Nicholas Hammond, the cities of Macedon were subjected to the rule of the central government, which consisted of the king and the assembly of the King's Men. Citizenship as 'Macedones' and membership in the assembly was held only by the King's Men, who had the honor of being the king's 'Companions.' The king selected his commanders and administrators from among them, whom he called his 'Friends.' He consulted them at his own discretion, but he was not bound to accept their advice. Many of the King's Men had graduated from the school of pages. Outstanding service was rewarded by the king, who granted a Friend an estate or other property at his discretion.

Macedon's infantry was organized as heavily armed troops only in *ca.* 369 BC. Ten years later, Philip II equipped them with his new weapon: a lethal pike that measured 5 to 6 m long, along with a small shield suspended from the neck and plate-armor greaves (i.e., protective shin guards that covered the legs from the knees to the ankles). Wielding the pike and maintaining the formation of the phalanx required intensive training and peak physical fitness. Like the hoplites of the city-states, the infantry fought in a full phalanx of men, shoulder to shoulder, 8 to 10 men deep. As Hammond remarked, the Macedonians' pikes so outreached the 2-m spears the hoplites wielded that their phalanx presented four pike-heads to a hoplite's single spearhead. While the Cavalry Companions provided their own mounts and equine equipment, the king supplied the Infantry Companions with pikes and equipment from his own resources.

In the spring of 358 BC, Philip II convinced the assembly of the King's Men that they should mount an offensive in the regions near his kingdom. In decisive battles, he inflicted a crippling defeat on Bardylis, established the eastern bank of Lake Lychnitis as his frontier, and freed Pelagonia, Lyncus, and the other tribal states of western Macedonia. Philip II then invited the peoples of these states to abolish their monarchies and enter the Macedonian Kingdom with rights equal to those of the Macedonians. He raised the standard of life in upper Macedon to that of lower Macedon, and toward that end he founded new towns in upper Macedon, which included an education and military training.

As these men graduated, he recruited the best of them to enter the king's army and become members of the assembly as Macedones. Philip II's innovations were so successful that from 358 to 336 BC, his Companion Cavalry rose from 600 to 2,800 riders, while his Companion Infantry rose from 10,000 to 27,000. Philip II's foresight and brilliant innovations would allow Alexander to inherit the most formidable army in all of Europe.

By using diplomatic skill and military opportunism, Philip II defeated the Illyrian tribes beyond his western frontier, forced the Paeonians to become his subjects, gained possession of Greek colonies on the coast, defended Amphipolis against the Athenians, defended Crenides (later renamed to Philippi) against the Thracians, and advanced his eastern frontier to the Nestus River, all by late 354 BC.

Philip II thus expanded his kingdom eastward and southward. He also managed to make a treaty with his powerful neighbor, the Chalcidian League of city-states, on the condition that neither party would enter into separate negotiations with Athens. During these years, he confirmed an alliance with Larissa in Thessaly by marrying Philinna, a lady of the ruling house. He also made an alliance with the Molossian royal house by marrying Olympias in 357 BC, in which year he was elected to replace Amyntas IV as Macedon's king. Onomarchus, the leader of the Phocian occupiers of Delphi, launched an offensive against Thebes in 353 BC, sending 7,000 mercenaries to support Pherae against the other Thessalians, which became Philip II's opportunity to lead Macedon into greatness. The reason is that the Thessalians appealed to him for aid, which he provided by helping them to win a great victory.

In 352 BC, Philip II and his Thessalian allies won a decisive victory over Onomarchus's army of 500 cavalry and 20,000 infantry, to the amazement of the leaders of the Greek city-states. After the battle, Philip II ordered 3,000 prisoners to be drowned because of their sacrilege against Apollo, the patron god for whom Philip II's troops went to battle wearing laurel wreaths in his honor. His generosity obviously had its limits, and this vicious act demonstrates the type of character that empire-builders typically possessed.

Philip II championed the cause of liberty and federalism (i.e., a system of rule that combines a national government with a regional government in a way that splits power and responsibility between them) against the dictators of Pherae, whom he then expelled together with their mercenaries. As a reward, he was elected president of the Thessalian League, which placed its forces and its revenues at his disposal.

Philip II sought to unify the city-states of Greece by creating *The Treaty of Common Peace* and forming a coalition of Greeks and Macedonians as its members. Despite his offers to establish this *Common Peace*, Athens, Sparta, and Thebes resisted in the name of freedom. He realized in 341 BC that force, instead of diplomacy, may be needed to subjugate the cities of Greece. Amphissa rebelled against him and persuaded Athens to join in the opposition. He attempted more than once to negotiate terms of peace, but these efforts were in vain. War simply could not be avoided, because these proud city-states had no intention of losing their freedom and independence, so the decisive battle was fought in Boeotia in August of 338 BC.

The troops of Boeotia, Athens, Megara, Corinth, and Achaea numbered 35,000 men, while the figures for Macedon and her allies are somewhat less. Alexander, at this time the crowned prince and commander of the Companion Cavalry, participated in the battle. As Hammond noted, when Philip II's tactics created a breach in the opposing phalanx, Alexander and his cavalry charged through the gap. He personally led the attack on the Sacred Band of 300 Thebans, a total victory for Macedon, and the Grecian league of city-states suffered terrible losses. Thebes was treated harshly for violating its oath to Philip II, while Athens was shown mercy.

As Philip II advanced into the Peloponnese, his enemies submitted, and his allies rejoiced. At this point, Sparta alone was defiant. On account of this, he ravaged Sparta's territory, without attacking the city itself, and gave some of her frontier regions to his allies. As he returned northward, the Amphictyonic League reduced the restrictions on the Phocians and approved the actions of the Macedonian king. The future of the city-states now was in his hands, prompting him to create "the Greek Community" (Greek: *to koinon ton Hellenon*), in which the Grecian city-states would swear to keep peace among themselves, maintain existing constitutions, and act against any violator of the Common Peace.

Philip II's proposal, tendered in autumn of 338 BC, was accepted by the city-states in spring of 337 BC. The ground and naval forces at the disposal of the council were defined: 15,000 cavalry, 200,000 infantry, and 160 triremes (i.e., large warships) manned by crews totaling some 30,000 men. The Greek Community far exceeded the Macedonian state in the size of the forces that they could deploy. The next step was the creation of a formal, military alliance between the Greek Community and the state of Macedon.

Because Macedon was at war with Persia already, the Common Council declared war on Persia late in 337 BC, and they voted that the commander of the joint forces should be Philip II. Within the community, he was given the title of *hēgemōn* (i.e., a type of commander), and the powers of his office were defined carefully. In the spring of 336 BC, the advanced guard of the joint forces crossed into Asia under the command of three Macedonian generals whom he had appointed, and arrangements were made for the stipulated forces of the coalition to follow that autumn, with Philip II as their supreme commander.

In 336 BC, the center of attention was the war in Asia Minor. The advanced forces of Macedon and the Greek Community won impressive victories under the commands of Parmenio, Attalus, and Amyntas. With a supporting fleet, they liberated the Greek cities of the western coast as far south as Ephesus, where a statue of Philip II was erected in the temple of Artemis. The Persians entrusted the defense of Asia Minor to Memnon, a Rhodian commander of Greek mercenaries, but there was no Persian fleet in the Aegean Sea to support him. The main Greco-Macedonian forces, with Philip II in command, were planning to land in Asia during autumn.

While the forces of the Greek Community were gathering, Philip II made the October festival at Aegeae an international occasion by inviting the envoys of the city-states and the leaders of the Balkan states to attend as guests. Just before dawn of the second day of the festival, the theater was packed with the leading Macedonians and the official guests of the Macedonian state. Some of Philip II's Friends, headed by Alexander, entered through the side entrance (Greek: *parodos*) and took their seats in the front row.

Philip II entered alone, wearing a white cloak, then stood in the center of the orchestra and acknowledged the cheers of the spectators. His seven Bodyguards had fanned out nearby. Suddenly, one of them, Pausanias, sprang forward, stabbed the king, and fled through the *parodos*. The king's Bodyguards killed Pausanias with their spears, but the Macedonian king lay dead in the orchestra. Many scholars are convinced that Pausanias was the king's spurned homosexual lover who was exacting revenge on him. Either way, Philip II's dream of conquering Asia ended abruptly, just when he was on the cusp of realizing it.

ALEXANDER III AS THE BUILDER OF THE GRECO-MACEDONIAN EMPIRE

As the crowned prince, Alexander was educated under Aristotle, beginning in *ca.* 342 BC. Philip II hired this great thinker to teach philosophy to his son, which embraced both practical and theoretical knowledge. These lessons and seminars usually were held in the open-air sanctuary of the nymphs near Mieza, a beautiful place that was visited by sightseers in Plutarch's day. The influence of Aristotle on Alexander III was profound. The boy embraced Aristotle's views on cosmology, geography, botany, zoology, and medicine. Due to this training under his respected tutor, Alexander took scientists with his army when he marched into Asia.

Alexander also was fascinated by Aristotle's lectures on logic, metaphysics, poetry, and the essence of politics. Above all, he learned from Aristotle to put faith in reason and the intellect. For this reason, he has been called the apostle of Hellenism, as he not only conquered nations but infused a cultural ideology into his subjects. In summer of 338 BC, Alexander attended the School of Pages, whose physically fit graduates entered the

Companion Cavalry as troopers. He emerged from the school with flying colors, winning distinction as a cavalryman mounted on his warhorse and by his fearless hunting ability. His future was promising, and he fully expected that one day the Assembly of the Macedones would elect him as its king.

After Philip II's assassination, as many of the King's Men as could be summoned assembled under arms in the theater to elect a successor. The Friends gathered around Alexander and chose him, so he followed in the footsteps of his father as the king of Macedon, becoming Alexander III. The force that the new king prepared for the conquest of Asia—when including various specialists and support personnel—is estimated at 90,000 strong, with at least half of them from the Greek Community and centers of mercenary recruitment in Greece, and less than one quarter from within the Macedonian Kingdom. This Macedonian contingent consisted of 1,800 Companion Cavalry and 12,000 phalangite infantry and lightly-armed troops. The Balkan contingent of Illyrians, Triballians, Agrianians, and Odrysians totaled 7,500 men.

At Amphipolis, the main Greco-Macedonian army met the expeditionary force under Parmenio, the loyal general under the king's deceased father, whose troops included 2,300 cavalry, 7,000 hoplites from the Greek Community, and 5,000 Greek mercenaries. The Macedonian fleet consisted of 22 triremes and 38 penteconters and triaconters (i.e., smaller warships), with crews totaling around 6,000 men. The Greek fleet, provided by the Greek Community, numbered 160 triremes, with crews of some 32,000 men. In addition to the warships, there were merchant ships that carried equipment and supplies that could maintain the army for a period of one month.

This army was the most formidable force ever to leave Greek soil, led by a youthful but battle-tested king who regularly led his troops into battle, and his Macedonian warriors were its indispensable nucleus. In spring of 334 BC, Alexander III led his fearsome army to the Hellespont, where they would cross the narrow waterway into Asia, which became the traditional event that signaled a European army's intent to conquer the East. Alexander III, the conspicuous horn of the Bible, thus began to fulfill the prophecy of Daniel: "While I was observing, take note, a male goat was coming from the west over the surface of the whole earth, without touching the ground, and the goat had a conspicuous horn between its eyes" (Dan 8:5).

Upon his arrival on the other side of the Hellespont, Alexander III, fully armed, was the first Macedonian to cast his spear into the ground in Asia. He leaped ashore and declared, "I accept Asia from the gods, won by the spear." Although the battles were waiting to be fought and the Medo-Persian army had yet to be bested by an opposing force, he was certain of the success that lay ahead of him.

Three days after his troops completed their landing, they advanced onto the plain alongside the Granicus River, having crossed the Dardanelles at Eleus. They adopted a strong defensive position on the eastern bank of the Granicus. The full army did not travel with him, but merely 13,000 infantry and 5,100 cavalry from his elite forces. The king was sure that his elite forces could defeat the superior numbers of the enemy.

After midday, his scouts galloped back to tell their king of the Persian position on the far side of the river. The Macedonian king issued his detailed orders, and his troops formed a frontal attack as follows: on the left, under the command of Parmenio, the units consisted of 2,400 Greek cavalry, a squadron of 150 Thracian cavalry, and three brigades of phalangites (4,500 men). On the right, under Alexander III's command, the units consisted of 500 Agrianians, 500 archers, the Companion Cavalry of 1,800 men, a squadron of 150 Paeonian cavalry, 600 lancers, 3,000 Hypaspists, and three brigades of phalangites totaling 4,500 men.

If the Macedonian cavalry was 10 horses deep and the infantry was 8 men deep, the length of the line was some 2½ km, which matched the length of the Persian cavalry line with a depth of some 16 horses, of which the rear ranks had plenty of room to maneuver on level ground. The Persian commanders kept their forces in the positions that they had adopted initially. Alexander III ordered the trumpets to blow, and the army went down into the wide riverbed. The initial assault was delivered to the left of Alexander III's position by one Companion Cavalry squadron, the Paeonian Cavalry, the lancers, and the royal brigade of Hypaspists.

Alexander III, who wore an iron helmet with white plumes, was a conspicuous figure at the front of the Royal Cavalry Guard. The Persian commanders moved to face him with their finest cavalry, but the Macedonian attack pinned down the opposing cavalry and held them at bay. The Companion Cavalry squadron that began the assault and inflicted casualties was being driven back. Seeing this, Alexander III ordered the general attack. At the head of the Royal Cavalry Squadron, he led a charge toward the enemy forces that would repulse the weakened Companion Cavalry squadron.

Amidst ferocious hand-to-hand combat, Alexander III and his entourage began to prevail. The Persians were losing ground all along the line. On the right, Alexander III's archers and Agrianians, who were attacking the Persian cavalry on the flank, were gaining position around the enemy's left wing, while the squadrons of the Companion Cavalry fought their way onto the top of the bank. To the left of Alexander III, the Royal Hypaspists and the phalangites achieved convincing results with their superior pikes.

According to the ancient records, "When the Persian center had given way, the cavalry on each wing broke and fled precipitately." Alexander III regrouped his men and surrounded the phalanx of the 20,000 Greek mercenary infantry that was employed by the Persians, but the Macedonian phalanx in formation shattered the Greek phalanx that was fighting under Persian hire. Alexander III thus fought his first battle against the Persian satraps who governed Asia Minor, routing their armies on the banks of the Granicus River.

The total defeat of the Persian forces at this battle was due primarily to the military genius of Alexander III. His immediate grasp of the situation tactically, his coordination of all of the arms in a planned attack, and his ingenuity in combining the initial assault with the extension of his line upstream to the right, all display marks of brilliant military strategy. His speed in deliberation and action left the Persian commanders with no chance to defeat the Macedonian cavalry and infantry separately, or to reorganize their forces. The spoils were collected, and Alexander III sent 300 sets of Persian armor to the acropolis of Athens for dedication to Athena.

Yet the decisive battle between the invading Greco-Macedonians and the Medo-Persian Empire of Asia would be fought at Issus, where the entire force of the Persian army would be present. Rounding the northeastern corner of the Mediterranean Sea, the Macedonians turned south and marched through the Pillar of Jonah, then came to Myriandrus. On the following day, Alexander III learned that the army of Darius III, the Medo-Persian king, was behind him to the north of the Pillar of Jonah. Alexander III sent some cavalry and archers to ascertain if the pass at the Pillar, which was over 6 km away, was controlled by the enemy. The pass was unoccupied, to Alexander III's relief, because the route followed along a narrow beach that was flooded when winds were adverse and was flanked by cliffs on the landward side.

The army was told to take its evening meal, then march to the pass, which they reached at about midnight. Fortuitously, the beach was not flooded. Sentries were posted on the clifftops, and the men slept for several hours. At dawn, the march began toward the Payas River. All that Darius III could do was to move his huge army, which was several times larger than Alexander III's army, to a defensive position on the right bank of the river. The Macedonian forces deployed from columns into battle lines and began to descend slowly onto the lower ground, as Alexander III was issuing orders to his commanders. He was about to confront the Persians on the narrow coastal plain to the south of Issus.

The Greco-Macedonian army numbered 5,300 cavalry and 26,000 infantry. Parmenio, who was told to stay close to the coast to keep his troops from being outflanked, commanded the left side of the line, while Alexander III commanded the right side. There was a second line behind his forces, which was shorter than the phalanx. Although the Medo-Persian army outnumbered their enemy by a ratio of nearly 4:1, the natural boundaries of the terrain prevented them from positioning more men along their front line than Alexander III could put along his front line, so the Persians' numerical superiority was neutralized.

Despite this logistical flaw, the position Darius III chose at Issus was exceptionally strong. He placed his best infantry on the top of the bank between the positions of the two modern bridges, and he strengthened any gaps with stockades. The Persian infantry was in an unusually deep phalanx. Darius III was behind them, along with 3,000 of his Royal Cavalry Guard. When the right side of Alexander III's line was some 80 m from the enemy, he led the Royal Infantry Guard double-time through the riverbed just above the first bridge, charged the Cardaces (i.e., foreign mercenaries of the Persians), and broke through their formation.

To Alexander's left, the Hypaspists and the phalanx-brigades entered the channel and engaged the enemy. To his right, the Companion Cavalry and the infantry beyond them crossed the riverbed, outflanked the enemy, and broke their position. Alexander III then joined the Royal Cavalry Guard in an attack against the flank and rear of the Cardaces, then the rear of the enemy Greek mercenaries who were conscripted by the Persians, being joined by the victorious troops on his right wing. Meanwhile, the phalangites, trying to storm the defensive position of the mercenaries and the Cardaces, suffered considerable casualties, but with extraordinary effort they maintained pressure on the Persians.

To the left, the Persian cavalry charged repeatedly, but the Thessalian and other Greek cavalry were holding their ground. The sudden advance of Alexander III toward Darius III then decided the issue. As Alexander III's infantry on the right wing attacked the flank of the Greek mercenaries who fought for the Persians, and behind them Alexander III and the Cavalry Guard forced their way toward Darius III, the Medo-Persian king turned his chariot around and fled, followed by his Cavalry Guard. Alexander III then pressed on toward the left wing, which compelled the Persian cavalry to join their king in retreat.

Only then did Alexander III order the pursuit by his cavalry, who covered a distance of 48 km until nightfall and inflicted extremely heavy losses on the Persian cavalry when they overtook them. The surviving Greek mercenaries escaped into the hills, some of whom later rejoined Darius III. The Macedonian losses were 150 cavalry and 300 infantry, and Alexander III was one of 4,500 wounded. The victory and the small number of casualties were due to his planning, his army's superior weaponry and armor, and their commitment to fight in formation despite the adversity and stress that they experienced throughout the battle.

The defeat of the Persian army was total. Maybe the numbers were inflated in the official reports by Callisthenes, so the figure of 110,000 casualties also may be somewhat inflated. Whatever was the true number of the Persian losses, the full strength of the empire failed utterly on the banks of the Payas River near Issus. By a daring cavalry attack, Alexander III had defeated his bitter enemy. He accomplished this by disrupting the Persian front line with his standard cavalry charge from the right and forcing their entire army into a panic-stricken retreat.

Darius III escaped with his life and fled to Persia, but he left so hastily that he abandoned his family—including his mother, wife, children, and some of his harem—and his treasure to the victorious Macedonians. When Alexander III heard of the capture of the royal family and their mourning for Darius III, whom they supposed to be dead, he sent Leonnatus to inform them that Darius III was alive, and that Alexander III was granting them "the status and the title of their royal rank." Such was the account of Ptolemy and Aristobulus, as noted in Arrian's *Anabasis*, which undoubtedly is correct. Alexander the Great treated the Persian royalty with the honor that befits royalty, a respectful form of behavior that was unknown to conquerors from the East.

As Hornblower and Spawforth pointed out, Alexander III did not pursue his fleeing rival, but instead turned southward to capture the Phoenician cities along the Levantine coast. Capturing Susa and pursuing Darius III before the Persians had a chance to recruit another imperial army may have been a tempting prospect after the total victory at Issus, but the young king granted his enemy this unchallenged retreat in order to accomplish a greater good. He chose to persist in his primary strategy of mastering the Persian fleet from the land, which Hammond insightfully perceived. To achieve this goal, Alexander III needed to control the entire Mediterranean coast. As long as the powerful Phoenician fleet remained loyal to Persia, it could cut off the communication and supply lines from Macedon to the army of her king.

Moreover, such Phoenician intervention could incite the Greek cities of Asia Minor to revolt. As Hammond rightly observed, the decision of Alexander III to follow this strategy would be epoch-making. The first step was to secure the coastal cities of the Levant, most of which submitted to the Macedonian king willingly. Tyre was the notable holdout, which required a protracted siege. Alexander III's army labored and fought for seven months against the Tyrian navy and defenses, until they completed a mole that joined the tiny island to the adjacent coast. The Tyrian fleet was defeated, and the city fell to the Macedonians in July of 332 BC. Due to the utter defiance of the Tyrians, Alexander III's army was ruthless with them in response.

As the record states, "The Macedonians went to all lengths in their anger, because they were enraged by the length of the siege, and by the Tyrian slaughter of Macedonians taken prisoner, and the throwing of their corpses into the sea in front of the Macedonian camp." About 8,000 Tyrians were killed during the siege, and the 30,000 survivors were sold into slavery or smuggled out by the Phoenicians. The Tyrian king, his nobles, and some Carthaginian envoys on a sacred mission were pardoned as suppliants at the altar of Heracles. The Macedonian dead were reported by Arrian to be 400, with the list of wounded probably exceeding 3,000, based on the proportion of the soldiers wounded at the Battle of Issus.

In December of 332 BC, the Greco-Macedonian army and fleet proceeded from Gaza to Egypt in seven days, averaging some 32 km per day due to efficiently planned logistics. The fleet entered Pelusium (i.e., a city on Egypt's northeastern coast) unopposed, and the army was welcomed by the priests and the people, as the Persian commander surrendered to Alexander III at Memphis. The fleet sailed on the waters of the Nile River, and a naval base subsequently was established at the site that would become Alexandria.

With the Levantine coast essentially secured, Alexander III could continue his strategy of mastering the Persian fleet from the land. By this time, the Persian fleet truly was suffering tremendously from the effectiveness of the plan, as reports had reached Alexander III that the Macedonian and Greek fleets—helped by uprisings among the islands—had driven away the remnants of the Persian forces and their supporters at sea (i.e., the "pirates" from the Aegean Islands), with fighting continuing only along the island of Crete.

Alexander the Great wintered in Egypt during the season of 332/1 BC, becoming a full-fledged Egyptian pharaoh. Hieroglyphic inscriptions reveal that they granted him the traditional royal titulary. While in Egypt, he began planning for the building of Alexandria, which would become a model city for the new Hellenistic kingdom in the East.

Citizens of all of the cities of his kingdom, including Alexandria, would learn skills in agriculture, land reclamation, capitalism, and—most importantly—the Greek language, which would become the official medium in every city. This language, based on a modification of the Attic dialect, originally was known as Hellenistic Greek. Later, it would be called the *koine* (i.e., "communal") Greek language, the word that describes the style of Greek used for composing the Greek Bible.

Before Alexander III began the complete conquest and Hellenization of the East, he had to finish the task of subduing the Medo-Persian Empire. The battle that was waged to end the war was fought at Gaugamela. With the victory over his bitter enemy at Granicus, Alexander III proved ready to face the massive Persian army in pitched battle on the open plain, challenging the old adage about the importance of avoiding involvement in a land war in Asia (i.e., against traditional Asian powers). The Battle of Gaugamela became the futile attempt of Darius III to prevent these Europeans from ripping his kingdom away from him.

In preparation for what would be the final battle, Darius III mustered the finest cavalry in the empire from Cappadocia to Pakistan, and the Sacae from beyond Persian borders. He armed some units with lances and swords, but most would fight in the traditional manner: with archery, javelins, and scimitars. He had 15 war elephants, but he left them in his camp, probably because the Indian horses alone had been trained to act with elephants. His elite infantry consisted of some 6,000 Greek mercenaries and 1,000 Persian Guards. Other infantry supported their cavalry units or formed a general reserve.

The lowest estimate that has been offered for the size of the Persian infantry is 400,000 men, although this figure may be inflated. Darius III also had a new weapon, the scythed chariot, which had razor-sharp blades that were attached to the chariot's turning wheels, chassis, and yoke-pole. He expected that a charge by 200 of these chariots would disperse a phalanx formation and expose the pikemen to close combat, during which time the pike would be more of a hindrance than a help. According to Hammond, Darius III was the first to reach his desired battleground, a stretch of flat pastureland and ploughland. He cleared three fairways for the scythed chariots and laid spikes to maim the enemy's horses.

The Macedonian army moved onto the plain with perfect precision. At first, the line was parallel to that of Darius III, and then they advanced to face the Persian right flank and part of the center. At a predetermined moment, the line made a right incline and advanced toward its right front, in an oblique formation, with the right wing in advance and the left wing behind. Darius III saw that Alexander III's army now was moving away from the prepared fairways of the scythed chariots, so he ordered the Bactrians and the Scythians to attack the Macedonians' right flank in order to halt their movement.

Alexander III counter-attacked with squadron after squadron, each in wedge formation. Meanwhile, he kept advancing to his right front. As Hammond observed, Darius III sent his scythed chariots into the charge before it was too late, but they proved ineffective because the Macedonians opened ranks to let the chariots pass through, while the Agrianian and Thracian javelin-throwers struck chariot-drivers and horses alike with their javelins, and the Macedonian troops made a tremendously loud sound that frightened the chariot-horses from their course.

While the scythed chariots were making their attack, Darius III ordered a general advance, and at the same time he sent some Persian cavalry to support the defeated Bactrians and Scythians. Alexander III ordered the last unit of his flank-guard, the 600 lancers, to charge into the Persian cavalry where it was leaving the Persian main line. When the lancers broke through and created a gap, Alexander III turned his line 90° to his left, formed a wedge with the Companion Cavalry and the infantry (Hypaspists), charged through the gap with a resounding battle cry, and swung left in the direction of Darius III.

In fierce fighting, the long pikes of the Companion Cavalry and the spears of the Hypaspists prevailed. As the enemy drew near, Darius III fled from the battle, visibly stricken with panic. The impetuous charge of Alexander III's wedge had been delivered at the precise moment when the attacking cavalry of the Persian right flank was bringing the left part of the Macedonian phalanx to a halt. A gap arose between that part of the phalanx and the brigades that were advancing in line with Alexander III's wedge.

The gap was created by Indian and Persian cavalry, but instead of wheeling and attacking, they rode to the Macedonian camp, which was guarded by only a small force of Thracians. Part of the second line of the halted phalanx turned around as they had been ordered, and they defeated the enemy within the Macedonian camp. Meanwhile, Alexander III's entire left wing, which had come under Parmenio's command, was hard pressed by attacks from all sides. According to Hammond, a request for help went out to and reached the king.

Although he must have been tempted to pursue Darius III, who was now fleeing, he turned the squadrons of Companion Cavalry to his left and fought his way through the cavalry of the Persian right-center that met him head-on in formation. Sixty Companions died, but Alexander survived. He was about to attack the Persian cavalry on the extreme right when it broke and retreated under the inspired charges of the Thessalian squadrons. The massive army of the mighty Medo-Persians was now on the run. Alexander III and the Companions led the pursuit, followed by Parmenio's troops. Capturing and eliminating the enemy would ensure that Darius III never again could raise an imperial army in Asia.

The young Macedonian king had prevailed, gaining the crowning victory of which he long had dreamed. This time, however, the Persians were outmaneuvered on chosen ground and unrestricted plain. In another show of military genius, Alexander III sacrificed his left wing, leaving it to be enveloped, while he extended the enemy line to the right, creating a gap that enabled his main cavalry forces to drive inwards and turn the course of the battle. When daylight failed, Alexander III camped until midnight, while Parmenio captured the Persian camp. Alexander III later carried the pursuit to Arbela (i.e., modern Erbil, in Iraq), where he confiscated the treasure and possessions of Darius III.

Darius III fled from Ecbatana to the Caspian Sea, where he was put to death by his closest entourage—led by Bessus, the satrap of Bactria—just a few hours before the Macedonians could reach the Persian camp. Alexander III honored his rival by giving him a proper soldier's burial, ending the war with Persia, and discharging his Hellenic troops *en masse*. "He [Alexander III] fought many battles, conquered strongholds, and put to death the kings of the earth" (1 Macc 1:2), with Darius III at the top of the list.

After Gaugamela, Alexander III was acclaimed as "king of Asia," and from the time of Darius III's death in 330 BC, his status was displayed in his court dress, which combined the traditional Macedonian hat (Greek: *kausia*) and cloak with the Persian diadem, tunic, and girdle. According to Hornblower and Spawforth, he even conducted Persian court ceremonies and promoted Persian nobles. As early as 331 BC, he had regarded himself as the proper ruler of the Medo-Persian Empire. This fact is confirmed by the writer of Maccabees: "After Alexander—son of Philip, the Macedonian, who came from the land of Kittim—had defeated Darius (III), king of the Persians and the Medes, he succeeded him as king" (1 Macc 1:1).

After Darius III's death, Alexander III continued his campaign through eastern Persia and advanced onto the steppes of Central Asia, stopping in Bactria to prevent Bessus from claiming the Medo-Persian throne. From Bactria, Alexander III moved into India at the invitation of the local dynasts of the Kabul valley and Punjab.

The spring of 326 BC found him at Taxila, east of the Indus River, poised for a campaign against Porus, who controlled the area around the Hydaspes River. After a series of diversionary maneuvers, Alexander III crossed the river under cover of a spring thunderstorm, defeating Porus, whose war-elephants could not compensate for his inferior cavalry.

Alexander III continued eastward, eventually crossing the rivers of the Punjab in the face of an increasing monsoonal deluge, until his troops' patience was exhausted. On the way to the Ganges Valley, they refused to cross the Hyphasis (a.k.a. Beas) River in India and invade the peoples along the Ganges River. In what Hornblower and Spawforth called an unprecedented move, the king reluctantly conceded, halting his advance to the east.

Yet still it could be said of him, "He advanced to the ends of the earth and plundered many nations" (1 Macc 1:3). He eventually returned to Mesopotamia from the East, with plans to use a war fleet of 1,000 ships to invade the Persian Gulf and Arabian littoral, which he intended to conquer and colonize. Yet in June of 323 BC, Alexander the Great died in Nebuchadnezzar II's palace in Babylon at only 32 years of age.

CHAPTER 9

CONCLUDING THOUGHTS

NIMROD'S BIOGRAPHY IN SUMMARY

NIMROD'S CONNECTION TO SARGON OF AKKAD

THE IDENTIFICATION OF BIBLICAL NIMROD WITH A historical personage has proven to be a challenge to commentators and scholars alike for centuries. Proof of the difficulty of this task is found in the healthy number of candidates who have been presented as options. From ancient times, fantastical renditions of Nimrod's deeds have fascinated many generations of readers of the Bible, some of which go beyond what the text strictly has to say about him, thanks in part to the uncertainty of his identity and when he lived. As far back as 1876, the American traveler John Philip Newman predicted, "The day may not be far distant when Nimrod's Biography [et al.] shall become standard works among the civilized nations of the earth."

Hopefully, the present study demonstrated that this day now has arrived, thanks to the two-edged sword of biblical exegesis and modern archaeological discovery. This was accomplished by sifting through the relevant data and the options for the candidate who matches Nimrod's biographical sketch with precision. The first step in the task was to present Moses's literary convention that places the Nimrod pericope within a larger timeline (Genesis 10), then follows it with the story of Babel and its tower (Genesis 11), which precedes Nimrod's lifetime on that same timeline. The second step in the task was to elaborate on how the Nimrod pericope fits into the greater context of Genesis 1–11.

The third step in the task was to review and critique some of the more popularly held opinions that scholars have proposed for the identification of Nimrod, which includes the consideration of Ninurta, Gilgamesh, and

Amenhotep III. Ninurta, the Šumerian god of war, was proposed as an option for Nimrod due to his being a great hunter, an Assyrian deity, and a warrior-king. Ninurta was rejected as a legitimate candidate due to the lack of his possessing a kingdom over Šumer and Assyria, along with his basic lack of humanity, because Nimrod should be connected genealogically to Adam, specifically through Cush and Ham. Also, the Nimrod pericope was shown to be devoid of any references to hunting in Gen 10:9, which word reflects a faulty—even if commonplace—translation into English.

Gilgamesh was presented as an option for Nimrod since he was a semi-divine hero, since the historical Gilgamesh was a king in the First Dynasty of Uruk, since he lashed out at deity for sending the universal flood, and since he possessed superhuman strength. However, Gilgamesh cannot be considered as a plausible candidate because there are no historical inscriptions attesting to his reign, because he did not overtake or build up any cities—either in Šumer or Assyria—and thus did not possess an actual empire, and because the Bible never describes Nimrod as having attempted to lash out at God for sending the flood.

An Egyptian king named Amenhotep III was proposed as an option for Nimrod because the African nation of Cush, also known as Nubia, was located immediately to the south of Egypt, and because this pharaoh was known for his great hunts and allegedly extending his rule to the Euphrates. Amenhotep III was rejected as a legitimate candidate because the Nimrod pericope is set in Mesopotamia, and not in Africa or west of the Euphrates, because Amenhotep III lived approximately 1000 years after these centers of power existed in southern Mesopotamia, and because Moses recorded Nimrod's biography no more than two years before this pharaoh took the Egyptian throne.

Amenhotep III's genealogical background traces back to Ham through Mizraim, and not through Cush. Another flaw in Amenhotep III's candidacy is that the starting point of his kingdom was the cities of Egypt, and not the centers of power in Šumer, as required by the biblical record. Plus, his army never actually reached anywhere close to the Euphrates.

The fourth step in the task was to present a working translation and the results of an investigation into the various lexical, grammatical, and syntactical features of the Nimrod pericope in Gen 10:7–12, which forms the foundation from which a fuller study could be launched. In fact, the most important part of the present study is an accurate understanding of the inspired biblical text that presents Nimrod's biography, because this is essential for understanding any biblical character properly. This step proved instructive, leading to at least the following certainties about Nimrod:

(1) Nimrod's genealogical background requires him to have been a distant descendant of Cush, and thus undisputedly a human being from the line of Adam, without the possibility of being Cush's son or grandson. (2) Nimrod's character is defined by his having profaned, meaning that he acted irreverently in order to become powerful on the earth, and by his having become a powerful slaughterer in the sight of He-who-is, meaning that he butchered an enormous number of people in plain sight of God. (3) Nimrod's exploits yielded him a kingdom, thus requiring him to be a king, whose domain began with the great power-centers of Šumer, which encompasses southern Babylonia. (4) Nimrod's kingdom expanded northward into Assyria, where he built up cities that eventually grew to be prominent seats of Assyrian power.

The fifth and final step in the task was to present the case for Sargon of Akkad as the proper candidate for Nimrod. The evidence for this connection consists of five arguments that were delineated and supported: (1) Sargon's geographical origin of Kish may be associated with Nimrod's genealogical origin of Cush. (2) Both Sargon and Nimrod were credited with bringing Akkad into prominence. (3) Both Sargon and Nimrod were involved in major building projects extremely early in Assyria's history. (4) Both Sargon and Nimrod had a lasting influence in Assyria. (5) Both Sargon and Nimrod were legendary for their military exploits and brutality.

The detailed evidence presented for each of these arguments leads the objective reader of the Bible and student of ANE history to the inescapable conclusion that Sargon of Akkad is not only the best candidate for historical Nimrod, but the only valid one. The candidacy of his grandson, Naram-Sin, also was examined, but this later Sargonid king's biography was shown to vary too significantly from that of Nimrod to be a viable option. The biography of Sargon of Akkad, now illuminated by the discovery and publication of inscriptional and material cultural evidence provided by epigraphy and archaeology, matches that of Nimrod perfectly. The human and divine authors of the Bible, knowing that Israel soon would be a monarchy, offered this vivid picture of how far a king could stray from God to if he gives himself over to an insatiable lust for power and a commitment to conquering kingdoms and foreign nations.

Nimrod, who rose to prominence as a cupbearer at Kish, surpassed the exploits and successes of all of the Mesopotamian kings who preceded him as great conquerors. Several cities of Šumer, the Bible's "land of Shinar," had risen to prominence in southern Mesopotamia, such as Eridu, Kish, and Uruk. Eridu was the ancient world's first urban center, and in a future publication (*The Forgotten Era: Illuminating Biblical History from the Tower of Babel to Abraham*) the present writer will attempt to prove that Eridu is equated with the Babel of Genesis 11. For now, it may be stressed that Eridu was abandoned long before Nimrod's lifetime.

The city of Kish, which thrived in the Early Dynastic Period, was led by powerful kings such as Enmebaragesi, the twenty-first king in the *Šumerian King List*, who is said to have confiscated the weapons of Elam. Nimrod served as the cupbearer of Ur-Zababa, the second king of the Fourth Dynasty of Kish and the man whose throne Nimrod usurped. Neither of these rulers achieved what Nimrod accomplished. Lugal-zege-si began as the king of Umma but conquered Uruk and became the only king of the Third Dynasty of Uruk. After he defeated the city of Lagash, he united Šumer into a single kingdom.

Yet Nimrod surpassed Lugal-zage-si's ambitious achievements, not only overtaking Šumer, but subduing all of central and northern Mesopotamia. In addition, he conquered peoples even beyond the land between the two rivers (i.e., the Euphrates and Tigris). To the east, he invaded Elam and Barakhshi. To the southeast, he incorporated Bahrain and the eastern coastland of Saudi Arabia. To the northwest, he overran Mari and parts of eastern Syria. To the north, he incorporated Assyrian and Hurrian lands into his empire. Sargon truly acquired more territory than any of the kings who preceded him, and the price that was paid to accomplish this feat is the loss of thousands of lives, in battle and by invasion.

It is for good reason that Moses wrote of how Nimrod became a powerful slaughterer in the sight of He-who-is, and that on account of his exploits a saying arose that future empire builders were "as Nimrod, a powerful slaughterer in the sight of He-who-is" (Gen 10:9). His imperialistic military victories were so epic in the ANE world that all future conquerors were compared to him, as they followed his blueprint for conquest and typified his insatiable desire to acquire more lands and more city-states. This type of excessive greed resulted in a thirst that simply could not be quenched. For Nimrod, more was never enough.

NIMROD'S SUCCESSORS AS ANCIENT EMPIRE BUILDERS

The first ruler to implement Nimrod's imperialistic blueprint was his own grandson, Naram-Sin, the last truly successful king of the Akkadian Empire that Nimrod had built. One of Naram-Sin's innovations involves a change to the Akkadian royal titulary. Whereas early in Naram-Sin's reign he referred to himself with the more modest title, "king of Akkad," during the middle of his reign he adopted the more boastful title of "the mighty one, king of the four corners" (of the world), which was incorporated by virtually every future king who attempted to exert universal dominion over Mesopotamia.

Naram-Sin implemented numerous administrative and domestic reforms, but his true goal was to prove himself a worthy successor to Sargon, which he accomplished by dominating a large portion of the ANE. His expansion of the empire included Purushkhanda in the northwest, Magan in the southeast, Lullubi to the east of Babylon and Akkad, and Subartu in upper Mesopotamia. Evidence of his campaigning comes from his votive and building inscriptions, such as those found at Nippur, Adab, Ur, Marada, Girsu, Tutub, Susa, Nineveh, Tell Brak, Bassetki, and Mari. At Tell Brak, the remains of the king's fortress/palace demonstrate that he intended his occupation of the area to be more than merely temporary.

Although the Akkadian Dynasty ended in *ca.* 2121 BC, this would not be the last of empire builders or their empires. In a mere 10 years after this (i.e., *ca.* 2111 BC), Ur-Nammu established the Third Dynasty of Ur at the site of Abram's earlier birth (*ca.* 2166 BC), which is located in Šumer. Ur-Nammu asserted the independence of Ur from Uruk, followed in Nimrod's footsteps by establishing an eponymic dating system at Ur, and assumed the title, "king of Ur." He then forced into submission the local rulers who had depended on the Gutians. By the end of his reign, he established control over most of Šumer and Akkad.

Ur-Nammu gained the loyalty of Ur's citizens by initiating a massive building program in honor of the two patron deities of the city: Nanna, the Šumerian moon-god, and Ningal, Nanna's female consort. Ur-Nammu also erected the great terrace of Ur and a giant ziggurat on top of it, a practice that dates back to the tower of Babel that is mentioned in Gen 11:4. Ur's ruins preserve these architectural plans, although the actual structures often were repaired or rebuilt after his death. Ur-Nammu also adopted the title, "king of Šumer and Akkad," but he is known mostly from his implementation of the world's oldest known law code.

Central Mesopotamia was not finished with significant empires centered there, as another empire with its capital there after the Akkadian Empire is the Old Babylonian (a.k.a. Amorite) Empire, located at Babylon under Hammurabi. He ascended to the throne as Babylon's sixth Amorite king and reigned from *ca.* 1792 to 1750 BC. According to Hammurabi's eponymic dating formulae, he captured Isin and Uruk in Year 6, which had been under Larsa's control. He attacked Emutbal in Year 7, which weakened his bitter enemy, Larsa. In Year 11, Hammurabi conquered Rapiqum, which was close to Mari.

Hammurabi spent Years 12 through 28 consolidating his kingdom, but he radically altered the Mesopotamian political landscape during the decade that followed. In Year 29, Elam attempted to turn him against Larsa's Rim-Sin, but when Hammurabi and Rim-Sin learned of this scheme, they became allies. Their short-lived alliance was joined by Amorite forces from Yamhad and Mari. This coalition defeated Eshnunna, Shubartu, and Elam, leaving Hammurabi with *de facto* control of southern Mesopotamia. In Year 30, Hammurabi conquered Larsa and annexed it into what was now the Old Babylonian Empire. He thus assumed the illustrious Sargonic title of "king of Šumer and Akkad."

Hammurabi's conquests and expansionism did not end there. In Year 31, he again defeated Eshnunna and its allies, and in Year 32 Babylon even defeated Mari. In Year 34, Babylon's armies reached from one edge of Assyrian territory to the other edge, making Hammurabi the dominant ruler between Elam and the Euphrates River. He subjugated Larsa, Isin, Kish, Uruk, Ur, Mari, Eshnunna, Shubartu, Malgium, Rapiqum, and numerous other city-states, incorporating them into Babylonia's new Amorite empire.

Hammurabi obtained the first empire concentrated in central Mesopotamia since that of the Sargonids, and his empire certainly rivaled Sargon's in size and breadth.

Egypt's one true empire builder, Thutmose III (1504–1450 BC), is known to modern historians as the Napoleon of Egypt. The boy-king shared the throne with Hatshepsut (1504/2–1483 BC), his stepmother and aunt, until she abdicated the throne in Year 22. Thutmose III then became sole regent, ruling into Year 54. He is known to biblical history as the king who chased Moses out of Egypt after the Hebrew killed an Egyptian.

Within only weeks after Hatshepsut's abdication, Thutmose III launched a campaign into western Asia to counter a rebellious coalition led by the king of Kadesh, and the conflict resulted in an Egyptian siege of Megiddo. The successful siege and subsequent Battle of Megiddo, which involved the largest number of forces that ever participated in Thutmose III's Asiatic campaigns, showcased his brilliance as a military tactician.

In subsequent Asiatic campaigns, Thutmose III penetrated further and further northward into the Levant. His 8th and most glorious campaign in Year 33 (ca. 1472 BC) was a direct attack on Mitanni, his fellow super-power within the ANE world. The Egyptian army ventured through Kadesh and Tunip but met Mitannian resistance near Aleppo. The Egyptians won three engagements, which allowed them to reach the Euphrates at Carchemish. The Mitannian army crossed over to the eastern bank of the river, then confiscated or destroyed all of the river-crafts in the vicinity. In an act of extreme brutality, Thutmose III showed no mercy to the local inhabitants, as his army burned down all of the towns along the Euphrates where they ventured.

The Egyptians crossed the Euphrates at Carchemish and entered Mitannian territory, where Thutmose III erected a boundary stele on the river-bank alongside that of his grandfather, Thutmose I. This act proved his intention for the conquest to be permanent, even though the dream never materialized. Nonetheless, the Egyptians received tribute for these accomplishments, as stated by Mitanni's vassal-states of Assyria, Babylon, and Cyprus. Thutmose III's venture to and along the Euphrates represents the greatest imperialistic expansion in Egyptian history. He launched 17 Asiatic campaigns in total, six of which were directed against Kadesh.

Scholars agree that Egypt's true arch rival was Mitanni, the other dominant ANE superpower of the day. The campaign of Year 33 proved that Egypt was the more dominant of the two superpowers during his rule. While Thutmose III essentially held onto the territory that he conquered over the balance of his reign and bequeathed it to his son, Amenhotep II (i.e., the exodus pharaoh), Egypt never again threatened to be the most powerful nation in the ANE world after the loss of the Egyptian army and all of Egypt's firstborn children at the time of the 10th plague on Egypt in 1446 BC. God so decimated Egypt's army and their male population that the empire ended much faster than it was built.

The first millennium BC experienced even greater empires than the previous millennium, with the first being the Neo-Assyrian Empire (911–609 BC). Esarhaddon, the young son and heir of Sennacherib, ascended the Neo-Assyrian throne in *ca.* 681 BC. Although his father had extended the territory of the empire that his forefathers had built, Esarhaddon expanded Assyria's dominion to the greatest extent that the kingdom ever would experience. He rebuilt the city of Babylon, which Sennacherib had destroyed, with construction evidently having begun in 678 BC and concluded in *ca.* 669 BC. This conciliatory act won him the loyalty of the Babylonians, who repulsed an Elamite attack in *ca.* 675 BC and helped Assyria against the son of Merodach-Baladan, the Chaldean tribal chief who attempted to recapture Ur.

Esarhaddon experienced resistance in Anatolia from *ca.* 679 to 669 BC and in the Levant from 679 to 677 BC. His army invaded Egypt in the winter of 673 BC with the intent of absorbing Egypt into the empire. This attempt failed miserably, as the Assyrians were routed in battle near Ashkelon by a Cushite pharaoh named Taharqa (690–664 BC). In 671 BC, Esarhaddon invaded Egypt with an even larger army and won both of the two encounters with the Egyptian army, which allowed the Assyrians to capture Egypt's capital of Memphis. Esarhaddon subsequently relocated many surviving Egyptians to the other side of his empire.

With the conquest of Egypt in 671 BC, the Neo-Assyrian Empire reached its maximum extent. Assyria's borders were Lake Van, the Kingdom of Urartu, the mouth of the Iris River, Cimmeria, Lake Tuz, the Kingdom of Phrygia, the northern part of Anatolia's Halys River, the eastern Mediterranean Sea, part of the way into Nubia/Cush, Sinai, the Persian Gulf, Elam,

Media, Mannaea, and Scythia. Esarhaddon's success sometimes came through ingenuity, such as how he solved the problem of the rebellious Babylonians without further bloodshed. As a military leader, he was popular and effective, although the foreign and domestic evidence reveals his brutality. Esarhaddon followed in the footsteps of Sennacherib, and Nimrod long before, both by his viciousness and by exalting himself with the title, "king of Šumer and Akkad."

The second great empire of the first millennium BC is the Neo-Babylonian Empire (626–539 BC), whose zenith was reached under Nebuchadnezzar II (605–562 BC). Although this empire did not even last a century, its power and presence were felt throughout the ANE. After Nebuchadnezzar II's accession onto the throne, he soon possessed most of the former territories of the Neo-Assyrian Empire. With the Medes unopposed to the rise of the Neo-Babylonians to their south and west, he concentrated the majority of his efforts on the Euphrates valley, the Levant, and Egypt.

Nebuchadnezzar II reestablished Babylonia as the leading power in Mesopotamia and the ANE, and his reign rivaled Hammurabi's in size and strength. Perhaps his imperialistic ambition is seen best in his extended siege of Tyre, along with his invasion and reinventing of Egypt in *ca.* 570 BC. His empire surpassed Hammurabi's in geographical dimensions, yet in Nebuchadnezzar II's inscriptions he prided himself more on his domestic building activities than his foreign conquests. His military campaigns were motivated largely to finance his ambitious rebuilding of Babylon and other Babylonian cities.

Nebuchadnezzar II invaded Judah three times. In 605 BC, he besieged Jerusalem, plundered the Temple articles, and captured Daniel and his friends. After a battle with the Egyptians in *ca.* 601 BC, in which both sides suffered great losses, Judah's king Jehoiakim suddenly switched allegiance from Babylonia to Egypt, believing that the Egyptians were more powerful. On 16 March of 597 BC, Nebuchadnezzar II's army captured Jerusalem, which was followed by the deportation of Jehoiachin and members of his royal family. On 27 January 589 BC, the Neo-Babylonians besieged Jerusalem, which fell on 29 August 587 BC. However, all of Babylonia's wealth and power acquired under Nebuchadnezzar II was lost by 539 BC.

The third great empire of the first millennium BC is the Medo-Persian Empire (*ca.* 550–334 BC), whose zenith was reached under Darius I (522–486 BC). Darius had served Cambyses II in Egypt as a spearbearer within an elite force of 10,000 royal soldiers. As king, Darius I effectively reorganized the empire, including the placement of a military commander and a tax official in each of the 20 Persian satrapies. He also created a network of roads to facilitate travel and communication within the empire. The king built a new palace at Susa in 521 BC, and he founded a new capital at Persepolis in 518 BC.

Darius I, known to history as Darius the Great, was legendary for his military exploits and foreign acquisitions. He expanded Medo-Persian rule over the Scythians, conquered the territory that would become the satrapy of Hindush (in modern Pakistan), invaded Egypt and constructed a temple to Amun there, built a canal between the Nile River and the Red Sea, and ruled the Ionian cities of Lydia through Greek tyrants. Darius I led the first Medo-Persian attempt to subjugate Greece, which culminated in the Battle of Marathon (490 BC). Thanks to the use of a classic pincer movement during the battle, the Greeks routed the Persians.

Darius I's losses totaled 6,400 men, while the Athenian and Grecian forces lost only 192. Despite the massive Medo-Persian loss at Marathon that prevented the conquest of Greece, Darius I procured the empire's maximum amount of imperialistic acquisitions. He ruled from the Indus and Jaxartes Rivers in the east to the Aegean Sea and Egypt in the west, and from the Persian Gulf in the south to the Caspian and Black Seas in the north. Throughout the next century-and-a-half (*ca.* 486–338 BC), his successors could be content with consolidating the vast empire that he had acquired and organized.

The fourth great empire of the first millennium BC is the Greco-Macedonian Empire, which was built by Alexander the Great (*ca.* 336–323 BC) of Macedon. In spring of 334 BC, Alexander III led his fearsome army to the Hellespont, where they crossed from Europe into Asia. Three days after the army landed, they advanced onto the plain alongside the Granicus River. After ferocious hand-to-hand combat along the banks of the river, Alexander III and his entourage prevailed. The total defeat of the Persian forces at this battle was due mainly to his strategic genius. He grasped the situation tactically, coordinated his troops and weaponry with precision, and ordered an assault that best utilized the terrain around his army.

The decisive battle between the Greco-Macedonians and the Medo-Persians was fought later at Issus, against the main Medo-Persian army rather than provincial troops. On the narrow coastal plain south of Issus, the Macedonian army deployed from columns into battle lines and descended slowly onto the lower ground, as Alexander III was issuing orders to his commanders. Despite the Greco-Macedonian army's numbers consisting of 5,300 cavalry and 26,000 infantry, their enemy outnumbered them by a ratio of nearly 4:1. Yet the natural boundaries of the narrow terrain prevented Darius III from positioning more men along their front line than Alexander III could put along his front line, neutralizing the Persian superiority in numbers.

The Persian cavalry charged time and time again, but the Thessalian and other Greek cavalry held their ground. The sudden advance of Alexander the Great toward Darius III decided the issue, and he forced his way toward the enemy king, who turned his chariot around and fled. Alexander III then pressed on toward the left wing, which compelled the Persian cavalry to join their king in retreat. The defeat of the Persian army was total. The figure of 110,000 Persian casualties may be inflated, but whatever their actual losses were, they utterly failed at Issus. Alexander III defeated his enemy decisively, while Darius III escaped to Persia.

The Greco-Macedonians did not pursue their rivals, but rather turned southward and captured the Phoenician cities of the Levant and Egypt, where Alexander the Great wintered in 332 to 331 BC and became a full-fledged Egyptian pharaoh. Before he could complete the conquest of the East, he had to eliminate the Medo-Persian Empire. The Battle of Gaugamela became Darius III's futile attempt to maintain his massive empire, as this battle settled the war with finality. He mustered the finest cavalry of the empire from Cappadocia to Pakistan, and his infantry consisted of about 400,000 men, according to the ancient record. Yet Alexander III's forces once again routed the Persians decisively. With this victory over his bitter enemy, the Macedonian king proved that his army could defeat the massive Persian army in pitched battle on the open plain.

After Gaugamela, Alexander III was acclaimed, "king of Asia," and he continued his campaign through eastern Persia and advanced into the steppes of Central Asia. From Bactria, he proceeded into India at the invitation of the local dynasts of the Kabul Valley and Punjab. The spring of 326 BC found him at Taxila, east of the Indus River, ready for a campaign against an Indian king named Porus. He crossed the river under cover of a spring storm and defeated Porus, whose war-elephants could not compensate for his inferior cavalry.

The Greco-Macedonian army continued eastward, crossing the rivers of the Punjab in monsoonal conditions, until their patience came to an end. Alexander III reluctantly conceded to their desire to stop fighting, as he halted his advance to the east. In just over a decade, the Greco-Macedonian army had conquered Asia Minor, the Levant, Egypt, the Medo-Persian Empire, and much of the East from Mesopotamia to India. In June of 323 BC, the young king died in Babylon at the tender age of 32. Although the empire was divided up immediately between his generals and the Macedonian elites, Alexander III had followed in Nimrod's footsteps by acquiring a vast empire and slaughtering a plethora of human beings in the sight of He-who-is.

NIMROD'S LEGACY IN MODERN TIMES

The present study has shown that the Nimrod of the Bible, whose biography is extremely abbreviated, was nothing less than a power-hungry ruler obsessed with conquering the world of his day. Most English translations fail to communicate this adequately in their rendering of Genesis 10:7–12, stating that Nimrod became a mighty one, instead of one who acted irreverently, and calling him a mighty hunter (i.e., of game animals), instead of a powerful slaughterer (i.e., of human beings). Nimrod certainly was no big-game hunter out on safari or the equivalent to David's mighty men who served the king by selflessly risking their lives to fight his enemies (2 Samuel 23; 1 Chronicles 11).

This significant inaccuracy in translation and interpretation has led many unwitting readers of the Bible to believe that Nimrod was an honorable statesman, or at least some sort of neutral figure. A closer look into the Hebrew terminology and the context of the passage has shown that Nimrod was a violent imperialist whose biography matches perfectly with that of the world's first empire builder, Sargon of Akkad. Nimrod indiscriminately killed armies of thousands of soldiers and expanded his kingdom by bloodshed and the overtaking of cities and nations by utilizing a strategy of shock and awe. He set his sights on ruling the ancient world of his day, and he subdued peoples in lands in every direction on the compass.

Nimrod's biographical profile, however, was not unique to him. Instead, he was merely the first of numerous empire builders who desired to acquire for themselves as much or more than he did. Just as the 20th and 21st centuries are marked by the glorification of evil on 'news' broadcasts that present ideas to viewers who then can go out and copy or surpass those criminal offenses in their own neighborhoods, so Nimrod's biography acted as a model and a measuring stick for the reigns of the likes of Naram-Sin, Ur-Nammu, Hammurabi, Thutmose III, Esarhaddon, Nebuchadnezzar II, Darius I, and Alexander the Great.

The world of the ANE possessed no great shortage of such empire builders. Yet this volume would be remiss if it were to say nothing about the empire builders of more recent times, as an addendum to the focus of the present study. The 20th century is as far back as a person of the present age needs to go to observe the legacy of Nimrod hard at work in the unbridled greed of a ruler obsessed with regional or global domination. The two tyrannical leaders who probably stand out the most are Adolf Hitler and Joseph Stalin, whose sinister regimes overlapped considerably during the first half of the century.

Adolf Hitler's dictatorship in Germany from 1933 to 1945 under the guise of the National Socialist German Workers' Party, known to the world as the Nazis, led to the conquest of most of Europe and northern Africa. In Europe, Hitler's forces overran or conquered France, Netherlands, Belgium, Denmark, Italy, Austria, Czechoslovakia, Hungary, Yugoslavia, Albania, Greece, Bulgaria, Romania, Poland, East Prussia, Lithuania, Latvia, Estonia, Finland, and parts of westernmost Russia. In northern Africa, Hitler acquired Tunisia, Libya, and northern parts of Algeria and Egypt. His ambitions for international conquest extended far beyond Europe and northern Africa, but his demise prevented even further imperialization.

Historian Nicholas Goodrick-Clarke analyzed the influence of occultic sects on Nazism in his book, *Occult Roots of Nazism: Secret Aryan Cults and Their Influence on Nazi Ideology*, which was published first in 1985. He contended that these sects espoused a mixture of popular nationalism, Aryan racism, and occultism to proclaim their advocacy of global rule by Germany. Goodrick-Clarke contended not only that these ideas and associated symbols exerted a profound influence on Heinrich Himmler's *SS*, but also that they had psychic roots and drew on occultic sects to devise the terrifying creation of Nazi concentration camps such as Auschwitz, Sobibor, and Treblinka.

Goodrick-Clarke and other atheistic historians have been quick to denounce any assertions that Nazism was connected to demonic influence and deception, calling these claims either sensational or under-researched. The reason for this denouncing, of course, is that admitting to the existence of angelic beings and demons compromises his atheistic worldview, and thus cannot be entertained as a legitimate possibility. However, the Bible is explicit about connecting the work of angelic beings to the ambitious offensives of empire builders.

Perhaps the most vivid example of this connection is found in Daniel 10:1–21. During the first month of Year 3 of Cyrus the Great (535 BC), an angelic being was sent to Daniel to reveal a vision regarding something that pertained to the future (Dan 10:12, 14). Although the angel was unnamed and featured a body like that of a man (Dan 10:5), his face appeared as lightning, his words were like the sound of roaring, his appearance caused Daniel's companions to flee and hide out of a great sense of dread (Dan 10:6–7), and his manifestation was in response to Daniel's prayer to God (Dan 10:12). Therefore, this individual who appeared to Daniel can be nothing else *but* an angelic being.

The angel recounted to Daniel how this angel's arrival was delayed due to being opposed for three weeks by "the prince of the Kingdom of Persia" (Dan 10:13), which contextually refers to an evil angelic being who was attempting to carry out some unspecified deeds of darkness through the powerful Medo-Persian Empire as his pawn. Evidently, the evil angelic being was doing his best to persuade the Medo-Persian leadership to perform some act(s) of violence, but the godly angel was there to oppose this deceptive scheme. What turned the tide for the godly angel, which freed him to visit Daniel, is that God sent Michael the archangel to help him (Dan 10:13). Daniel's angel even told him that no one stands with him firmly against these forces, except for Michael (Dan 10:21).

The fact that Daniel referred to Michael as "one of the chief princes" (Dan 10:13), clearly the same godly archangel who disputed with Satan about the body of Moses (Jude 1:9) and in the end times will wage war with his angels against the dragon (Rev 12:7), validates the conclusion that "the prince of the Kingdom of Persia" is an evil angelic being rather than a human being. As a result, evil angelic beings sought to manipulate a world empire (i.e., Medo-Persia) into performing their bidding, while godly angelic beings joined the battle in order to oppose this exploitation. If this type of spiritual warfare existed in the days of an ancient world empire, there is every reason to believe that opposing angelic beings were fighting over the Nazis' performing of heinous acts of evil and violence during the days of Hitler's empire in Europe, Asia, and Africa.

Joseph Vissarionovich Stalin, who rose to power even before Hitler, led the Union of Soviet Socialist Republics beginning in 1924, the same year in which Vladimir Lenin died. From the late 1920s, he essentially ruled as a dictator, which continued until the time of his death in 1954. The republics that were under his control include Latvia, Estonia, Lithuania, Belorussia, Ukraine, Moldova, Georgia, Armenia, Azerbaijan, Kazakhstan, Turkmenistan, Uzbekistan, Kyrgyzstan, and Tajikistan.

By the end of World War II, Stalin's Soviet army controlled virtually all of eastern and central Europe, which prompted him to create the title of *Generalissimus* for himself, a rank with roots in the imperial Russian army of an earlier era. The Russians essentially liberated the Balkan nations of eastern Europe from the Nazis, so Stalin had the power to incorporate them into the USSR as satellite nations. This list of eastern European nations includes Poland, East Germany, Czechoslovakia, Hungary, Romania, and Bulgaria. Yugoslavia was aligned with the USSR until 1948, at which time it became an independent socialist nation, and Albania was aligned with the Soviets until 1960.

The empire that Joseph Stalin built was a considerable force, especially because the Russians exploited the economic resources of all of these former nations and people groups for decades after World War II. Stalin was one of the most vicious empire builders of all time, following in the footsteps of Nimrod. Almost three million prisoners of war were abducted by Stalin's troops, and when they were brought into the USSR, they were taken to filtration camps at first. There, they were interrogated to determine if they would be considered disloyal to the republic, clearly a subjective criterion at best. Almost half of these prisoners were relocated to labor camps, while nearly 150,000 Balkans were deported.

Internally, Stalin was just as brutal to ethnic nationalities in Russia and the USSR as he was to foreign prisoners after the war. As Otto Pohl wrote in 2000, Stalin's regime systematically deported 13 nationalities to remote areas within the USSR from 1937 to 1951. The Soviets ruthlessly cleansed these ethnic groups from strategic areas within the nation, without any concern for their human rights.

Those who were uprooted from their traditional areas of settlement include Koreans, Finns, Germans, Karachays, Kalmyks, Chechens, Ingush, Balkars, Crimean Tatars, Meskhetian Turks, Georgian Kurds, Khemshils, and Pontic Greeks. Over two million people were deported due to internal exile. Many of them died from disease before arriving at their destinations, and the overall death count from genocide and other forms of death is an astounding 264,086 people.

One argument made within this volume is that Moses wrote the story of Nimrod in Genesis 10 for an important purpose: knowing that future kings would arise over Israel, he included Nimrod's biography about a renowned king's lust for power and appetite for world domination in order to deter any eventual Israelite king from following in the footsteps of this savage empire builder. Nimrod's story validates the old adage that John Dalberg-Acton, a British lord and historian, coined in 1887: "Absolute power corrupts absolutely." Nimrod proved this to be true in and around ancient Mesopotamia, and countless political rulers have followed his example ever since. Yet the truth is that this principle is not just true for empire builders, but for anyone in a position where power has come into his or her hands.

A wise seminary professor once taught his students that the three things a person should do with power that has been placed in one's hands are to (1) divest it, (2) divest it, and (3) divest it. In other words, push away that power, and do not hold onto any of it for another moment. Such power has corrupted countless pastors of churches and administrators of Christian colleges, universities, and seminaries. They no longer resemble the people they once were before gaining such power or prominent positions. For this reason, when the present writer became a church-planting pastor in Russia, he declined to take any type of power for himself within that church, instead allowing only the principles in the Bible to wield power.

If an issue with any member of the church could not be solved by consulting the Bible for God's perspective on the issue, he refrained from taking a definitive position one way or the other. He controlled no one. Why is this matter so crucial? Every church or Christian institution belongs only to Jesus Christ, not to any pastor, elder, or administrator, so leaders have no right whatsoever to usurp the power that belongs only to the head of the church. Divest the power. Divest the power. Divest the power. Nimrod's legacy as the architect of shock and awe is a blueprint that must be avoided for every person, in any position of authority.

SELECTED PUBLICATIONS
BY THE AUTHOR

2006   Amenhotep II and the Historicity of the Exodus Pharaoh. *Master's Seminary Journal* 17/1: 81–110.

2008   The Dating of Hazor's Destruction in Joshua 11 by Way of Biblical, Archaeological, and Epigraphical Evidence. *Journal of the Evangelical Theological Society* 51/3: 489–512.

2013   Identifying Nimrod of Genesis 10 with Sargon of Akkad by Exegetical and Archaeological Means. *Journal of the Evangelical Theological Society* 56/2: 273–305.

2013   Toward Pinpointing the Timing of the Egyptian Abandonment of Avaris during the Middle of the 18th Dynasty. *Journal of Ancient Egyptian Interconnections* 5/2: 9–28.

2015   The Ophel Pithos Inscription: Its Dating, Language, Translation, and Script. *Palestine Exploration Quarterly* 147/2: 130–145.

2016   Tayinat's Building XVI: The Religious Dimensions and Significance of a Tripartite Temple at Neo-Assyrian Kunulua. Unpublished dissertation. University of Toronto.

2016   *The World's Oldest Alphabet: Hebrew as the Language of the Proto-Consonantal Script.* Jerusalem: Carta.

2019   Determining the Precise Length of the Israelite Sojourn in Egypt. *Near Eastern Archaeological Society Bulletin* 64: 21–41.

2021   Connecting Khirbet Qeiyafa to the Proper Israelite King: Sauline Stronghold or Davidic Fortress. *Journal for the Evangelical Study of the Old Testament* 7/1: 82–118.

2022   The Lachish Milk Bowl Ostracon: A Hebrew Inscription from Joshua's Conquest at Lachish. *Bible and Spade* 35/1: 16–22.

MORE ABOUT THE AUTHOR

PROF. DOUGLAS PETROVICH CURRENTLY SERVES AS ADJUNCT Professor of Biblical History and Exegesis at Brookes Bible College, which is located in St. Louis, Missouri. He teaches remotely and resides in Richmond, Texas. From 2017–2022, he served as full Professor of Biblical History and Exegesis at The Bible Seminary, in Katy, Texas. Professor Petrovich was born and raised in Akron, Ohio. He has lived in California (twice), Illinois, Siberia (Russia), Toronto (Canada), and Texas. He is passionate about pouring his life into those whose lives God has given him the opportunity to influence, whether in the setting of the local church or an academic environment. He is committed to modeling his life after that of the incarnate son of God, Jesus Christ, albeit quite imperfectly. He has been married to his wife, Sherri, since 1991, and they have three adult children.

Soon after graduation from The Master's Seminary with a Master of Theology degree in New Testament, he and his family moved to Akademgorodok (in Siberia) under missionary status with Slavic Gospel Association, in order to build and launch a seminary from scratch for a Christian denomination in Russia. While at Novosibirsk Biblical-Theological Seminary, he served as the assistant to the seminary president, academic dean, and an assistant professor who taught many courses. In 2008, having turned over the leadership of the seminary to Russians whom he and his colleagues had trained to replace them, his family moved to Canada, where he pursued a M.A. and a Ph.D. from the University of Toronto.

Prof. Petrovich's Ph.D. includes a major in Syro-Palestinian archaeology, a 1st minor in (Middle and Late) Egyptian language, and a 2nd minor in ancient Near Eastern religions. He has participated in archaeological digs at Hazor, Tell Tayinat, and Shiloh, which reflects his love for seeing how ancient history converges with the events and people of the Bible. He was ordained as a pastor in 1998, having begun as an assistant pastor at a church in California.

For the majority of his 10 years in Siberia, he served as a church-planting pastor in Berdsk. He has appeared in two documentary films, the more recent being *Patterns of Evidence: The Moses Controversy* (2019), which features his unexpected discovery that the world's oldest alphabetic script is the Israelites' initial national script. The earlier film in which he appears is entitled *Is Genesis History?* (2017), which became the most watched documentary film on Netflix during the summer of 2018. In that film, he identifies the correct location for the city of Babel in Genesis 11, as well as its famous tower.

Please visit the author's YouTube channel, Illumining the Path (with Prof. Douglas Petrovich), to catch his free videos (best viewed with a computer or tablet) and shorts (best viewed with a smart phone). Here is the QR code to access his channel with electronic devices: